Determinants of Democratization

What are the determinants of democratization? Do the factors that move countries toward democracy also help them refrain from backsliding toward autocracy? This book attempts to answer these questions through a combination of a statistical analysis of social, economic, and international determinants of regime change in 165 countries around the world in 1972–2006, and case study work on nine episodes of democratization occurring in Argentina, Bolivia, Hungary, Nepal, Peru, the Philippines, South Africa, Turkey, and Uruguay. The findings suggest that democracy is promoted by long-term structural forces such as economic prosperity, but also by peaceful popular uprisings and the institutional setup of authoritarian regimes. In the short-run, however, elite actors may play a key role, particularly through the importance of intra-regime splits. Jan Teorell argues that these results have important repercussions both for current theories of democratization and for the international community's effort in developing policies for democracy promotion.

JAN TEORELL is Associate Professor of Political Science at Lund University. His most recent publications have appeared in *Studies in Comparative International Development*, *European Journal of Political Research*, *Journal of Democracy*, *Governance*, and *Political Research Quarterly*.

Determinants of Democratization

Explaining Regime Change in the World, 1972–2006

JAN TEORELL

CAMBRIDGE
UNIVERSITY PRESS

University Printing House, Cambridge CB2 8BS, United Kingdom

Cambridge University Press is part of the University of Cambridge.

It furthers the University's mission by disseminating knowledge in the pursuit of education, learning and research at the highest international levels of excellence.

www.cambridge.org
Information on this title: www.cambridge.org/9780521139687

First published 2010
5th printing 2014

A catalogue record for this publication is available from the British Library

ISBN 978-0-521-19906-3 Hardback
ISBN 978-0-521-13968-7 Paperback

For Lina

Contents

List of tables

List of figures

Acknowledgments

Although the usual disclaimer of course applies (that all remaining shortcomings are my own responsibility), this book owes several intellectual debts to various persons and institutions. My first and most serious debt is to Axel Hadenius, with whom I started out on this journey, and who also raised the initial research grants that made it possible. Axel's previous work on democratization (as published in his Cambridge University Press book from 1992) was also an early inspiration for my work, but even more important have been our intellectual conversations on these topics throughout the years (including the publication of Teorell and Hadenius [2007], which is a previous version of the large-*n* approach adopted here). Early versions of different parts of the book were presented at a working conference in Uppsala in 2004, in Istanbul 2005 and in Lund 2006; at research seminars in Gothenburg and Lund in 2004; and at the annual meetings of APSA in Chicago 2004, in Washington in 2005 and in Philadelphia in 2006. I owe gratitude to several persons for helpful comments at these and other occasions, most notably Jason Brownlee, Valery Bunce, Barbara Geddes, Staffan Lindberg, Karen Remmer, Alfred Stepan, Kaare Strøm and Nicolas van de Walle. Jens Bartelson and Bo Rothstein contributed greatly to the introductory chapter, and two anonymous reviewers for Cambridge University Press provided insightful criticism and encouragement at the latest stage of the work. I finally owe thanks to Emilie Anér and Michael Wahman for excellent research assistance, and to the Swedish Research Council, the Bank of Sweden Tercentenary Foundation and the Quality of Government Institute in Gothenburg for funding. I dedicate this book to you, Lina, for making it all worth the while.

Introduction

Why do some countries become democracies and others not? Why do some countries remain more democratic whereas others slide back toward authoritarianism? Are social, economic or international forces the key determinants of these processes? Are some types of authoritarian regimes more prone to democratize than others? Do actors influence democratization, or is that a structurally determined outcome? Do the same determinants affect democratization in the short-run as in the long-run? What lessons can be learned for international efforts at promoting democracy from comparative democratization studies?

In this book I address these questions by drawing on evidence from the extraordinary improvement in the realm of democracy the world has witnessed in the past 35 years or so. Starting in the Mediterranean area in 1974, Greece, Portugal and Spain overthrew longstanding dictatorships and installed popularly elected governments. After military juntas came down in Ecuador and Peru in the late 1970s, democracy profoundly swept the Latin American continent during the 1980s with the establishment of democracy in Bolivia, Argentina, Uruguay, Brazil and Chile. In Asia, the Philippine dictatorship of Ferdinand Marcos was toppled, followed by the inauguration of competitive multiparty elections in South Korea, Nepal and Bangladesh.

By this time, the disintegration of single-party rule in the former Soviet bloc was well under way. Starting in Poland, the incumbent one-party regime in February 1989 commenced round-table talks with the opposition movement, which led to elections in June where the Communists suffered a disastrous defeat. Meanwhile, in Hungary the Communist Party was formally dissolved and multiparty elections proclaimed. In the fall of that same year, massive anti-government rallies appeared all across Eastern Germany, eventually forcing the government to resign and the wall to come down. Czechoslovakia followed suit, and before the end of 1989 the Communist one-party system had been dismantled in Romania as well. Less than two years later, after a failed coup, the

Soviet Union dissolved into fifteen independent states, quite a few of which soon held competitive multiparty elections.

Meanwhile, in Africa south of the Sahara "the wind from the East" started "shaking the coconut trees," as noted by a local observer (cited in Kurzman 1998, p. 55). On the eve of the revolutionary year 1989, Frederick Chiluba, then Chairman of the Congress of Trade Unions in Zambia, proclaimed: "If the owners of socialism have withdrawn from the one-party system, who are the Africans to continue with it?" (cited in Bratton and van de Walle 1997, pp. 105–6). Only 10 months later, the one-party system in his country crumbled as Chiluba was elected president of Zambia in the first free and fair election for decades. Across the African continent, from South Africa and Namibia in the south to Benin, Mali, Guinea-Bissau in the west, including the island states Sao Tome and Principe, Cape Verde, and Madagascar, rows of dictatorships transited toward democracy in the following first years of the 1990s.

Toward the turn of the millennium, democracy made further significant inroads around the globe, such as in Croatia and Serbia in Europe, in Mexico, Ghana and Senegal in the South, and in Taiwan and Indonesia in the East. In this latest decade renewed hope for democracy arose in the wake of the 2002 elections in Kenya, the so-called "colored revolutions" in Ukraine, Georgia and Kyrgyzstan, and with the return of seemingly competitive elections in Lebanon in 2005.

This tidal change in the establishment of democratic practices around the globe has been referred to as the "third wave" of democratization (Huntington 1991), following the first and second waves culminating after World War I and II, respectively. Depicted in quantitative terms in Figure 0.1, the average level of democracy in the world has been steadily on the rise since the late 1970s, with a significant peak in the speed of change around 1990. Beneath the general trend of democratization, however, the third wave has also been marred by serious undercurrents pulling in the opposite direction. In Latin America democratic deterioration in the 1990s significantly struck longstanding democracies such as Colombia and Venezuela. Following a short opening after the breakup of the Soviet Union, democratic politics in the former republics eroded quickly in Belarus, and – although at a slower pace – in Russia. In Africa, a coup in 1994 ended decades of multiparty competition in Gambia, and backsliding into authoritarianism infected several other polities on the continent, including the Democratic Republic of Congo, Zambia and Zimbabwe. In some years, as the lower part of Figure 0.1

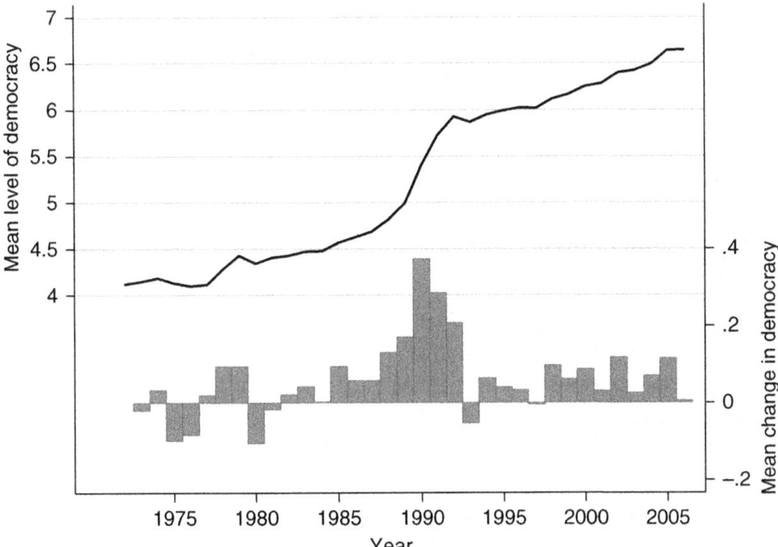

Figure 0.1 The Third Wave of Democratization
Note: The graph is based on the combined Freedom House and Polity measures of democracy (to be introduced in Chapter 1) on a global sample of 196 countries.

makes clear, this authoritarian undercurrent even outweighed the generally democratizing trend of the third wave. Within certain countries over time, such as in Haiti, Turkey, Thailand, Pakistan and Niger, swift changes toward and away from democracy have occurred repeatedly. Yet in other countries, most notably in the Middle East and in Northern Africa, authoritarian regimes have been left more or less untarnished by the global wave of democratization.

What forces drove these patterns of regime change and stability within countries across the globe? Were the same factors that drove democratization also responsible for hindering de-democratization? To what extent are the causes of democratization and de-democratization even intelligible?

Turning to the most prominent theories of democratization in the field, four distinct answers to these questions suggest themselves. Modernization theory (Lipset 1959) alleges that democratization in the last three decades is the upshot of a general trend toward furthered economic development, deepened industrialization and educational expansion. With knowledge on these structural parameters, movements toward and away from democracy should be fairly easy to predict. By the account of the so-called "transition paradigm" (Carothers 2002), in contrast, democracy has been brought about from above through the strategic skills, and at times sheer luck, of elite actors maneuvering under profound uncertainty (Rustow 1970; O'Donnell and Schmitter 1986). With idiosyncratic factors playing such a decisive role, our understanding of the general factors driving democratization is severely limited. If instead the "social forces" tradition (Bellin 2000) were to prove correct, democratization during the third wave has been triggered by mass mobilization from below, most notably by the working class (Rueschemeyer *et al.* 1992; Collier 1999). In accordance with the new economic approach to explaining democratization, however, democratic institutions have been granted by the rich as a concession to the poor. This should have been made possible through weakened fear of redistribution resulting from eroding economic inequality (Boix 2003; Acemoglu and Robinson 2006).

In this book I shall argue that while each of these approaches to explaining democratization during the third wave contains a grain of truth, they are nonetheless incomplete and in many respects simply at fault. These novel findings have been reached by a combination of an improved large-*n* study design and a more systematic employment of in-depth case studies. Starting with the former, using a combination of two predominant democracy indices I intend to explain variations in democracy over time across 165 countries over the period 1972–2006. These analyses break new ground on several accounts. First, in terms of the range of explanatory variables entered, I outperform most, if not all, earlier studies in the field. Second, I present some novel findings pertaining to factors hitherto untested on a global scale. These particularly concern the democratizing effects of mass protest, a posited determinant which has so far attracted limited attention in large-*n* studies. Third, I will test whether there is variation in how determinants affect movements in different directions along the graded democracy scale. In other words, I endeavor to separate the effects on movements toward as well as reversals away from democracy. Fourth, I systematically explore the effects as well as the overall predictive performance of these determinants in both the short-run and long-run perspective. To the best of my knowledge, the third and fourth endeavors have never before been thoroughly undertaken. Fifth, and finally, I systematically assess intermediary links in the hypothesized chain of causation connecting each determinant to democratization.

The second methodological innovation of this book is the way it combines statistical with case study evidence. From Bolivia, Argentina, Uruguay and Peru in Latin America, the Philippines and Nepal in Asia, Hungary in the post-communist region, Turkey in the Middle East, and South Africa on the African mainland, I draw on first-hand scholarly knowledge on processes of democratization from all corners of the globe. These cases are carefully selected for being instances where particular determinants impacted on democratization, which makes them especially suitable for explorations of the causal mechanisms at work.

Factors driving and not driving the third wave

Drawing on this comprehensive research design, I make several new findings in this study. The predominant approach to testing modernization theory has become the use of simple proxies such as energy consumption or national income. I instead revive the tradition initiated by Seymour Martin Lipset (1959) according to which socioeconomic modernization is a broad, coherent syndrome underlying several societal processes, such as industrialization, education, urbanization and the spread of communications technology. Applying this broader measure, I evidence a robust effect which, contrary to recent claims (Acemoglu *et al.* 2005; 2007; 2008), even applies within countries over time. However, modernization affects regime outcomes by hindering authoritarian reversals rather than promoting transitions toward democracy. If democracy is a ladder, modernization does not help countries scale upwards; it helps them avoid falling downwards. By and large, I thus confirm the argument by Adam Przeworski *et al.* (2000), although I base my finding on a graded measure of democracy and use a larger set of controls.

Moreover, I find that the most effective component of the syndrome of modernization is not education, as some would have it (Glaeser *et al.* 2007), nor is it industrialization, as others would claim (Boix 2003; Acemoglu and Robinson 2006). Somewhat surprisingly, the strongest bite in modernization's assemblage is exerted by media proliferation. As radios, TVs and newspapers spread in the population, anti-democratic coups are either deferred or aborted. This is probably one of the most undertheorized facets of the modernization syndrome. On my interpretation, however, media proliferation as the most prominent mechanism behind the modernization effect helps explain its asymmetric nature. As opposed to increased national income, industrialization or educational expansion, the democracy-promoting effects of the media cannot materialize under authoritarian conditions. More specifically, for the media to work as a safeguard of democracy, some freedom of the press has to be established. What this implies is that the effect of media proliferation on democratization increases with the level of democracy already achieved. For this reason, widespread access to media outlets defers backsliding from these achieved levels rather than triggering movement toward more democracy.

Whereas societal modernization accompanying long-term economic development thus helps sustain democracy, the effect of short-term growth on the prospects for democratization is exactly the opposite. Economic upturns help sustain autocracies, whereas economic crises trigger transitions toward democracy. As evidenced from case studies in Latin America and the Philippines (Haggard and Kaufman 1995), deteriorating economic performance, and the austere policy measures it provokes, undercut the power bases of authoritarian regimes. It drives a wedge between the regime and economic elites, encouraging the latter to withdraw from the authoritarian bargain, and between hardliners and softliners within the regime elite itself, eventually subverting its hold on power.

Deteriorating economic conditions also help fuel the mobilization of mass protest against the regime. Despite numerous assertions from area specialists of the import of popular mobilization for understanding transitions to democracy (Bratton and van de Walle 1997; McFaul 2002; Bunce 2003), no systematic study has hitherto tested its impact on a global scale. I document a significant influence – but, critically, not from all forms of mass protest. Only peaceful demonstrations are effective in promoting democratization, whereas the use of violent means such as rioting or even armed rebellion proves largely ineffectual. Inquiring more closely into the unarmed resistance movements toppling authoritarian regimes in the Philippines, South Africa and Nepal reveals why this is the case (Schock 2005). Violent opposition is usually a strategy reserved for marginalized groups that helps autocracies close the lines and legitimize its use of repression, making it more successful in quelling the resistance. Peaceful protest, by contrast, may arouse larger segments of the population. When the regime chooses to confront protest through the barrel of a gun, moreover, moral outrage spurs further counter-regime mobilization, both domestically and internationally. A successful popular challenge eventually disrupts the material and other support bases of the regime. Intra-elite divisions are thereby exacerbated, preparing the scene for a democratic takeover.

I find that democratization is rooted in economic and social conditions not only within the boundaries of the nation state, but also within the international system. As the "wave" metaphor itself would suggest, there is evidence of democratic diffusion effects. Authoritarian regimes during the third wave behaved like falling dominoes (Starr 1991), in that the fall of one affected the likelihood that among neighboring countries others would fall. This pattern holds despite the fact that I control for a significantly greater number of possible common background factors than do the latest contributions to this field of inquiry (Brinks and Coppedge 2006; Gleditsch and Ward 2006). In other words, it appears that authoritarian dominoes influenced each other's fall, not simply because some simultaneous process "shook the table" on which they were standing.

Disentangling the mechanisms responsible for neighbor diffusion is, however, a thornier issue, and more case study work on its operation on the ground is called for. The same applies for Jon Pevehouse's (2005) claim that regional organizations may promote democratization among their member states. I find support for this in my large-*n* study, and by tracking the influence of, primarily, the Council of Europe in Turkey, and the Organization of American States in Peru, I find that regional organizations may encourage democratization by pressurizing authoritarian regimes. But the evidence in other cases is weaker, again drawing attention to the fact that international explanations for democratization seem to rest on less robust foundations.

I also challenge several predominant theoretical perspectives on democratization by showing that their pet explanatory factors do not work as expected. Despite widely held beliefs to the contrary (e.g., Bernard *et al.* 2004), I find colonialism to have no systematic effects, either as a phenomenon in its own right, or in the form of distinct experiences depending on colonial origin. My argument is thus supportive of the alternative claim that the importance of colonialism in the history of the developing world may have been exaggerated (Herbst 2000). Moreover, despite having access to the largest dataset on income disparities hitherto assembled, my findings do not substantiate the core assumption of recent economic theories of democratization (Boix 2003; Acemoglu and Robinson 2006). That is, democratization during the third wave did not ensue from increased economic equality. My data also belies cherished assumptions about the nature and consequences of identity politics (Rabushka and Shepsle 1972; Horowitz 1985). Heterogeneous populations did not hurt democracy during the third wave.

Having a predominantly Muslim population, or being dependent on foreign trade, are both factors that appear to impede democratization. However, neither can be easily explained. Although I find that the Muslim gap in democracy is mostly an "Arab" gap (Stepan and Robertson 2003; 2004), separating the Middle East and North Africa from the rest of the world, this gap cannot be explained in terms of superior economic performance in this region, nor is it due to oil wealth or, as Fish (2002) suggests, to female subordination. Even more importantly, since individual Muslims in various parts of the world express democratic sentiments no weaker than those of people belonging to other religious denominations, the cultural interpretation of the Muslim gap rests on shaky micro-foundations. Finally, the fact that countries relatively independent of trade have been more likely to democratize would at first sight seem to support classical "dependency theory" (Bollen 1983). I show, however, that a core assumption in this theory is faulty. Countries whose trading patterns are heavily geared toward the capitalist core of the world system, such as toward the US and Europe, were *not* less likely to democratize during the third wave.

Institutions under authoritarianism

For a long time a dubious assumption haunted most prevalent theories of democratization: the notion that all authoritarian regimes face similar constraints on and opportunities for democratization. Much as democracies vary among themselves in terms of the institutions that structure their mode of operation, different dictatorships have different institutional setups. Some dictators are crowned; others wear a uniform. Some organize a ruling party and stage single-party elections; others maintain a façade of controlled multiparty competition. While a new literature has recently emerged on how to classify autocracies, as well as the "hybrid" regimes located in the gray zone between democracy and autocracy (Geddes 1999; 2003; Diamond 2002; Levitsky and

Way 2002; Schedler 2002b; 2006), no systematic attempts have been made to assess whether distinguishing among types of authoritarian regimes really pays any dividends for the understanding of democratization.

Relying on the improved classification of authoritarian regime types in Hadenius and Teorell (2007), I undertake such an assessment. I find that military dictatorships, according to expectations (Geddes 1999; 2003), are more prone to democratize than single-party regimes. Most importantly, however, I develop and test a theory of when and why non-democratic regimes that still allow multiparty elections – termed multiparty autocracies – are more prone to democratize than other species of the authoritarian brand. This theory moves beyond established deductive models of authoritarian regime types (Wintrobe 1998; Geddes 1999; 2003; Bueno de Mesquita *et al.* 2003), which do not even make the distinction between single- and multiparty autocracies.

My theory starts from the assumption that competition in multiparty autocracies is a dual battle, where the incumbent elites and the opposition simultaneously compete for votes in the electoral arena and struggle over the very rules that shape this arena (Schedler 2002a). Either through efforts to reform the electoral system, which is often rigged in the incumbent party's favor, or by struggling to establish independent institutions for impartial electoral governance and resolution of post-election disputes, the opposition attempts to pull the electoral contest toward greater uncertainty. The incumbent party, which loathes uncertainty, struggles to resist such reforms. The end result could be change in either the opposition's or the regime's favored direction, making autocratic multiparty competition an inherently unstable equilibrium.

The logic of these unstable dynamics, however, tends to push multiparty autocracies in the direction of democratization. To begin with, the incidence of elections in which not only the ruling party participates creates an arena unavailable under other institutional conditions in which rival party factions can voice grievances. Multiparty elections, however controlled, rigged and unfair they may be, thus fuel intra-regime divisions, a condition favorable to democratization. Moreover, these divisions may improve the incentives for what may be divided opposition parties to join forces and challenge the ruling party under a unified banner – an additional condition favorable to democratization. These two processes – divisions within the incumbent regime and unification of the opposition forces – reinforce one another.

These dynamics are of course not set in motion by sheer necessity. They are more likely to be triggered when the multiparty autocracy faces exogenous shocks, be they domestic or international. An economic downturn, for example, drains the resources available to the regime to secure electoral support. As the chances of winning electoral contests on the opposition's ticket thus increases, intra-elite divisions are exacerbated. The challenge of popular mobilization triggers similar dynamics, again by driving the wedge deeper between the softer and sturdier elements of incumbent elites, and also by questioning the viability of the regime in the eyes of potential supporters of the opposition. My theory thus not only furnishes an account of how electoral authoritarianism differs from other ways of institutionalizing autocracy. It also specifies the circumstances under which multiparty autocracies are more likely to democratize.

In an unprecedented test of these expectations, I show on the basis of a global sample of countries that multiparty autocracies are by themselves more prone to democratize than other authoritarian regime types, even when all other putative determinants of democratization are held constant. Moreover, multiparty autocracies are significantly more likely to democratize as a response to exogenous shocks such as economic downturns, popular mobilization and even foreign interventions.

Theoretical implications

How far, then, can these determinants take us in terms of explaining democratization? When the entire range of putative determinants is taken into account, my statistical models at best explain some 10 percent of the yearly change in democracy during the third wave. This means, for example, that by knowing the geographical size, the religious denominations and diversity of a country in a given year, by knowing its economic performance, its level of popular mobilization, trading patterns and international environment in terms of neighbor diffusion and membership in regional organizations, the incidence of democratization in this country over the coming year would still be a more or less unpredictable event. In other words, structural theories are not very successful at explaining short-term democratization.

With a longer time horizon applied, however, this situation radically changes. If we think of these same structural conditions as determining a long-run equilibrium level of democracy, to which countries would gravitate in the absence of short-term perturbations, their explanatory performance is improved considerably. By knowing the point of departure and structural prerequisites of countries at the beginning of the third wave, for example, my models explain some 40 percent of the variation in their level of democracy at the end of this period. This of course still rules out any claims for determinism. Even over the long haul, some countries deviate far from their structurally predicted long-run equilibrium levels of democracy. There is thus considerable room left for non-structural, country-specific and even chance factors to affect the long-run dynamics of democratization. As compared to explanatory performance on a yearly basis, however, structures explain a whole lot more over the longer time horizon.

Returning to the stylized versions of the four most prominent theories of democratization, I may thus first conclude that processes of socio-economic modernization played a role during the third wave, but not in the way originally conceived by Lipset (1959). Rather than pushing countries toward democracy, modernization – mostly in the form of media proliferation – hindered them from sliding back toward autocracy. At the same time, the broader structural approach originating from Lipset's seminal work (1959) is fairly successful at explaining the degree of democracy reached in a country over the long haul. This success is not only due to domestic or economic determinants, but to an equal extent to international factors such as democratization among neighboring countries and pressure from democratic regional organizations. The future challenge for structural theories will be to more clearly furnish their predictions with accounts of the causal mechanisms at work, and to improve their ability to forecast eruptive regime change.

The strategic approach heralded by Guillermo O'Donnell and Philippe Schmitter (1986), by contrast, is quite on target in predicting the unpredictability of short-term change. Uncertainty surrounds the transitional moment, even when a vast range of underlying structural forces are taken into consideration. The structure- and actor-centric approaches to explaining democratization may thus be made compatible by applying different time horizons. In addition, my case study evidence repeatedly underscores the short-term importance of divisions within the authoritarian regimes for understanding democratization, as originally predicted by O'Donnell and Schmitter (1986, p. 19). Nevertheless, the theoretical clout of the strategic approach has suffered from an excessive focus on explanatory factors too proximate to the outcome, and a lack of understanding of the conditions under which different elite actors appear, and what determines their interests.

Moreover, the drama of democratization is not simply driven by elite actors. The social forces tradition is right in stressing a key influence by the general public as it successfully mobilizes against the regime. Democratization not only occurs from above; it also critically hinges on popular mobilization from below. By contrasting episodes of popular protest in Asia and Africa during the third wave with the European and Latin American experience, however, I cast serious doubt on the assertion that these uprisings were driven by opposing social classes (Rueschemeyer *et al.* 1992; Collier 1999). People taking to the streets in Asia, in Eastern Europe and across most of the African continent were a loose blend of actors from various spheres of society, not distinguishable in terms of a specific social class. The critical feature of these popular insurgencies was not their social origin, but their use of nonviolent tactics. This failure to recognize the mode of mobilization, and why it matters, as the key to explaining democratization is a serious flaw in the social forces tradition.

I thus argue that a successful future theory of democratization needs to incorporate elements from all these three approaches: structural conditions, strategic interaction among elite actors, and popular mobilization from below. The key virtue of the fourth, economic approach is exactly the integration of these elements into a coherent theoretical model. Structural conditions affect the regime preferences of the general public, whose action (or threat of action) is responded to (or anticipated by) elites in office making decisions on regime change (Boix 2003; Acemoglu and Robinson 2006). The predictions from Carles Boix's (2003) model in particular, which also includes a critical element of information uncertainty, are well in line with a number of my empirical findings. This supportive evidence includes the impact of popular mobilization, the fact that smaller countries seem to have been more likely to democratize during the third wave, that economies free from state incursion were more likely to sustain democracy, and my support for Michael Ross' (2001) much-cited notion that natural resource abundance in terms of oil hinders democracy.

Nevertheless, the economic approach appears too preoccupied with conflicts over income distribution. As already mentioned, its core prediction – that decreasing income inequality triggers democratization – is not borne out in my data. Moreover, these economic models have hitherto failed to take the nature of authoritarian institutions into account. Moving away from the obsession with redistributive politics and toward a focus on the various "authoritarian bargains" (Haggard and Kaufman 1995) or "dependency relations" (Schock 2005) that structure the workings of different types of autocracies thus ought to be the preferred strategy for future modeling attempts in this tradition.

Policy implications

Although the direct purpose of this book is not to issue policy recommendations, some implications for policy do follow from my results. To begin with, the structural indeterminacy of democratization in the short-run affords domestic actors considerable room for maneuver. This implies that foreign assistance with democracy promotion, targeted at domestic pro-democracy forces, may pay dividends (Finkel *et al.* 2007).

More specifically, democracy promoters must develop a two-pronged strategy, sensitizing their reforms to the democratic context of the various recipients of assistance. In countries that have already made some progress toward democratization, these reforms may be safeguarded by widening media access through the spread of radio, TV and newspapers among the population. When censorship has lifted and some freedom of the press has been attained, this works as an antidote to anti-democratic coups d'état. In more authoritarian settings, by contrast, efforts to mobilize non-violent popular insurgencies against the incumbent regime should be promoted. This strategy will prove particularly rewarding where there are intra-regime splits between hardliners and softliners to exploit, and when mobilizing tactics can be found that damage the material and other support bases of the regime. Economic sanctions or violent military intervention have dubious consequences for democratization. However, it is worthwhile supporting multiparty elections, even when these elections may fall short of international standards for freedom and fairness. When an authoritarian regime has begun to pursue the path of multiparty competition, the odds are more often than not stacked in the opposition's favor. In addition, the regime becomes more vulnerable and more likely to respond by democratizing when facing exogenous shocks such as economic crises or peaceful popular mobilization.

According to my findings, however, promoting economic development under authoritarian regimes would not be an advisable strategy for fostering democracy. To begin with, democratization is spurred on by short-term economic crises, not growth. Secondly, long-term development does not affect the prospects for democratization, but the chances of sustaining democratic reforms that have already been enacted. This suggests a possible trade-off, at least in the short-run, between the foreign policy goals of promoting development and fighting poverty on the one hand, and that of promoting democracy on the other.

Plan of the book

The book is organized as follows. In Chapter 1, I review the four predominant theoretical approaches to explaining democratization. Given a set of ideal standards, I show that no such thing as a perfect theory of democratization exists. Furthermore, the three predominant strategies for testing these theories – based on statistics, historical-comparative or single-case studies – have not been successful on their own. The stance taken in this book, based on theoretical eclecticism and a combination of methodological approaches, follows from these observations.

In Chapters 2–6 I then concentrate on one group of explanatory factors in each, drawing both on large-*n* analyses and, where applicable, case study evidence. In Chapter 2 I review the literature and evidence with respect to how historical legacies, such as colonial origin, religious denomination, social diversity and country size, may shape the fate of democracy. Here I find that small countries were more likely to democratize during the third wave, and that a large proportion of Muslims in the population impeded democratization, but I am not able to uncover any explanatory mechanisms for these findings.

Chapter 3 is devoted to economic determinants, including socioeconomic modernization, abundance of natural resources, and economic performance, inequality and freedom. I find that freedom from state incursion in the economy and socioeconomic modernization hinders reversals toward authoritarianism, and that the socioeconomic mechanism works through the importance of media proliferation in deterring or derailing coups. Moreover, I find that oil dependence hinders democracy, whereas economic crises trigger democratization. I then trace the democratizing mechanisms resulting from economic crisis in the cases of the Philippines, Bolivia, Argentina and Uruguay.

In Chapter 4 I turn to the international determinants of democratization, and find that trade dependence hinders, whereas neighbor diffusion and membership in international organizations that attract members from particular world regions foster democratization. Neither of these international determinants, however, is supported by clearly designated causal mechanisms. Not even the case study evidence explaining the importance of membership in democratic regional organizations in Turkey, Hungary and Peru is unambiguous. International capital flows do not have any significant impact, whereas the consequences of foreign intervention are varied.

Chapter 5 moves the analytical focus from the international scene to the forces that bring about democracy from below. I find that peaceful demonstrations trigger democratization, whereas strikes, violent riots and domestic armed conflict do not. The explanatory mechanisms responsible for the impact of peaceful demonstrations are then traced through case study evidence from the Philippines, South Africa and Nepal.

Chapter 6 then addresses the question of whether the prospects for democratization differ among different types of authoritarian regimes. I first derive a set of hypotheses on the propensity of one-party, military, monarchical and multiparty autocracies to democratize, both in and of themselves and as a response to exogenous shocks. I then test these expectations, with the exogenous shocks operationalized as popular mobilization, economic performance and foreign intervention (either military intervention or economic sanctions), again using my global estimation sample of countries during the third wave of democratization.

In the concluding Chapter 7, I summarize my findings and evaluate the combined explanatory performance of all determinants taken together, in the short- and long-run perspective. I end by discussing the implications of my findings: for theory, for the future study of democratization, for strategies of democracy promotion, and for the real world of democratization itself.

1 *Explaining democratization*

Ideally, an explanatory theory of democratization should fulfill several criteria.[1] It should be sufficiently general to encompass the regularities in patterns of regime change across both time and space, but without sacrificing concreteness and the ability to account for complex causal mechanisms at work in singular instances. It should transcend the structure and agency divide by specifying how and when structural constraints affect the desires and beliefs of social actors, while at the same time providing some logic for understanding why these actors make decisions the way they do, and how the interaction of these decisions produces an outcome in terms of regime change. This ideal theory should be capable of explaining both short-term and long-term dynamics in regime trajectories over time, and both why autocracies turn into democracies and why some democracies become autocracies again. It should be probabilistic by nature, and thus leave the possibility of perfectly determined outcomes as a limiting case under extreme circumstances rather than as an inherent quality of the theory itself. It should be integrated and internally consistent: if consisting of more than one explanatory factor (which seems likely), these should not be mutually contradictory. Finally, this theory should be empirically corroborated, that is, it should be supported by as broad a body of empirical evidence as possible.

Perhaps not very surprisingly, all theories of democratization to date fall short of these standards. Social scientists have employed various theoretical and methodological approaches in order to explain democratization. The territory has been charted by sociologists, political scientists and economists alike, drawing on in-depth case study knowledge, comparative-historical analysis and statistics. Most work has

[1] On ideal criteria for explanatory theories in general, see King *et al.* (1994, pp. 99–114), and Gerring (2001, chap. 5); on such criteria in the case of explaining democratization, see Coppedge, forthcoming, chap. 3.

been based on informal theory, largely developed inductively, but more recently formal, game-theoretic and deductive approaches have come to the fore. Beneath these conspicuous differences, however, one may discern three intellectual traditions that have forged the landscape of democratization studies. These are the structural and strategic approaches and the social forces tradition. To this we must now also add the more recent economic approach to explaining democratization. In this chapter I shall review these four approaches in turn, assessing their respective theoretical strengths and weaknesses. Equipped with these insights, I conclude by defending the particular approach to explaining democratization that will be adopted in this book.

The structural approach

Undoubtedly one of the most well-known propositions in comparative politics is Lipset's (1959) claim that countries having undergone a more extensive process of societal modernization are more likely to be democratic. Partly drawing on Daniel Lerner (1958), Lipset sustained the idea that countries tend to undergo a large number of more or less parallel and simultaneous processes, most notably industrialization, urbanization, increasing levels of education, rising national income and a continued spread of communications technologies – all of which may be viewed as different aspects of modernization. Democracy, then, is but the tip of an iceberg composed of these larger processes at work in society.

Lipset's hypothesis posits what is still one of the most well-established, and yet – probably for that very reason – most controversial relationships within studies of comparative democratization (see, e.g., Przeworski *et al.* 2000; Boix and Stokes 2003; Epstein *et al.* 2006). But Lipset's work is also paradigmatic in the way it has inspired an outburst of structural accounts of what explains democratization. The last decades have seen tremendous growth in the number of structural factors added to the list of democracy's hypothesized determinants. Pertaining to aspects of the domestic economy other than modernization, these include state involvement in the economy (Brunk *et al.* 1987; Burkhart 2000), income inequality (Muller 1988; Burkhart 1997), economic crises (Gasiorowski 1995; Bernard *et al.* 2001; 2003), and natural resource abundance (Ross 2001; Dunning 2008). Conjectured non-economic but still domestic structural influences on democratization include country size (Dahl and

Tufte 1973), religious composition (Lipset 1994), societal fractionalization (Dahl 1971; Rabushka and Shepsle 1972; Horowitz 1985), colonial heritage (Bernard *et al.* 2004), social capital (Paxton 2002), and mass political culture (Inglehart 1997; Inglehart and Welzel 2005). There are also structural accounts that suggest various international determinants of democratization, including economic dependency (Bollen 1983) – nowadays rephrased in terms of globalization (Li and Reuveny 2003; 2009; Rudra 2005) – democratic diffusion (Starr 1991; Brinks and Coppedge 2006) and regional organizations (Pevehouse 2005).

What distinguishes these theories is that they locate the most significant triggers of democratic advancement in social or economic structure, that is, beyond the immediate reach of human agents. In many instances there are not even any actors or agents specified within these explanatory models. The causal process conveyed is largely mechanical: a structural shift occurs in the "environment" that precipitates change in the political regime. True, this mechanical view rarely, if ever, reflects an ontological position. Most theorists within this camp – definitely including Lipset himself – would agree that only through the behavior of individual and collective actors could the process of regime change actually occur. But in terms of the explanatory properties they specify in their theories, the role of human agency is "black boxed." The distinguishing features of structural theories of democratization, then, are (a) that structural factors are given causal primacy, and (b) that questions on how, why and which social actors are motivated to produce specific regime outcomes are left underspecified.

Much the same could be argued about studies on the institutional determinants of democracy. These include a renewed interest for some of the classic debates in how varying constitutional frameworks, such as forms of government and electoral systems, may affect democratic stability (Gasiorowski and Power 1998; 1998; Bernard *et al.* 2001; Cheibub 2007; Norris 2008). As of late there has also been a growing interest in how different authoritarian institutions may affect the prospects for democratization (Bratton and van de Walle 1997; Snyder and Mahoney 1999; Hadenius and Teorell 2007; Magaloni 2008; Brownlee 2009). Although institutional explanations by and large are more sensitive to problems of agency (in particular, see Geddes 1999; 2003), they still bear a strong resemblance to the structural theories of democratization by locating causal primacy in institutional conditions exogenous to human agency.

The structural approach to explaining democratization contains both strengths and weaknesses. On the positive side, most structural theories are highly general and, as a result, have been subject to extensive empirical testing, mostly from within the probabilistic worldview of statistics. On the downside, however, the palette of suggested structural determinants of democratization has grown out of proportion and is in great need of theoretical synthesis and integration. The black-boxing of causal mechanisms also means that most structural theories of democratization lack micro-foundations. In Samuel Huntington's (1991, p. 107) famous words, the structural approach is thus in great need of moving from "causes" to "causers" of democratization.

The strategic approach

In a widely cited article Dankwart Rustow (1970, p. 340) criticized Lipset and the wider structural literature on democratization for neglecting the "genetic question of how a democracy comes into being." To address this neglect Rustow furnished a process model of democratization, highlighting certain "phases" – the preparatory, decision and habituation phases – through which all countries pass on their way from authoritarian to democratic rule. It would take another 26 years, with the publication of O'Donnell and Schmitter (1986), before Rustow's model (1970) would reappear in a form that literally transformed the study of comparative democratization. The key components of this emerging "transition paradigm" (Carothers 2002) were, however, already present in his original contribution. Most notably, these include the idea of democratization as a process occurring according to a certain sequence of "phases," the notion that (almost) no structural prerequisites exist for the initiation of this process, and the key part played by agency and strategic decision making, particularly among political elites.

In O'Donnell and Schmitter's (1986) terminology, which is now the most well known, Rustow's (1970) "preparatory" phase is called liberalization, the "decision" phase is democratization, and the "habituation" phase is consolidation.[2] The installation of a democratic regime is

[2] Although O'Donnell and Schmitter (1986, pp. 11–13) originally termed this third phase "socialization," they also used the word "consolidation" at various places in their book, and this was the term that stuck (see, e.g., Schedler 1998).

again largely explained through a process of elite interaction. The actors involved, drawing a highly influential distinction, are primarily the "hardliners" and the "softliners" of the incumbent regime, although the opposition is also to some extent taken into account. The result of these elite interactions is conditioned to a high degree by the bargaining skill of the actors involved. In addition a number of random conditions and unexpected events have the potential to determine the outcome. Although O'Donnell and Schmitter (1986, pp. 4–5) acknowledged the possibility that long-run trajectories of regime change were shaped by structural forces, they stressed the indeterminacy of the short-term dynamics. Whereas both *virtú* and *fortuna* played an influential part of their theory, they thus gave short shrift to Machiavelli's third determinant of events: *necessità*.

Similar to Rustow, O'Donnell and Schmitter (1986) discerned one common denominator of all democratization processes (although a different one): "that there is no transition whose beginning is not the consequence – direct or indirect – of important divisions within the authoritarian regime itself." In other words, no transition to democracy could be forced solely by an opposition facing a cohesive, undivided authoritarian regime (1986, pp. 19–21). Democracy, in other words, is installed through an elite-driven process from above, with other segments of society playing at most an "ephemeral" role (1986, p. 55). In essence, this means that the process of transition itself determines its outcome. Apart from this proposition, the most widely held generalization from the transitions project is that there is no generalization about the "prerequisites" of democratization (see, e.g., Karl 1990; Karl and Schmitter 1991; Shin 1994). Democracy may crop up under extremely varying historical, institutional and structural conditions.[3]

The strategic approach to explaining democratization has had an enormous impact, both within and outside the scholarly community. Bringing actors and agency to the analytical fore was a substantial contribution at a point in time when the structural approach was perceived as presenting a deterministic stranglehold on the prospects for democratization, not least for real-life pro-democratic forces in

[3] Considering the centrality of elite actors and strategic decision making in this approach to explaining democratization, it is no surprise that some of its insights have been amenable to game-theoretic interpretations (Przeworski 1991; Gates and Humes 1997, chap. 5; Weingast 1997; Crescenzi 1999; Swaminathan 1999; Colomer 2000; Sutter 2000).

countries under authoritarian rule (see Przeworski 1991, pp. 97–98). The work of Juan Linz (1978) and others has shown that the opposite process of democratic breakdown is also amenable to similarly voluntaristic theorizing (Cohen 1994; Alexander 2002). Moreover, the generalization that democratic transitions always originate from above through a split in the authoritarian regime is still high on the research agenda (Geddes 1999; Bratton and van de Walle 1997; McFaul 2002). Even the "no prerequisites" proposition has received empirical support in a large-scale statistical analysis showing that whereas the survival of democracy appears to be largely affected by structural forces, transitions from autocracy to democracy occur almost haphazardly (Przeworski *et al.* 2000) – although that finding is contested (Boix and Stokes 2003; Epstein *et al.* 2006).

Nevertheless, the strategic approach suffers from several theoretical shortcomings. It concentrates on the short-term calculations of a narrow set of actors during a condensed period of time. The approach almost by definition thereby excludes the possibility of long-term forces shaping the outcome. In addition, it has never adequately addressed the question of what it is that conditions the presence of certain sets of actors in certain circumstances, and what determines their preferences, interests and beliefs.[4] For this reason, the explanatory factors that enter the strategic model are usually very proximate to the outcome they should explain. Explaining democratization with reference to characteristics of the process leading to that outcome borders on tautology.[5]

[4] Notable attempts to overcome this voluntaristic bias include Snyder (1998) and Brownlee (2002).

[5] A clear example of these shortcomings comes from a comparative study of regime outcomes in no fewer than twenty-four transition processes across the globe between 1973 and 1990 (Casper and Taylor 1996). Despite an unusually sophisticated research design compared to other work within the strategic tradition, the nature of the strategic approach severely affects the quality of Gretchen Casper and Michelle Taylor's conclusions. One of their main "findings," for example, is that when incumbents acquiesce to the democratic demands of the mass public, the probability of a successful transition to democracy increases. But this conclusion is simply a way of answering the question of what explains democratization by posing a new one: what explains why incumbents sometimes acquiesce to popular demands, and sometimes not? Casper and Taylor's (1996) analysis clearly shows how little explanatory leverage is gained by moving the explanatory factors too close to the outcome that is to be explained. This demonstrates that the basic flaw in the strategic approach is theoretical and cannot be solved through a more elaborate research design (*cf.* Kitschelt 1992, p. 1,028; Rueschemeyer *et al.* 1992, pp. 32–33).

The social forces tradition

Alongside the structural and strategic approaches another vibrant tradition has evolved that instead seeks the origins of democratic rule in the characteristics of and relationships among social classes in society. As with the former approaches, its roots can be traced back to one seminal contribution, this time by Barrington Moore (1966). Moore's main concern was the role of the landed upper classes and the peasantry in explaining why the transformation from agrarian to industrial societies ended in democracy in some countries and in left-wing or right-wing dictatorships in others. Ironically, however, Moore's fame has not primarily been based on his analysis of these two social classes, but on his remarks on another more peripheral, collective actor in his book: the middle class. Moore's dictum "No bourgeois, no democracy" (1966, p. 418) is still among the most widely cited phrases within the entire literature on democratization.

Although empirically challenged,[6] Moore's way of theorizing the societal conditions that bring democracy about has attracted many followers. Key to this approach is a focus on class-based definitions of collective actors, primarily driven by material interests. These collective actors are thus "most likely to champion democracy when their economic interests put them at odds with the authoritarian state" (Bellin 2000, p. 177). Democracy is conceived of as forged from below, through a power struggle among social forces with competing economic interests. While this approach is actor-centric, in sharp contrast to the structural approach, it paradoxically lacks a theory of agency. Psychological perception or calculation is never an integral part of its explanatory scheme, which of course makes it quite distinct from the strategic approach.

All of these ingredients are clearly present in the most renowned contribution to this tradition after Moore: the book by Dietrich Rueschemeyer *et al.* (1992). Foreshadowed by the insightful observations of Göran Therborn (1977), Rueschemeyer *et al.* argue that the working rather than the middle class, or bourgeoisie, is the foremost champion of democracy. On the other extreme stands the landlord, who – following

[6] For an excellent review of the mixed and conditional support received by the Moore thesis in later comparative-historical work, see Mahoney (2003). Two important contributions that in various ways complement and refine Moore's approach and findings are Luebbert (1991) and Downing (1992).

the logic of Moore – resists democracy by any means. The bourgeoisie in Rueschemeyer *et al.*'s account takes a more ambiguous stance toward democracy. With this set of class actors in place, and their stance toward democracy defined, the approach to explaining democratization becomes a model of "relative class power." What largely explains the rise and survival of democracy is conjectured to be a set of twin factors: the strengthening in size and density of the organization of the working class, and the weakening in size and power of the large landowners. According to Rueschemeyer *et al.* (1992), this pattern also explains the correlations between indicators of socioeconomic development and democracy unraveled by the modernization school (1992, in particular pp. 46–61).

Incorporating actors into the structural approach, tying the strength of these actors to structural conditions, and including some general assumptions on the interests that motivate these actors, are probably the main achievements of the social forces tradition. These notwithstanding, there are several blind spots or other weaknesses in need of elaboration. First, this theoretical approach still awaits testing based on systematic evidence collected through both space and time. Its empirical foundations are hitherto dominated by case studies, and primarily from Western Europe and Latin America. Second, this approach smacks of determinism. By tracing the roots of democratic development to the presence or absence of a more or less complex series of "conditions" – most notably the strength or weakness of this or that social class or class alliance – adherents of the social forces tradition come close to providing deterministic explanations of regime outcomes.[7]

Third, despite efforts to relate the basic class interests to characteristics of the regime, the social forces tradition has problems in clearly specifying under what conditions different classes support or oppose democracy. Rueschemeyer *et al.* (1992) move in the right direction by stressing that labor's embrace of democracy is socially constructed – not predetermined by class position in the class structure. However, they fail to point out the same predicament for other social classes, and they lack a theory for explaining the process of preference formation even for labor (*cf.* Bellin 2000). Another problem in the social forces tradition also indicates a

[7] Nowhere is this tendency more evident than in Gregory Luebbert's (1991, p. 306) assertive claim that "leadership and meaningful choice played no role in the outcome."

need to dovetail strategic and class-based theories of democratization: the lack of a theory of how organized class action from below interacts with elite decisions from above to bring about regime change or stability. An important attempt in this direction is Ruth Berins Collier's (1999) bridging approach, in which both class and elite actors, protest activity and negotiation, moves by excluded groups and responses by regime incumbents, are incorporated into the same analytical framework.[8]

A fifth weakness of the social forces tradition is its relative neglect of non-class collective actors or of non-material collective identities more generally. Social forces other than economic class actors, such as university students, human rights activists, church leaders and regional elites, which have been professed to play a part in the popular mobilization surges behind recent democratization elsewhere in the world (Bratton and van de Walle 1997, 107), do not fit easily into a class theory of collective action (Slater 2009). Although traditionally not committed to the study of democratization, the literature on social movements has recently made some promising steps toward such a broader theory of collective identities, and their links to organized protest and democratization (Markoff 1996; Tilly 2004). Moreover, the broader study of "civil society" could contribute to the social forces tradition on this score (Gill 2000; Bermeo 2003a; Kopecký and Mudde 2003).

The economic approach

The latest approach to explaining democratization uses the tools of economics to understand regime transitions and democratic stability. There are three key components of this approach. First is the incorporation of a wider set of actors than merely regime elites and opposition groups. Basically, the preferences of the entire population matter for regime outcomes, and, critically, non-elites may exert important influence over regime outcomes through the organization of protest action. Second, the economic approach purports to explain the preferences of these actors in terms of structural preconditions and material resources.[9] The third component is the use of deductive formal

[8] In a similar vein, Nancy Bermeo (1997) discusses how elites calculate the risks of sustained mobilization by marginalized groups.

[9] Both these features set the economic approach apart from the simpler game-theoretic accounts of democratic transitions following in the tradition of

modeling: explicitly stated assumptions and mathematically deducted corollaries from these assumptions in the form of predictions derived from equilibrium conditions.

Although they lack this third component, Stephan Haggard and Robert Kaufman (1995; 1997) may be seen as an early precursor to this emerging literature. While retaining its actor-centric essence, they explicitly criticize the transition paradigm for failing "to address the factors that shape actors' political preferences, the conditions under which these preferences change, and even the identity of pivotal actors" (Haggard and Kaufman 1995, pp. 5–6). The first more fully blown contribution, however, is that of Boix (2003). Firmly based in the tradition of formal economic theory, Boix assumes that people only care about their income, and hence evaluate their preferences for democracy or autocracy in terms of this. By implication, the fundamental struggle over democracy occurs between the rich and the poor. Based on the median voter theorem and the assumption that the median voter is poor, it follows that under democracy the poor set a positive tax rate in order to redistribute income (in the tradition of Meltzer and Richard 1981). Under (right-wing) dictatorship, by contrast, policies are not determined by the median voter but by the rich themselves, who choose a zero tax rate and no redistribution. Thus, the poor generally prefer democracy whereas the rich prefer (right-wing) dictatorship.

Two fundamental parameters may, however, alter this scheme of things. The first is income inequality: the more equally distributed the level of income is to begin with, the less the rich have to fear from conceding democracy to the poor.[10] The second is capital mobility, or asset specificity: the less productive an asset is at home relative to abroad, the lower the tax rate will have to be in order to avoid capital flight. This means that the cost of democracy to the rich decreases as asset specificity decreases.[11] From these simple assumptions, Boix

Przeworski (1991), where preferences are taken as given and only elite actors are being analyzed.

[10] Peter Rosendorff (2001) presents a model similar to Boix's (2003) in structure and outcome with respect to the relationship between income distribution and democracy, but also derives predictions for the effects of the size of capital stock and size of the workforce.

[11] Interestingly these two fundamental parameters parallel Bellin's (2000) discussion of two factors that determine the stance toward democracy among the capital class: fear (of redistribution) and state dependence (the latter, among other things, leading to low capital mobility). The same two factors

(2003) develops a simple static game-theoretic model in which the rich may choose to repress (sustain autocracy) at a certain cost or not repress (allow democracy), and the poor may choose to revolt (mobilize against the regime) or acquiesce. The two most important observable implications from the model concern income inequality and asset specificity: as they decrease, the likelihood of democracy increases.

Although in large part based on the same fundamentals, Daron Acemoglu and James Robinson (2006) make another contribution to this emerging literature. In a setting basically made up of the same actors (rich and poor), and with the same preferences for policies (tax rate) and regime outcomes (dictatorship and democracy) as in Boix's model, Acemoglu and Robinson ask why it is that the elite would concede democracy under the threat of revolution and not simply switch to a more redistributive policy. Their explanation stresses the importance of democracy as a solution to a commitment problem. As long as those wielding political power (the rich) are not themselves the beneficiaries of redistributive policies, they will not make a credible commitment to honour in the future the promise of such policies made in the past under the threat of revolution. With democracy, however, this problem is solved since the wielders of power and the beneficiaries of redistribution are the very same actors (the poor). Following this logic, Acemoglu and Robinson (2006) propose a dynamic model of democratization much richer in subtle technical detail than the simple static setup of Boix (2003).

There are two key virtues of this new and emerging theoretical approach to democratization. The first is consistency and integration. The deductive tools of formal theory ensure that these theories in themselves are not self-contradictory. When different causal factors are discussed in tandem, their inter-linkages are fully explored. But even more importantly, the economic approach integrates all of the three previous approaches to democratization. This approach provides structural conditions (such as the level of income inequality), it relates these to the preferences (such as the demand for redistribution) and actions (such as popular mobilization) of "social forces," and it models how these conditions affect the strategic choices made by political elites (such as the decision to extend the suffrage). This integrative effort links to the second virtue: transcendence of the structure and agency divide.

also appear to have shaped the shift in interests of business elites in El Salvador and South Africa prior to democratization (Wood 2000).

By virtue of their appeal to micro-foundations of macro-phenomena, these theories satisfy all three criteria Jon Elster (1983, p. 86) once stipulated as ideals for a "general sociological theory":

> (i) the explanation of individual action in terms of individual desires and beliefs, (ii) the explanation of macro-states in terms of individual actions, and (iii) the explanation of desires and beliefs in terms of macro-states.

The greatest drawback of the economic approach, to date, is its relative lack of empirical corroboration. Following Rebecca Morton (1999), we may distinguish among three types of tests of formal models: evaluation of predictions, assumptions and alternative models. The economic theories of democratization have hitherto been almost exclusively evaluated in terms of their empirical predictions. The most systematic effort in this regard is Boix's large-*n* and historical analyses (2003, chap. 2–3), whereas Acemoglu and Robinson (2006) almost exclusively provide anecdotal evidence. Neither, however, provides much evidence for the Meltzer–Richard theorem on which their models rely – namely, that tax rates increase with inequality under democracy, and that tax revenues in democracies are really used to redistribute income to the poor. There is even ample evidence that these predictions are not quite as robustly borne out as expected (Perotti 1996; Gradstein and Milanovic 2004; Mulligan *et al.* 2004; Ross 2006).

With respect to assumptions, there have been far fewer, if any, efforts toward empirical corroboration. The most crucial assumptions in the economic approach to democratization are the ones concerning information and preference formation. The world of Acemoglu and Robinson's (2006) model is populated by individuals that are fully informed: of the preferences of all other individuals, of the (assumed) redistributive consequences of dictatorship and democracy, of the costs of repression, of the share of society's economic resources that would be destroyed by a revolution, and so on. These are of course extremely unrealistic assumptions.[12] With respect to what determines individuals' preferences over outcomes, people in both Boix (2003) and Acemoglu and Robinson (2006) are only concerned with their personal income. They thus evaluate their preferences regarding democracy vs. dictatorship solely in terms of

[12] True, they are relaxed in Boix's (2003) model, but only with respect to one piece of information: citizens are assumed to be uncertain about the elite's repression costs.

the net material benefit that would accrue to them from living under each type of institution. To the best of my knowledge, however, there have been no attempts to empirically validate these assumptions.[13]

The third type of empirical evaluation – testing alternative theories – has similarly not been paid much attention in the economic literature on democratization. Few, if any, attempts have been made to pit more than one formal model against another. The greatest need for this arises when different models tell different stories about the underlying mechanisms responsible for the same empirical regularity, such as the correlation between democracy and economic modernization (see, e.g., Chen and Feng 1999; Feng and Zak 1999; Zak and Feng 2003; and Glaeser *et al.* 2007).

The present approach: theoretical eclecticism, methods combined

In sum, the field of comparative democratization studies is inchoate, diversified and incoherent. Neither the structural, strategic nor social forces traditions have succeeded in stating a generally acceptable theory of democratization. And although the more recent economic approach contains the seeds of a much-needed theoretical integration, it has thus far relied too much on unverified assumptions and empirical predictions. On top of this, methodological divides have even further widened the existing gulfs in our theoretical understanding of democratization. Statistical methods applied to a large number of countries have dominated the structural approach from its inception, and in so far as they have been systematically assessed, this goes for the economic models of democratization as well. The *Transitions from Authoritarian Rule* edition that epitomized the strategic approach (O'Donnell *et al.* 1986), by contrast, was empirically designed as single-country studies, whereas the social forces tradition has primarily relied on historical-comparative analysis of country trajectories over long stretches of history. Studies crossing these boundaries are, however, a rare species. In other words,

[13] Using World Value Survey data, Torsten Persson and Guido Tabellini (2009) find that the cumulative experience of democracy at home and abroad (termed "democratic capital") is positively related to aggregate support for democracy in a cross-section of countries. This lends support to one of their assumptions about preference formation, but not to the larger assumptions of Boix (2003) and Acemoglu and Robinson (2006).

the extant literature on comparative democratization is deeply divided between tables of causal effect estimates and close-up case narratives that rarely speak to each other.[14]

Given the relative merits and drawbacks of each methodological approach, this is of course no ideal state of affairs. The general strength of statistics include claims of generality, probabilistic estimates of causal effect magnitudes, and the ability to incorporate multiple putative causes simultaneously, thereby also controlling for confounding factors behind each cause. Case studies, whether comparative or single-case, are at a relative disadvantage in these regards. They tend to be concentrated in time and space, thereby both impairing generality and the range of confounding factors that can be held constant across cases compared. Case studies instead thrive on sensitivity to temporality, agency and process. Whereas statistical analysis, with data over time, may provide insights into temporal priority, the results tend to be sensitive to untested assumptions about the length and equality of causal lags. Statistical approaches are also not capable of tracing causal mechanisms in terms of intervening variables, but these mechanisms tend to be devoid of actors, action and processes of interaction.

Departing from this depiction of the current state of affairs, in this study I will deploy two strategies to further the field of comparative democratization: theoretical eclecticism, and a combination of statistical with case study methods. The theoretical ambiguity as to what forces drive democratization implies that no particular approach may be elevated above the others in terms of testing priority. Thus, I will not test any singular explanatory approach, but rather a vast range of theoretical predictions stemming from several approaches. This eclectic strategy will, as a first step in each of the following five substantive

[14] An exception has in recent years evolved among area specialists studying democratization within different world regions, such as Sub-Saharan Africa (Bratton and van de Walle 1997), the post-communist countries (Fish 1998; Bunce 2000; McFaul 2002), and Latin America (Mainwaring and Pérez-Liñán 2003; 2005a). The virtue of this regional specialization is that it combines deep contextual knowledge from comparative case studies with systematic statistical analysis. What these studies never make quite clear, however, is that as long as they rely on cross-country variation they can only uncover factors that explain variations in democracy among countries *within* specific regions. What they fail to assess is the extent to which these same factors have affected democracy in the region as a whole. This latter question can only by addressed by making comparison *between* regions – that is, more or less global analyses.

Chapters 2–6, favor the statistical approach to how to take theory to data. The large-*n* empirical strategy is simply better at weeding out the unsuitable candidates from a long list of theoretical predictions. As far as is possible, this statistical framework will then also be employed in an effort to trace the intermediary links in the chain of causation. Yet since statistical and case study methods have relative but complementary merits, they should be dovetailed in order to maximize the overall quality of our inferences instead of favoring just a few of them. I will thus also complement the extensive study of a large number of cases with an intensive examination of just a few of them. This will bring me closer to the question of agency in processes of democratization.

Although all empirical investigations must contain both deductive and inductive elements, my inferential strategy will in one sense be dominated by the inductive logic: moving from theoretically informed observations of the data to implications for theory. When I eventually turn to institutional determinants of democratization in Chapter 6, however, the deductive approach will come more to the fore as I develop formalized hypotheses before accessing the data.

In the remaining sections of this chapter I develop the methodological specificities of my approach. More specifically, this entails my strategies for conceptualizing and measuring democracy and democratization, for statistical estimation and for the selection of cases. The non-technically oriented reader may skip this part and turn directly to the next chapter, where the unfolding of the substantive argument begins.

Conceptualizing and measuring democracy and democratization

I shall in this book be following the mainstream approach in the field of comparative democratization by defining democracy in terms of its basic criteria (see, e.g. Hadenius 1992; Hadenius and Teorell 2005a; 2005b). This implies the holding of periodic, free, fair and effective elections to the legislative and/or chief executive offices of state, together with a bundle of continually upheld political rights, most notably freedom of association and opinion. By implication, autocracy or authoritarianism means the absence of these basic characteristics (although I will in Chapter 6 introduce some important distinctions *among* autocracies). Beyond the basic criteria, there is profound disagreement over the meaning of democracy. Terms such as "responsive," "participatory" and "deliberative" democracy, for example, have been coined in efforts to highlight some of the most distinguished dividing lines in this debate (see, e.g., Teorell 2006). At the level of basic criteria, however, students of democracy are more in agreement on what the term means (O'Donnell 2001).

A more contested conceptual issue, however, concerns whether to conceptualize democracy as a continuous or discrete phenomenon (Collier and Adcock 1999). Is democracy a property that can be graded in terms of having more or less of it, or is it an either/or phenomenon? I have argued elsewhere that methodological concerns speak in favor of the graded approach, refuting the dichotomous conception due to loss of information and reliability (Hadenius and Teorell 2005a; 2005b). To this I would now like to add an even more fundamental argument: that there is a lack of a *theoretical* definition of democracy (or autocracy) stated in solely qualitative or dichotomous terms.

Take, for example, the famous definition provided by the most forceful proponents of the dichotomous view: Przeworski *et al.* (2000). These authors define democracy as "a regime in which those who govern are selected through contested elections," where "contested" means the presence of "an opposition that has *some chance* of winning office" (2000, p. 16, italics added). What does "some chance" in this definition imply? Any probability larger than zero? A probability of .001? Of .00001? Even theoretically, it arguably means some positive real number along a continuous probability scale. In other words, *even theoretically* a cut point has to be established somewhere. The same goes for other famous categorical definitions of democracy, where democracy is defined by having achieved a *certain amount* of some underlying continuous property such as competition, suffrage or political freedom (Gasiorowski 1996; Mainwaring *et al.* 2001; Reich 2002). Democracy is thus *in theory* not something qualitatively different from autocracy. The difference is a difference in degree.

Democracy will in this book be conceptualized accordingly: as a graded phenomenon. If we by a "regime" imply "the patterns ... that determine the channels of access to principal governmental positions" (O'Donnell 2001, p. 14), democracy is thus a regime, the features of which any country can approximate more or less well at any given time point. The concept of democratization, then, can be understood as one form of regime change.

Most obviously this implies the process through which countries become more democratic. In this book, however, I will be using the term democratization generically to also refer to the absence of the reversed process, or what Tilly (2004; 2007) pertinently terms "de-democratization": that is, movements from democracy toward authoritarianism. This is not to imply that the distinction between these two processes, or directions of change, is unimportant. On the contrary, as argued below I will be careful to distinguish the two in my empirical analyses by separating movements upwards in the level of democracy ("upturns") from movements downwards ("downturns"). Since there is no general agreement in the literature on what to call these twin processes, however, I shall be using the word "democratization" to denote both movements toward democracy and the absence of movements backwards, toward autocracy.

In terms of a distinction that has pervaded the strategic approach in particular, this means I will be dealing both with "transition" and "consolidation" (see, e.g., Schmitter 1995). I have, however, several reasons to prefer not to use this terminology. To begin with, the term "consolidation" has many usages in the literature, muddying its general meaning (Schedler 1998). Moreover, the distinction between "transitions to democracy" and the "consolidation of democracy" at least implicitly hinges on a dichotomous conceptualization of democracy. And this is, as argued above, a conceptual position I take issue with. I am not in this book trying to predict the demise of authoritarian regimes and their replacement by an alternative that is "democratic" in a qualitative sense, nor am I simply interested in understanding the survival of the latter. What I aim to do is to explain the extent to which different countries implement and sustain gradual democratic reforms – be they small or large in nature. In other words, some of the regime changes I try to predict may be very limited, such as lifting a minor ban on newspapers or increasing the regime's tolerance toward the organization of opposition groups. Other changes may, however, be of greater consequence, such as the holding of competitive elections for the first time in a long period. In the jargon of the strategic approach, this implies that I am not only interested in explaining "transition," but also in "liberalization" (see, e.g., O'Donnell and Schmitter 1986, pp. 9–11). Again, I find the generic term democratization more suitable, and clarifying, to capture the phenomenon under study.

How should democracy be measured? Favoring a continuous measure of democracy does not settle this matter, since even then there are several to choose from. In Gerardo L. Munck and Jay Verkuilen's (2002) broad conceptual and methodological assessment of most empirical measures of democracy in use to date, the two most favored graded indices were Michael Coppedge and Wolfgang Reinicke's (1990) "polyarchy" scale, and Axel Hadenius' (1992) "index of democracy" (Munck and Verkuilen 2002, p. 27). These are both purely cross-sectional measures, only covering a single year in the 1980s. They are thus not suitable for an assessment of what explained changes in democracy around the world during the third wave. In a recent study conducted with Hadenius, however, we reached a more workable solution based on two well-established graded measures of democracy – the average scores of political rights and civil liberties reported by Freedom House (2009), and the revised combined autocracy and democracy scores derived from the Polity IV data (Marshall and Jaggers 2009) – both of which have extensive coverage across time and space. By using the Hadenius (1992) measure as an independent yardstick on a sample of seventy-six country year observations with large discrepancies between the Polity and Freedom House scores of democracy, we found systematic measurement error in both sources' data, albeit in opposite directions. While Polity tended to overestimate the degree of democracy in a country, the Freedom House score suffered from underestimation. By taking the mean of the two indices, however, these offsetting biases could be eliminated. Moreover, the precision of the resulting democracy score, gauged in terms of the variability around the mean score, was enhanced (Hadenius and Teorell 2005b).

Hence, the preferred measure of democracy in this book is this combined index. I thus first transform the Freedom House and Polity to vary between 0 ("least democratic") and 10 ("most democratic"), and then average them. In the robustness tests included as Appendix C, however, I also include the main results when using the component parts of this composite index.

Statistical estimation strategy

The statistical results reported in this book are based on regression analysis, using yearly changes in the combined democracy index just presented as the dependent variable, and a series of measures of potential determinants of democratization as independent variables (see Appendix A for a detailed description of the data). Although I give a more detailed account of the statistical model used in Appendix B, I will highlight some critical features of this model here.

First, I make important use of the temporal dimension of the data. To begin with, for all years I include the measures of the independent variables from the year before the dependent variable is measured. This is done in order to mitigate the problem of "reversed causation," that is, that the explanatory variables at least in part are also being caused by the dependent variable. I also include measures from previous years of the dependent variable itself in the model. There are both theoretical and methodological reasons for this. It makes theoretical sense to include this control for the past experience of democracy in a country, since democracy is a fairly sticky phenomenon: neither democracy nor autocracy is invented anew each year in every country. There is a lingering presence of the past, or "path dependence": having democracy (or not) today positively impacts on the incidence of having democracy (or not) tomorrow. Methodologically, the presence of this control also "proxies" for a host of other potential determinants of democratization that cannot be measured but still might have affected a country's level of democracy at earlier time points.

The inclusion of previous levels of democracy in the model is also the key to my distinction between short-term vs. long-term effects and explanatory performance. Since the level of democracy in the previous year represents all changes in the dependent variable up until that time point, the direct estimates of the effects of all other explanatory variables only pertain to the change in democracy over the yearly time horizon. This is my definition of a short-term effect. Democracy being a sticky phenomenon, however, the effect of a change in one independent variable also makes itself felt in more years to come. If the system of government in a country is perturbed by a shock in a given year, say a deep recession, then the effect of this shock will slowly dissipate, being strongest at the outset and then gradually losing its strength over the years. The sum of all these yearly effects of a hypothetical change in a given independent variable is my definition of a long-term effect. How long it takes for such an effect to reach its limit depends on the degree of stickiness in the dependent variable, and is thus an empirical question. According to my estimates in the analyses that follow, it takes approximately 50 years for the full long-run effects in my models to occur (see Appendix B).

Moreover, as argued above I will take seriously O'Donnell and Schmitter's (1986, p. 18) assertion that "what brings down a democracy is not the inverse of those factors that bring down an authoritarian regime." As argued in more detail in Appendix B, this distinction is not easily operationalized in the context of a graded measure of democracy. However, I will here interpret it to imply that if a determinant has, for example, a positive impact on movements toward democracy, the absence of that determinant does not necessarily imply more reversals away from the democratic end of the scale. Since the yearly change in level of democracy may be either positive ("upturns") or negative ("downturns"), I simply run the same analysis after having set all downturns to zero in order to estimate the effect on upturns, and by setting all the upturns to zero in order to estimate the effects on downturns. By comparing these results together with the result when both upturns and downturns are considered jointly, I draw conclusions as to whether a particular determinant exerts most of its influence in either or both directions.

Finally, where possible I attempt to test proposed causal mechanisms based on the large-*n* evidence. Given the heavy concentration in methodological writings on "process tracing" as the method designed to deal with this issue (George and McKeown 1985; Brady and Collier 2004; George and Bennet 2005), it may even come as a surprise for some readers that this is actually possible within a statistical framework. The intuition behind the case study and statistical approaches to tracing causal mechanisms is, however, very similar. The idea behind process tracing is that specific causes leave uniquely discernable traces in the historical record of a particular case. To the extent that these intermediary steps may be traced, they should fully account for the original relationship between cause and effect. In terms of Alexander George and Andrew Bennett's (2005, pp. 206–7) domino metaphor, if the first and last of a line of dominoes lie flat, pointing in the same direction, one would tackle the question as to why the fall of the one led to the fall of the other by observing the characteristics of the intervening dominoes. If they are all aligned in a sequence, pointing in the same direction as the first and last domino, this would suggest that the intervening dominoes fully account for how the fall of the first domino could cause the fall of the last one. Similarly, if a variable in a large-*n* analysis appears to affect a temporally succeeding variable, one can ask *why* this is the case by controlling for intervening variables. If the original relationship between putative cause and effect vanishes under such controls, one has successfully uncovered the entire chain of causal mechanisms linking the two.

As the domino example suggests, this procedure also works as an additional test of *whether* the temporally antecedent variable causes the other. As captured by Judea Pearl's (2000) so-called "front-door criterion," one could even perfectly identify a causal effect to the extent that the intervening variables constitute an isolated and exhaustive path connecting cause and effect. By implication, the failure to uncover any mechanisms at work should weaken our belief in a causal hypothesis.

In sum, after taking missing data into account my general estimation sample in this book consists of 3,795 annual observations in 165 countries of the world from 1972 to 2006.[15] In some exceptional cases I allow for a smaller estimation sample due to more restricted data availability. Even though I will present results for different groups of variables in the chapters to come, all figures in the first table of each chapter are drawn directly from one general estimation with all determinants included. Thus, I do not claim to make any distinctions between direct and indirect effects. At the present level of theorizing I can justify no general claims as to a causal ordering among the determinants.

Integrating statistics with case studies

Since the publication of *Designing Social Inquiry* (King *et al.* 1994) and its follow-up (Brady and Collier 2004), there has been a growing awareness among comparativists in general that neither the statistical nor the case-oriented approach to studying politics by themselves satisfy ideal standards of inference. Relying on the two methodological approaches' relative but complementary strengths, the ideal strategy for research thus ought to combine them in what has been termed a "nested analysis" (Coppedge 2005; Lieberman 2005).

Although this is the approach commonly preached, it is, however, rarely put into practice. This applies for the study of comparative democratization as well. In a recent analysis of more than three hundred

[15] As a robustness check, however, I have in Appendix C also included the results from a multiple imputation model where there are no missing data, covering fully 196 countries over the same time period.

articles published in the three leading journals in comparative politics from 1989 to 2004, no more than 14 percent of the articles on political regimes relied on a combination of quantitative and qualitative methods (Munck and Snyder 2007, p. 17). There is thus a dearth of mixed-method strategies applied within the field of comparative democratization studies.

When the two methodological approaches are combined, moreover, they are not sufficiently integrated. In Pevehouse's (2005) prominent study of regional organizations and democratization, for example, large-*n* quantitative analysis is interfolded with thick descriptions of events in six country case studies. This is a laudable study, an exemplar of clarity and versatility. However, the extent to and ways in which the cases fit into the larger statistical picture are not well understood. Since the results from the statistical analysis are never used to throw light on the selection of cases, Pevehouse fails to make the mixed-method design amount to more than the sum of its parts.

In this book I address these drawbacks in the literature by combining large-*n* statistical analysis with case study evidence from nine countries. The ambition is, however, not simply to muster just any supportive case study evidence. I also want to highlight the extent to which the particular cases explored fit with the larger statistical evidence. This raises the critical issue of criteria for case selection. If one wants to trace a causal mechanism able to explain why a certain determinant appears to exert an effect in a multiple regression model, what kind of cases should be selected? Despite the general move toward integrating statistical and case study methods in political science, there is surprisingly little methodological advice given on this in the literature. Evan Lieberman (2005) aptly summarizes the conventional wisdom on the subject: select a case "on the regression line" if you want to trace the causal mechanism underlying the statistical relationship in question; select a case "far from the regression line" if you want to explore what other, unaccounted for sources of variation might add to your understanding of the phenomena under study. What this conventional wisdom does not take into account, however, is the fact that the regression "line" is usually a multidimensional surface determined by multiple independent variables. If one selects a case that is well accounted for by the statistical model (being close to the regression surface), should one expect the causal mechanisms for *all* causal variables entered into the model to be equally present in that case? The reasonable answer is no, since one single variable could be responsible for that particular case's closeness to the regression surface. Moreover, even if one expects multiple causal mechanisms to account for a single case, that would severely limit one's ability to use the method of process tracing to uncover this fact, since the strength of that method generally depends on having strong theoretical predictions for a *singular* causal path.

To the best of my knowledge, John Gerring and Jason Seawright's (2007) notion of a "pathway case" provides the only guidance in the literature on how to select a case from a multiple regression analysis that is suitable to trace the mechanism pertaining to a single causal variable. Simply put, the more a specific determinant contributes to explaining the outcome in a specific case, the better that case fits the criterion of a pathway case for that determinant. In Appendix D I present a refined version of this "pathway criterion" that also takes the amount of change in the dependent variable into account. In the chapters to come, I will then make use of this criterion in order to evaluate the extent to which the particular cases selected fit the statistical evidence for that particular determinant.

2 *The shadow of the past: social determinants*

It is a commonly held belief that democracy can only take root in fertile soil. Countries vary in their historical origins. Some countries were more or less always free, whereas others gained independence from colonial rule only recently. Since the characteristics of the colonizing countries also vary, not even former colonies are all alike. Some countries share a Christian legacy, whereas others have inherited Islamic, Buddhist or Hindu traditions. In some countries people share the same language and ethnic background, whereas in others they are composed of a multitude of such groups. And depending on the historical circumstances under which the state was formed, some countries are big whereas others are small.

Did these historically inherited circumstances affect the prospects for democratization during the third wave? In this chapter, I first review the extant literature on historical factors, here termed domestic social determinants. I then consult the data to test which legacies did have an impact on my full sample of 165 countries in 1972–2006. It turns out that in the main two historical legacies mattered: the share of Muslims in the population, and geographical country size. While still relying on the large-*n* data, in the final two sections of the chapter I investigate the mechanisms through which these two effects occurred.

The literature on domestic social determinants

There is a long tradition of trying to explain democratization with reference to the history or demographics of a country. To begin with, a longstanding debate concerns the consequences of colonialism. This literature has pointed to the fact that colonialism has been associated with underdevelopment and high levels of social fractionalization, which in turn impede democratic development, but other mechanisms are also suggested. Usually the effect of colonialism is not assumed to be constant across different colonial powers. Most importantly, a British colonial legacy has been understood to be more conducive to democracy than the effect of other colonizers. On most accounts the British were supposedly better than the French or the Spanish at nurturing self-government and a more independent civil society in their colonies (Bernard *et al.* 2004, pp. 227–32).[1] Skeptics, however, argue that colonialism was too short an interlude in the history of the developing world to have any sustainable impact (Herbst 2000).

Another social determinant of democracy is religious tradition. Various scholars have asserted that Catholicism, Orthodox Christianity, Islam and Confucianism should be expected to negatively impact on the prospects for democracy, whereas Protestantism should be positively linked with democracy. According to Lipset, "[t]hese differences have been explained by (1) the much greater emphasis on individualism in Protestantism and (2) the traditionally close links between religion and the state in the other four religions" (1994, p. 5).

The religious heritage by far most discussed in recent years has been Islam. Most authors agree that Islam is negatively correlated with democracy, but few agree on how to interpret this finding. An influential argument has been put forward by Fish (2002), who suggests that the anti-democratic effect of Muslim countries is due to female subordination. Fish denies any scriptural basis for why this could be the case, arguing that the Koran does not prescribe female subordination. Instead, he tentatively suggests sociological, psychological and demographic reasons for why Islamic gender inequality may inhibit democracy. Repressive and patriarchal family relations may create a culture of dominance that could spill over into social and political life in general. To the extent that women are more supportive of democratic principles and practices, their social marginalization may inhibit overall popular support for democracy. A patriarchal society may also "create conditions under which young men are more likely to join militant groups

[1] In two much-cited articles, Acemoglu *et al.* (2001; 2002) argue that colonial origins determine a country's institutional quality and long-run levels of growth. There are two reasons I do not address this theory. First, Acemoglu *et al.* only purport to explain variations *among* former colonies, whereas my assessment includes non-colonies as well (in both the developed and the developing world). Second, Acemoglu *et al.* do not discuss different legacies of specific colonial powers, such as differences between British, French and Spanish colonial rule, which is what the democratization literature on colonialism has been mostly concerned with.

and engage in threatening, anomic behavior that provokes official repression" (Fish 2002, pp. 30–31, 37).

Others have, however, taken issue with this claim. Perhaps most importantly, Ross (2008) argues that it is oil wealth, not Islam, that impinges on gender equality, both in the Middle East and across the globe more generally. By implication, Islam is therefore not likely to affect democratization through this specific mechanism (Dunno and Russett 2004). Moreover, the argument has been made that the seemingly negative impact of a Muslim majority on the prospects for democracy is a contextual effect peculiar to the Arab world, and nothing inherent in the religion itself (Ross 2001; Stepan and Robertson 2003; 2004).

Another well-established presumption is that democracy's prospects are dimmed by social heterogeneity. Two influential treatments have dealt with the subject extensively. Alvin Rabushka and Kenneth Shepsle (1972) outline a theory of "democratic instability" based on social choice analysis of the problems involved in aggregating intense and incompatible preferences, such as those they assume characterize divided societies. Coupled with a set of assumptions about the behavior of political entrepreneurs, "whose quest for the perquisites of political office provokes appeals to ethnic passions," they argue that ethnicity soon turns into the most salient dimension of competition in such a setting. This leads in turn to a situation of outbidding among competing parties, the disappearance of brokerage institutions such as a multiethnic ruling coalition, and in the end "the decline of democratic competition, a result of electoral machinations and political violence" (Rabushka and Shepsle 1972, pp. 91–92, chap. 3). In a similar vein, Donald Horowitz (1985) summarizes the problems of party competition in ethnically divided societies: a propensity to form ethnic parties, which may lead the dominant multiethnic party to close down competition by creating a single-party regime. Alternatively, multiple ethnic parties contest divisive elections, conducive to violent opposition, which again may lead to one-party rule, military coups or outright civil war. In his own gloomy summary: "Whether party leaders terminate elections, military leaders reverse election results, or separatist leaders attempt to constrict the area in which those results will prevail, it is clear that ethnic divisions strain, contort, and often transform democratic institutions" (Horowitz 1985, pp. 681–82).

Drawing on the experiences from the post-communist transitions to democracy in Eastern Europe, however, Mark Beissinger (2008) argues that under certain circumstances ethnic diversity can bolster democratization by enabling nationalist mobilization against an authoritarian regime. Since social diversity might thus both impinge upon and engender democratization, others have suggested that its net effect is close to zero (Fish and Brooks 2004).

There is, finally, an old school of thought rooted in ancient Greece arguing that democracy should be more likely to prosper in smaller countries. Most accounts of this relationship link smallness to an enhanced likelihood of sustaining democratic institutions once installed. Robert Dahl and Edward Tufte (1973), in a classical treatment, asserted that democracy should be more likely to thrive in small countries by way of taking government closer to its people. This should enhance citizen participation, security and order, as well as loyalties to the state and the development of a common interest. Arendt Lijphart (1977, p. 65) similarly predicted that small countries should stand a greater chance of sustaining democracy by virtue of developing a stronger "spirit of cooperativeness and accommodation" (also see Diamond 1999, pp. 117–21).[2] There are fewer accounts of why size should matter for the introduction of democratic institutions. A rare exception is Boix, whose theory of capital mobility (see Chapter 1) predicts smallness to increase the chances of democratization: "The larger the geographical area controlled by the state, the higher the costs of moving abroad ... Accordingly, in large countries, the owners of capital may have a much stronger incentive to control the policy-making process" (2003, p. 44; *cf.* Rogowski 1998).

In an oft-cited study, Robert Barro (1999) tested the effects on democratization of all of these domestic social determinants, once the level of socioeconomic development was controlled for. He found only a marginally significant negative effect of ethnolinguistic fractionalization, and no effect of country size or colonial history. The only fully significant predictor in this set of variables turned out to be the size of the Muslim population, which had a markedly negative impact. Barro's findings may now be assessed on the basis of a substantially larger number of countries, and in the presence of far more controls.

[2] Some have made similar causal claims but with reference to insularity (or island status) rather than smallness. I will return to the relationship between size, insularity and democratization below.

Empirical results

I now turn to the first empirical results, presented in Table 2.1. Results are presented separately for the general effect on democratization, the effect on upturns and downturns, and the long-term effects. To indicate

Table 2.1 ***Domestic Social Determinants***

	Short-run			
	General	Upturns	Downturns	Long-run
Democracy at t–1	.018	.035	–.017	–
	(.049)	(.030)	(.025)	
Democracy at t–2	–.098**	–.091***	–.007	–
	(.048)	(.029)	(.025)	
British colony	–.014	–.005	–.009	–.177
	(.039)	(.029)	(.025)	(.487)
Spanish colony	–.061	–.005	–.056**	–.762
	(.055)	(.043)	(.027)	(.671)
French colony	–.029	–.025	–.004	–.363
	(.048)	(.040)	(.034)	(.607)
Portuguese colony	.079	.034	.045	.989
	(.085)	(.075)	(.029)	(1.044)
Dutch/Belgian/Italian colony	–.111	–.016	–.096	–1.392
	(.106)	(.078)	(.067)	(1.257)
Protestant population	–.024	–.021	–.003	–.303
	(.040)	(.026)	(.025)	(.507)
Christian-Orthodox population	.053	.017	.036	.665
	(.067)	(.062)	(.023)	(.847)
Other Christian population	.019	–.052	.071	.240
	(.144)	(.095)	(.089)	(1.798)
Muslim population	–.211***	–.109***	–.102*	–2.64***
	(.071)	(.042)	(.052)	(.804)
Buddhist population	–.132	.071	–.203*	–1.653
	(.137)	(.071)	(.106)	(1.744)
Hindu population	–.048	–.025	–.022	–.596
	(.145)	(.086)	(.114)	(1.834)
Population of other religion	–.047	–.138**	.090*	–.590
	(.083)	(.055)	(.050)	(1.041)
Non-religious population	–.247**	–.206**	–.041	–3.09**
	(.109)	(.087)	(.052)	(1.299)

Table 2.1 (*cont.*)

	Short-run			
	General	Upturns	Downturns	Long-run
Ethnolinguistic fractionalization	.051	.105**	–.055	.632
	(.060)	(.043)	(.037)	(.752)
Religious fractionalization	–.118	–.054	–.064	–1.474
	(.088)	(.057)	(.050)	(1.097)
Log(area)	–.014*	–.015***	.002	–.172**
	(.007)	(.005)	(.005)	(.080)

* significant at the .10-level, ** significant at the .05-level, *** significant at the .01-level.

No. of observations = 3,795; no. of countries = 165; mean years observed per country = 23.0.

Note: Entries are unstandardized regression coefficients with panel-corrected standard errors in parentheses. Non-colonized countries are treated as the reference category for the colonial dummies, the share of Catholics for the religious denomination variables. All models also include the determinants in Table 3.1, 4.1 and 5.1 as controls. Size (the log of area) has been lagged one year.

the importance of the more recent past, this table also reports the estimates for the two lagged values of the level of democracy. Since the dependent variable in these analyses is the yearly *change* in level of democracy, the parameter estimate for prior democracy (meaning at t–1 and t–2 jointly) is 1+.018–.098, that is, around .920. In other words, democracy moves extremely sluggishly over time. The extent to which democratic institutions have been implemented today in a country very closely matches the extent to which they were implemented yesterday. The fact that this match is not perfect (i.e., that it is less than one), however, indicates that there is mean reversion at work, implying that high levels of democracy at any given year tend to fall, whereas low levels tend to rise. If perturbed, democracy in a country tends to gravitate toward its long-term equilibrium level.

The social determinants for which effects are reported in Table 2.1 are with one exception (country size) measured as country constants (that is, they do not vary over time). The colonial origin of a country has been recorded for the last spell of colonial rule (that lasted more than 10 years), the religious denominations at around 1970, and the fractionalization measures at different time points in different countries. Turning to the results I find, in line with Barro (1999), that democracy during the third wave did not fare significantly better in former British colonies than in countries of other colonial origin. Nor do I find that there was any general negative democratic legacy of being a former Western overseas colony. Colonial heritage, at least in this sense, simply does not add to our understanding of the third wave of democratization.[3]

With respect to religious denomination, my results show – contrary to the earlier literature summarized by Lipset *et al.* (1993), but in line with Barro's (1999) findings – that during the third wave different forms of Christianity had no significant effects on democratization. In other words, Protestant countries had no democratizing advantage. On the other hand, societies dominated by Muslims suffered from an evident anti-democratic propensity. This effect is fairly substantial. If one compares two hypothetical countries, one with 100 and one with 0 percent Muslims, the Muslim-dominated country had an estimated democratization rate of .211 less in the short-run, and a long-run equilibrium level of 2.64 less on the 0–10 democracy scale. In terms of the direction of change, it appears that Muslim societies were both significantly less likely to make upturns toward democracy, and (although only marginally significant) more likely to make downturns toward authoritarianism.[4]

As shown in the Appendix C, the Muslim population factor is robust to most alternative specifications. It is even strengthened in the imputed global sample of 196 countries, and it affects all three constitutive components of my index of democracy (the Polity scores and both Freedom House's civil liberties and political rights ratings). However, when I control for regions, that is, take into account the difference

[3] This also applies if a general colonial variable, coded as 1 for all Western overseas colonies, is included in the model. As can be seen from Table 2.1, however, there is one minor exception: former Spanish colonies appear to have a stronger tendency to de-democratize than non-colonized countries (i.e., being a Spanish colony has a significant and negative impact on downturns). However, this effect hinges on the inclusion of one influential outlier: Argentina in 1976, a former Spanish colony suffering a devastating coup. When this observation is excluded, no significant effect remains for this colonial dummy.

[4] I get the same finding as Barro (1999) with respect to the fraction of *non*-religious people in the population: although this factor at first seems to exert a significantly negative impact on democratization, the result vanishes once China, an extremely influential outlier, is excluded from the analysis. I also find that the proportion of people belonging to the "Other" denomination (mostly including miscellaneous East Asian religions) has a significant and negative impact on upturns. Since there is no obvious interpretation for this finding, I leave it without further consideration.

between, most critically, Middle Eastern and North African countries on the one hand and the rest of the world on the other, the coefficient for the Muslim population is reduced substantially and rendered insignificant. I shall return to the interpretation of this in the following section.

Countries with a population that is heterogeneous in terms of ethnolinguistic composition, contrary to Barro (1999) and much of the previous literature, were *not* significantly more prone to move in either direction on the democracy scale.[5] The same goes for religious diversity, which does not appear to have had any significant impact on democratization during the third wave.

Finally, size – measured as the log of the country area at any given year – had a statistically significant and negative, although not very substantial, impact on democratization. Contrary to most of the literature, however, there is no net association between size and downturns. In other words, it is not the case that smaller countries were less prone to authoritarian backsliding. What drives this result instead turns out to be the fact that smaller-sized countries, in line with Boix's (2003) argument, experienced somewhat larger upturns in their democracy scores compared to larger countries. The coefficient of –.015 means that by comparing two countries A and B, where A is twice as big as B, the yearly propensity to democratize was ln(2)*.015, or approximately .010 larger for country B. This effect, while small, is robust to most robustness tests in Appendix C.[6] One could perhaps argue that the causal arrow points in the opposite direction: that democratization in this time period led to secessions (Alesina and Spolaore 1997), or that autocracies enjoyed stronger incentives to expand the territory under their control (Hiscox and Lake 2001). With the lagged dependent variable in place, however, these possibly distant historical patterns cannot explain my finding for the third wave.

In sum, I find evidence for only two robust determinants of democratization among the sociohistorical legacies: the size of the Muslim population, and country size. I now turn to an exploration of what mechanisms could explain these two findings.

5 Ethnolinguistic fractionalization has a significant and positive (!) effect on upturns, which, however, turns out to be caused by one extremely influential country: Suriname.

6 The main exception is the country-fixed effects specifications. Given the general rarity of territorial expansion and contraction of states, however, demanding within-country evidence in support for this determinant may be demanding too much on a 35-year horizon.

Islam and democracy

There has been some controversy over how to interpret the negative relationship between Islam and democracy. Is there something inherently undemocratic about Islam as a religious doctrine, or the way Islamic societies are organized? Or is the share of Muslims in the population merely picking up some other structural feature that negatively impacts on democratization? In support for his argument in the latter camp, Fish (2002) runs a series of cross-sectional regressions showing that the gap in level of democracy between predominantly Islamic countries and the rest of the world shrinks when the relative station of females, such as the female-to-male literacy gap or the share of women in government, is being controlled for. Daniela Donno and Bruce Russett (2004), however, take issue with Fish's findings. They show that the negative effect of size of the Muslim population does not diminish substantially when a long series of female subordination measures – also including the percentage of women in parliament, and the female-to-male education and life expectancy ratios – are being controlled for.

To the best of my knowledge, there is hitherto no test of Fish's argument in a dynamic setting, trying to explain the effect of Islam on democratization over time. The results of such a test are presented in Table 2.2. Since the Muslim effect is general, affecting both the likelihood of upturns and downturns, I may safely ignore that subdistinction here. I start in model (1) by replicating my finding from the previous table: despite the numerous controls applied in these extensive tests, the share of Muslims in the population exerts a negative impact on democratization. Can one eliminate or at least reduce this negative impact by controlling for measures of the station of women? Since there are several such measures I could apply, I have in model (2) opted for the measure of *social* female subordination that (a) correlates most strongly with the share of Muslims in the population, and (b) maximizes country coverage. This turns out to be the female-to-male secondary school enrollment ratio, which correlates with the share of Muslims at –.36.[7] Adding

[7] A qualitatively improved measure of the education ratio, based on Robert Barro and Jong-Wha Lee's (2000) data on total years of education achieved by men and women of age 15 or over, correlates at –.51 with the share of Muslims, but covers substantially fewer countries and years. Other measures of the social station of women, such as the female-to-male life expectancy ratios, are more weakly correlated with the share of Muslims (at –.32), but have a somewhat expanded

Table 2.2 *Explaining the Muslim Effect (general)*

	Model			
	(1)	(2)	(3)	(4)
Muslim population	–.211***	–.212***	–.295***	–.126
	(.071)	(.074)	(.099)	(.078)
Female-to-male education ratio		.028		
		(.094)		
Women in parliament			–.022	
			(.195)	
Middle East & North Africa				–.114
				(.079)
Gambia in 1994				–7.115***
				(.404)
No. of observations	3,795	3,610	2,817	3,795
No. of countries	165	161	149	165

* significant at the .10-level, ** significant at the .05-level, *** significant at the .01-level.
Note: Entries are unstandardized regression coefficients with panel-corrected standard errors in parentheses. All models use change in the level of democracy as the dependent variable and include two lags of the level of democracy and the determinants in Table 2.1, 3.1, 4.1 and 5.1 as controls. Both the female-to-male education ratio and women in parliament have been lagged one year.

this factor to the model, however, does *not* reduce the negative impact of Muslim population (rather it is increased!), the simple reason being that the education ratio itself does not impact on democratization. In model (3), I control instead for the measure of *political* female subordination that fulfills the same criteria: the share of women in the legislature (which correlates at –.30 with the share of Muslims in the population). The result is, however, again not in line with Fish's (2002) argument. The negative impact of Muslim population is not diminished, again for the simple reason that female representation in the legislature is not significantly related to democratization.[8]

country and time coverage. Adding any, or all, of these measures as controls does, however, not affect the impact of Muslim population on democratization.

8 These results do not change if I hold the number of observations constant, that is, if I look at the impact of Muslim population on the sample of non-missing observations for the education ratio and share of women in parliament.

If female subordination cannot explain the Muslim effect, what can? It may first be worth mentioning the numerous determinants of democratization controlled for already in model (1) of Table 2.2, which thus can immediately be taken off the list of potential suspects. The Muslim effect can, for example, not be explained with reference to underdevelopment or superior economic performance in Islamic countries, nor is it due to oil wealth. It is also not explicable in terms of a lack of neighbor diffusion, weak links to democratic regional organizations, or the absence of popular mobilization.

Moreover, the entire body of cultural interpretations of the negative Muslim effect must be cast in doubt when checked against individual-level evidence. In the last decade, the international survey industry has made significant inroads into the Islamic world, meaning that we now know a lot more about how ordinary people in these countries think and feel about democracy. Three approaches predominate in this growing body of literature: some compare the democratic outlook of more and less pious Muslims *within* predominantly Muslim societies in the Arab world (Tessler 2002a; 2002b); others compare Muslims with non-Muslims in religiously divided societies (Rose 2002; Hofmann 2004); and yet others compare predominantly Muslim societies, taken as a whole, with non-Muslim societies (Norris and Inglehart 2004; Tessler and Gao 2005). Interestingly, regardless of the approach used one significant finding is shared by all of these studies: there is *not* less support for democratic principles among people professing Islam. If Islamic culture somehow explains the negative impact on democratization, it is thus not because Muslims are more bent toward supporting authoritarianism than are supporters of other religions.[9]

[9] Another finding that flies in the face of any simplistic cultural interpretation of the Muslim effect is when the *change* in the share of Muslims over time is taken into account. If an authoritarian culture among Muslims is to blame, then countries with a growing Muslim population should become less, whereas countries with a diminishing Muslim population should become more democratic over time. This is, however, not the case. Although the within-country variation in the share of Muslims between 1970 and 2000 (with data from Barrett *et al.* 2001 in both cases) is small, it is *positively* correlated with the change in level of democracy between 1972 and 2002. This finding is also in line with the positive (and, in this case, significant!) coefficient for Muslim population in a fixed effects vector decomposition model (not reported), which separates out the within-country variation in democratization (see Plümper and Troeger 2007).

Another deterrent to believing in the democratizing force of religion is the fact that still in the early 1970s, Catholicism was considered a cultural hindrance to democracy. Then Southern Europe and Latin America democratized. In the 1980s, Confucianism was to blame for democracies' scant progress in Eastern Asia. But then South Korea and Taiwan democratized. In other words, religious obstacles to democratization have been cited before, only to be disproved by history at a later time point.

As a final word, there *is* one feature that does seem to make the Muslim effect dissipate: adding a dummy variable that controls for all countries belonging to North Africa and the Middle East. As model (4) of Table 2.2 shows, together with a control for one extreme outlier (Gambia in 1994), this reduces the Muslim effect to about half of its original magnitude, and renders it statistically insignificant. What this means is that there is something peculiar about this predominantly Muslim region (together with the geographically proximate case of Gambia), rather than the share of Muslims in the population in and of itself, that hindered democratization during the third wave. Thus, my results by and large confirm Alfred Stepan and Graeme Robertson's (2003; 2004) claim that the "Muslim" gap is mostly an "Arab" gap.

True, this is not much of an "explanation" since it begs the question *why* there is an "Arab" or Middle Eastern gap to begin with. Yet I believe this insight can help future scholars wishing to explain the Muslim effect by reframing the question to be asked. What we need to know is not why Islamic countries in general have been less inclined to democratize, but why this has been the case in North Africa and the Middle East. Of course, Islam as a religion could still be a part of the answer to this question, but then only those features of Islam that are unique to this particular region.

Why are small countries more likely to democratize?

As noted upon already in the previous chapter, Boix's (2003) theory of capital mobility presents an explanation for why size should have a negative impact on democratization, the idea being that fixed assets are more easily transferred out of geographically small countries, which reduces capital holders' fear of democracy. However, apart from the proxies for capital mobility already incorporated in my composite measure of modernization (such as industrialization and education),

Table 2.3 *Explaining the Size Effect (upturns)*

	Model			
	(1)	(2)	(3)	(4)
Log(area)	–.015***	–.017***	–.012	–.016***
	(.005)	(.006)	(.008)	(.005)
Island		–.026		
		(.023)		
Log(population)			–.007	
			(.010)	
Log(population density)				–.027
				(.111)

* significant at the .10-level, ** significant at the .05-level, *** significant at the .01-level.
No. of observations = 3,795; no. of countries = 165; mean years observed per country = 23.0.
Note: Entries are unstandardized regression coefficients with panel-corrected standard errors in parentheses. All models use upturns in the level of democracy as the dependent variable, including two lags of the level of democracy and the determinants in Table 2.1, 3.1, 4.1 and 5.1 as controls. All explanatory variables in the table have been lagged one year.

or in terms of natural resource abundance, this mechanism is not easily amenable to empirical testing. What I am able to provide in this section instead is something less ambitious: an inquiry into different interpretations as to what might be driving the negative effect of size on democratization.

First, several scholars have argued that insularity, or island status, is what makes small countries more conducive to democracy rather than their size (Hadenius 1992, pp. 125–27; Anckar and Anckar 1995; Anckar 2002; Clague *et al.* 2001). Since island states are usually small (size and insularity correlate at –.60), this could very well be the case. As model (2) of Table 2.3 shows, however, the effect of size is not at all reduced by controlling for island status (defined as a country sharing no land or river border with any other country). In effect, insularity does not promote democratization.

Another interpretation is that what matters is the size of the population, rather than the geographical reach of a country. In Ronald Rogowski's (1998) asset mobility theory of democratization, for example, it is the mobility of human rather than physical capital (as in Boix's theory) that matters. Since small country populations tend to belong to small linguistic groups, they are likely to know more foreign languages, and may thus more easily move abroad. Exit being an easier option for these populations when not satisfied with their government, their rulers are more likely to grant voice, that is, to democratize. Geographical and population size being strongly correlated (at .79), this is again a plausible rival interpretation of the size effect. As model (3) makes clear, however, neither the geographical nor the population size effects remain statistically significant when entered simultaneously to the model (although both are if entered alone). The correlation between geographical and population size is simply too strong to allow us to efficiently tease out the independent effect of each. It is notable that the geographical effect does trump the demographic one in terms of magnitude (since both are on logarithmic scales, their coefficients can be compared). But longer time periods would be needed to reach a more firm conclusion in this regard.

Since the interaction of geographical and population size produces population density, I finally test this third interpretation in model (4). One conjecture, following Herbst (2000), would be that state power is more easily broadcast over densely populated areas, and that state capacity, in turn, positively affects the prospects for democratization. Although the latter assertion has been challenged (Way 2005), there is an established tradition within comparative sociology arguing that, at least over the long haul, state formation tends to promote the development of representative institutions (Moore 2004; Ross 2004; Tilly 2004; 2007). Since smaller countries are more densely populated (as a rule), perhaps this is what explains the size effect? As can be seen, however, this is not the case. Population density in and of itself does not affect democratization, which still leaves the negative impact of size unexplained – at least in terms of observable characteristics for I which I have been able to collect data.

Conclusion

In sum, democracy during the third wave of democratization arose and sustained itself under variegated sociohistorical circumstances. Countries lacking a colonial history did not fare any better than former colonies, and the origin of the colonial power did not seem to have mattered much. Moreover, democratization seemingly struck diverse and homogenous countries alike, and almost regardless of religious traditions. The one exception in this regard is the negative impact of Islam, but this effect was almost exclusively restricted to the Middle East and North Africa. Country size also mattered, smaller countries being more likely to democratize.

Apart from the effect of Islam in the Middle East, and of geographical size, then, the past cast little shadow over the fate of democracy during the third wave.

3 *The power of prosperity: economic determinants*

It only takes a quick glance at the world to reach the conclusion that democracy and prosperity are related. Richer countries are no doubt on average more democratic. But is this relationship causal? More specifically, were prosperous or socioeconomically more developed countries during the third wave more likely to democratize? What then about short-term fluctuations in economic performance: was that a prosperity-enhancing factor moving in the same direction? It takes no more than a second quick glance at the world to find an obvious exception to the relationship between prosperity and democracy: the oil-rich autocracies in the Middle East. Were oil or other sources of natural resource abundance a more general impediment to democratization during this time period?

In this chapter I will address these questions in an attempt to systematically assess a series of economic determinants of democratization. These are divided into two sections: one on economic determinants observed in my full estimation sample of 165 countries; the other on determinants observed for a more restricted sample. I find statistical support for four economic determinants: the level of socioeconomic modernization, short-term economic growth, oil abundance, and freedom from state incursion in the economy. Through both large-*n* analysis and case study evidence I then assess the mechanisms that underlie the first two of them.

Modernization, performance and resource abundance

Since Lipset's (1959) seminal argument, summarized in Chapter 1, there have been countless studies confirming that one of the most stable determinants of democracy across the globe is the level of socioeconomic modernization. That said, Lipset's thesis still faces several unaddressed challenges. To begin with, the empirical support for his proposition has for the most part been based on measures of modernization in terms of economic development, such as energy consumption and GDP per capita. This pertains both to earlier cross-sectional studies (for an overview, see Diamond 1992) and to the more recent tests based on pooled time-series data (Burkhardt and Lewis-Beck 1994; Helliwell 1994; Londregan and Poole 1996; Gasiorowski and Power 1998; Barro 1999; Przeworski *et al.* 2000; Boix and Stokes 2003; Epstein *et al.* 2006). However, in Lipset's (1959) original account, as well as in the early studies following in its wake (Cutright 1963; Neubauer 1967; Olsen 1968; Winham 1970), a much wider range of indicators of socioeconomic development was employed. Apart from national income they included industrialization, education, urbanization and communications. According to modernization theorists these developmental processes should be viewed as parts of one underlying syndrome, "socioeconomic modernization," which eventually enhances democratic development (Lerner 1958; Deutsch 1961). This broader theoretical underpinning for the Lipset hypothesis has received surprisingly little attention in the more recent comparative democratization literature. I will try to remedy this situation below by treating socioeconomic modernization as a coherent syndrome with multiple observable indicators.

Secondly, there is the widely cited finding by Przeworski *et al.* (2000) that socioeconomic modernization does not trigger transitions to democracy, but instead helps to sustain democracies once installed. This finding has been both confirmed (Persson and Tabellini 2009) and criticized (Boix and Stokes 2003; Epstein *et al.* 2006) on empirical grounds, but mostly based on a dichotomous measure of democracy.[1] By separating the effects on upturns from those on downturns, in this chapter I will perform a systematic test of this finding using a graded democracy scale.

A third challenge comes from recent work purporting to show that the effect on democratization of both economic income and education only applies across countries at a given point in time, but not within countries over time (Acemoglu *et al.* 2005; 2007; 2008; Robinson 2006). The authors of this series of papers instead argue that different societies may have embarked on divergent political-economic

[1] The one exception I am aware of is Acemoglu *et al.* (2007), who (in tables 3–4) make use of the same technique as I in order to separate the effects of transition toward and away from democracy.

development paths at certain critical junctures some 500 years ago, with some countries following a high income-high democracy path, others a low income-low democracy path, but without the two ever being causally related. In the robustness tests supplied in Appendix C, I address also this challenge, again based on my broader measure of socioeconomic modernization.

A theoretical argument developed alongside the modernization hypothesis has been concerned with the impact of economic performance. Both autocracies and democracies, the argument goes, are more likely to break down when facing temporary performance crises, since this means "a reduction in the resources available to political elites for sustaining bases of support" (Haggard and Kaufman 1995, p. 29; 1997). The large-*n* empirical support for this contention has mostly been based on yearly growth rates as the measure of performance, and again mostly on dichotomous conceptions of the dependent variable, simply indicating whether regimes are authoritarian or democratic. Two findings have been predominant. On the one hand that growth is negatively related to transitions from authoritarian to democratic rule – or, inversely, that authoritarian regimes fall under the pressure of economic crisis (Gasiorowski 1995; Remmer 1996; Przeworski *et al.* 2000). On the other hand growth has been shown to positively affect democratic survival, implying that democracies too are vulnerable to economic crises (Przeworski *et al.* 2000; Bernard *et al.* 2001; 2003). These results do not translate easily into contexts where graded measures of democracy are being used. They could, however, imply that the coefficients for economic performance should be differently signed depending on the direction of change in the democracy scale, which might explain why the few studies that have tested them on graded measures have produced weak and inconsistent results.[2]

A more robust finding appears to be the anti-democratic effect of natural resource abundance. In a set of regressions predicting the development of democracy over time, Ross (2001) found that both the abundance of oil and of other non-fuel minerals as the primary sources of national exports had a markedly negative effect on the prospects for

[2] Using the same democracy index (Polity), but different controls, John Londregan and Keith Poole (1996) found a negative but small short-term impact of growth on democratization, whereas Quan Li and Rafael Reuveny (2003) found no effect of growth but a positive effect of inflation that decreased over time.

democratization. Earlier studies claiming to show the negative impact of oil had only made cursory remarks on the poor performance of democratic governance in a few oil-producing countries on the Arabian Peninsula (Helliwell 1994; Barro 1997; 1999). Ross (2001), by contrast, was able to show that the effect occurred on a global scale, and pertained to other sources of strongly profitable materials. According to Ross the relationship is due to the development of a "rentier state" in countries rich in natural resource wealth. Regimes that are predominantly reliant on such vast resources are capable of using both the carrot (tax cuts and patronage) and the stick (repression) to hold contestation at bay.[3]

Turning to my empirical results in Table 3.1, I first replicate the finding from some 50 years of comparative research on the positive relationship between socioeconomic modernization and democratization. As already noted, this result is based on a composite measure of the entire process of modernization, not simply on one of its macroeconomic subcomponents. Interestingly, moreover, during the third wave the effect of modernization should according to my estimates *not* be interpreted as a tendency among modernizing countries to advance toward democracy. Rather, there was a tendency among less modernized countries to revert toward authoritarianism. True, this tendency is not very strong. A standard deviation change in the modernization index – which is approximately equivalent to a move from the level of Somalia (at the very bottom) to the level of Namibia, or from El Salvador (at the mean) to the level of Ireland – according to these estimates results in an expected decrease of .061 in the propensity of democracy to backslide toward authoritarianism the following year. The impact on (the absence of) downturns is, however, statistically significant, unlike the effect on upturns.

This pattern bears a striking resemblance to the finding by Przeworski *et al.* (2000) and Persson and Tabellini (2009) that socioeconomic modernization does not effect transitions to democracy, but hinders reversals from authoritarianism. Moreover, the finding is highly robust to alternative specifications. As Appendix C makes clear, even the

[3] Thad Dunning (2008), in a recent contribution, adds an important caveat to Ross' (2001) argument by observing that when non-resource wealth is unequally distributed, resource abundance could actually foster democratization (or hinder de-democratization) by mitigating conflicts over redistribution.

Table 3.1 *Domestic Economic Determinants*

	Short-run			
	General	Upturns	Downturns	Long-run
Socioeconomic modernization	.038*	–.023	.061***	.472*
	(.021)	(.019)	(.015)	(.242)
Growth	–.184	–.540***	.356**	–2.30
	(.259)	(.195)	(.171)	(3.210)
Inflation	–.002	–.001	–.001	–.025
	(.004)	(.003)	(.002)	(.051)
Fuels	–.228*	–.189***	–.039	–2.85**
	(.120)	(.073)	(.080)	(1.447)
Minerals	–.034	.053	–.087	–.424
	(.230)	(.156)	(.182)	(2.872)

* significant at the .10-level, ** significant at the .05-level, *** significant at the .01-level.

No. of observations = 3,795; no. of countries = 165; mean years observed per country = 23.0.

Note: Entries are unstandardized regression coefficients with panel-corrected standard errors in parentheses. All models also include two lags of the dependent variable and the determinants in Table 2.1, 4.1 and 5.1 as controls. All explanatory variables in the table have been lagged one year.

within-country evidence (applying country-fixed effects) supports the view that modernization during the third wave decreased the expected level of backsliding toward authoritarianism. This, in turn, means that I do not find support for the argument by Acemoglu *et al.* (2005; 2007; 2008) that modernization only influences the cross-country correlations.[4]

When looking at short-term macroeconomic performance, I find no effect of inflationary crisis on regime change. Growth, however, negatively affected upturns toward democracy during the third wave. Since growth rates are measured in fractions, the coefficient of –.540 implies that for a country whose economy contracted by, say, 10 percentage

[4] True, when I apply both country- and year-fixed effects (robustness model 6 of Appendix C), the coefficient for modernization fails to reach statistical significance. This is, however, an extremely demanding test for a slow-moving characteristic such as socioeconomic modernization.

points, the propensity to democratize the following year increased by .054. This finding, although substantively small, turns out to be highly robust to alternative specifications,[5] and is consistent with Haggard and Kaufman's (1995; 1997) argument that authoritarian regimes are more likely to democratize when suffering from recessionary crisis. The coefficient for downturns, however, while appearing to be statistically significant, hinges on the inclusion of two extremely influential outliers.[6] I thus find no robust support for the supplementary view that economic growth kept democracies from backsliding. But the fact that the impact of growth on downturns is positively signed explains why there is no effect of growth on democratization in the general model, nor any discernable impact on the long-run equilibrium democracy level.

Despite the fact that I control for a much larger set of determinants, my results confirm Ross' (2001) findings on the anti-democratic effect of oil (or fuels more generally). According to my estimates the discovery of oil, increasing the export share of oil from 0 to 100 percent of GDP, would have led during the third wave to an expected decrease of .228 in the level of democracy the following year, and to a downward shift of 2.85 in the long-run equilibrium level of democracy. This effect is primarily caused by a tendency among oil-dependent countries to resist increases in their level of democracy (or, by implication, a democratizing tendency among countries not dependent on oil). Probably due to the fact that so few oil-rich countries have reached higher levels of democracy, however, the effect of oil as a trigger of downturns is weak and insignificant.

Whereas I thus confirm Ross' (2001) primary finding with respect to the effect of natural resource wealth, there are some qualifications. The fuels variable is to begin with not robust to all alternative specifications (see Appendix C). Most notably, oil dependency cannot explain movements in the level of democracy within countries (that is, taking into account country-fixed effects). Nor does it exert a significant impact in the imputed sample of all 196 countries across the globe. I thus cannot exclude the possibility that the oil effect is sample dependent. Finally,

[5] The only exception is that growth only affects upturns in political rights (according to Freedom House) and the Polity scores, not in civil liberties (see Appendix C). There is also a relatively extreme influential outlier, Panama in 1989, but the impact of growth on upturns is robust to excluding that case.

[6] These are Nigeria in 1984 and Suriname in 1980, two cases of devastating military coups staged the year after a serious economic recession hit each country.

contrary to Ross, I do not find any significant negative impact of non-fuel metals and ores.

Economic inequality and freedom

I now turn to two tests where I accept a somewhat smaller estimation sample due to the theoretical significance of the propositions involved. A key prediction from the economic models of democratization, presented in Chapter 1, is that democratization should be negatively linked to income disparity. More unequally distributed income means more pressure for redistribution, which autocratic elites are inclined to avoid by use of repression. Similarly, under high levels of income disparity the rich elites have a larger incentive to stage a coup against democracy to avoid future redistribution. We should thus expect income inequality to be negatively related to movements toward democracy, but positively related to movements away from democracy (Boix 2003; Acemoglu and Robinson 2006).

Most previous studies on the democratizing effects of inequality have been inconclusive, mostly due to scarce and unreliable income data (see, e.g., Bollen and Jackman 1985; 1995; Muller 1988; 1995a; 1995b). The most ambitious attempt on cross-sectional time-series data is Boix (2003), who finds that income inequality negatively impacts on the probability of transitions to democracy and positively impacts on democratic stability. Both these results appear to be highly sensitive to specification, however, and only apply to a sample of at best some 1,000 observations from 50 countries. Due to a novel dataset on economic inequality (measured through the Gini coefficient) I am in Table 3.2 able to test its impact on democratization in a sample about twice as large (and on a graded measure of democracy).

It turns out, however, that no coefficients for income inequality are statistically significant. This also applies to the lower panel of the table, where I allow for curvilinear effects. Ross Burkhart (1997) finds a non-monotonic relationship between income distribution and democracy, where the most democratic countries are located at intermediate levels of income inequality. This is actually in line with Acemoglu and Robinson's (2006) more nuanced theoretical prediction, according to which the poor have less incentive to stage a popular revolt against dictatorship in highly equal societies. Together with the elite effect (that fear of redistribution should be decreasing in the level of economic

Table 3.2 *Income Inequality*

	Short-run			
	General	Upturns	Downturns	Long-run
Linear:				
Income inequality	.271	.171	.100	2.36
	(.612)	(.446)	(.352)	(5.34)
Curvilinear:				
Income inequality	2.644	3.229*	-.585	22.8
	(3.238)	(1.949)	(2.288)	(28.2)
Income inequality^2	-2.745	-3.538	.793	-23.7
	(3.930)	(2.288)	(2.798)	(34.1)

* significant at the .10-level, ** significant at the .05-level, *** significant at the .01-level.
No. of observations = 1,829; no. of countries = 114; mean years observed per country = 16.0.
Note: Entries are unstandardized regression coefficients with panel-corrected standard errors in parentheses. All models also include two lags of the dependent variable and the determinants in Table 2.1, 3.1, 4.1 and 5.1 as controls. All explanatory variables in the table have been lagged one year.

equality) a curvilinear effect would be the expected pattern. Adding the square of income inequality to my model, however, again produces only insignificant results. In sum, despite the theoretical elegance of the economic models of democratization, income inequality appears not to have been a significant determinant of democratization during the third wave.

This result also runs against the first of Bellin's (2000) twin factors affecting capitalist elites' calculations regarding the net gains and losses of a democratic regime. This first factor is fear of redistribution, which, again, should be positively related to the level of economic inequality. There is, however, also a second factor in Bellin's theory, which similarly should affect the calculations of labor, namely economic dependency on the state. The more economic actors (capital or labor) depend on state subsidies and sector-specific regulations, the argument goes, the less inclined will they be to oppose an authoritarian regime. This factor also fit into Boix's (2003) framework in terms of capital mobility, since heavy state subsidies should increase the costs of moving capital abroad.

There is a tradition of studies related to this proposition that inquires into the relationship between democracy and "economic freedom," that is, freedom from state incursion in the economy. Previous studies have found intermediate levels of economic freedom to be most conducive to democracy (Brunk *et al.* 1987; Burkhart 2000) and that economic liberalization triggers democratization (Fish and Choudhry 2007) – although the direction of causality between economic liberalization and democratization may be questioned (Giavazzi and Tabellini 2005).

In Table 3.3 I assess the extent to which state dependence affects democratization through a measure of economic freedom ranging from 0 to 10. Although I again draw on data with widest possible coverage, this is the second test where I must accept a reduced estimation sample (this time restricted to 119 countries). But this time I do find an impact in the expected direction. As the coefficient for downturns in the upper panel indicates, countries with less state incursion in economic activity were during the third wave significantly less likely to backslide toward authoritarianism. The effect magnitude implies that by comparing a relatively state-dependent economy such as Zimbabwe, with an average of 4.74 on the economic freedom index during the estimation period, to economically freer Botswana, with an average of 7.19, leads to an average decrease in the tendency to backslide the following year by .042*(8.51–3.85), or approximately .099. Although there are some extreme outliers influencing this finding, it is robust to their exclusion.[7] As indicated in Appendix C, moreover, the economic freedom effect passes all robustness checks save one (it does not hold in the imputed sample of 196 countries). This, however, does not apply for the estimates of a curvilinear effect reported in the lower panel of Table 3.3. Although there is a tendency that downturns are most effectively avoided at intermediate levels of economic freedom, this finding is highly sensitive to a small number of extremely influential outliers.[8]

[7] This includes three extremely influential confirming outliers (Ghana 1981, Argentina 1976, and Peru 1992), as well as one extremely influential disconfirming outlier (Haiti 1991).

[8] The marginally significant effect of the squared index on upturns falters once a single influential outlier, Zambia in 1991, is excluded from the estimations sample. Excluding two relatively influential outliers, Ghana in 1981 and Argentina in 1976, renders the impact on downturns marginally significant.

Table 3.3 *Economic Freedom*

	Short-run			
	General	Upturns	Downturns	Long-run
Linear:				
Economic freedom index	.024	–.018	.042***	.252
	(.025)	(.017)	(.015)	(.245)
Curvilinear:				
Economic freedom index	.083	–.142**	.225***	.856
	(.100)	(.071)	(.070)	(1.04)
Economic freedom index^2	–.005	.012*	–.017***	–.057
	(.008)	(.006)	(.006)	(.089)

*significant at the .10-level, **significant at the .05-level, ***significant at the .01-level.

No. of observations = 2,827; no. of countries = 119; mean years observed per country = 23.8.

Note: Entries are unstandardized regression coefficients with panel-corrected standard errors in parentheses. All models also include two lags of the dependent variable and the determinants in Table 2.1, 3.1, 4.1 and 5.1 as controls. All explanatory variables in the table have been lagged one year.

Socioeconomic modernization and democratic recalcitrance

I will now turn to an assessment of the causal mechanisms underlying two of the economic factors that were linked to democratization during the third wave: socioeconomic modernization and economic crises. There are two reasons motivating the choice of these particular two. The first is theoretical. The putative mechanisms explaining why natural resource abundance hurts and economic freedom helps democracy are relatively unambiguous and well developed theoretically, a point that I shall return to in the concluding chapter. This is, however, not the case for socioeconomic modernization and economic performance, where there is instead a multitude of potential and not fully fleshed-out explanations alluded to in the literature. The second reason is empirical. For oil and minerals, Ross (2001) has already performed some empirical tests of hypothesized mechanisms. To the best of my knowledge, however, there have been no similar tests performed for the mechanisms of socioeconomic modernization or economic crisis. For economic performance, moreover, the most influential study uncovering mechanisms is based on case studies (Haggard and Kaufman 1995), the connection to large-*n* studies of which are largely unknown. Both theoretical indeterminacy and empirical shortage thus speak in favor of an attempt to unravel the mechanisms explaining these particular economic determinants.

So why then are socioeconomically modernized countries less likely to de-democratize? While the literature is replete with suggestions as to what explains the general connection between modernization and democracy, there have been few attempts to address this particular question.[9] Drawing on the more general literature, however, I may still work out some testable propositions.

Five ideas have dominated this literature, four of which were actually already present in Lipset's (1959) seminal article. First, according to Lipset development affects the nature of the class struggle in society. Most importantly, it helps develop a vibrant middle class, turning "the shape of the stratification structure so that it shifts from an elongated pyramid, with a large lower-class base, to a diamond with a growing middle class. A large middle class plays a mitigating role in moderating conflict since it is able to reward moderate and democratic parties and penalize extremist groups" (1959, p. 83). Although it has been argued that the working class rather than the middle class are the staunchest champions of democracy (Rueschemeyer *et al.* 1992; Collier 1999), the idea that modernization affects democracy through its impact on *socio-economic inequality* has been widely accepted in the literature, and as of late incorporated in the newest formal models of democratization (Boix 2003; Acemoglu and Robinson 2006).

Second, Lipset argued that economic development helps foster intermediary organizations in society – or, to use the catchword that has popularized this theme, to strengthen *civil society*. A society with a multitude of voluntary associations, the argument goes, helps check

[9] Among the rare exceptions are Przeworski (2005), Benhabib and Przeworski (2005), and Bueno de Mesquita *et al.* (2003, pp. 388–92), all of whom develop formal models based on the idea that wealthier societies are more likely to succeed in developing redistribution schemes acceptable to all parties. Another novel interpretation is Persson and Tabellini's (2009) "endogenous selection" interpretation: that income affects the survival of democracy more strongly than the transition from autocracy because countries more productive as democracies are over-represented among democracies. This latter theory does not easily extend to the non-economic components of the modernization syndrome that I study, however, and the former theories are not easily amenable to empirical testing.

and balance the power of the state, "serve to train men in the skills of politics" and "help increase the level of interest and participation in politics" (1959, p. 84). This theme has also been picked up and expanded more recently by, for example, Graham Gill (2000).

Third, Lipset (1959, pp. 83–84) argued that development helps foster democracy by enhancing certain political values, that is, by strengthening *political culture*. These values, or this culture, are according to Lipset primarily characterized by tolerance toward opposing views and, in general, a more moderate, restrained and rational style with respect to politics and political opposition. Piecemeal reform is preferred over radical change and social revolution. A recent book-length treatment by Ronald Inglehart and Christian Welzel (2005) shows that this tradition is also very much alive in the current debate on how to explain the modernization effect.

Fourth, and related to this, Lipset (1959, pp. 79–80) claimed that one component of the general modernization syndrome has special prominence, namely *education*. Mostly through its effect on the aforementioned democratic values, education raises the prospects for democracy. This idea is echoed in a recent economic theory arguing that human capital raises the benefits of political participation and draws relatively more people to actively support democracy (Glaeser *et al.* 2007).[10]

The one notion that is not easily traced back to Lipset's work, and thus is more genuinely new, is Boix's (2003) theory of asset specificity, and Acemoglu and Robinson's (2006) narrower but related concept of the capital-to-land ratio. Both accounts operate through the expected tax level under dictatorship and democracy. As society modernizes, in Boix's theory, assets become less specific and hence less easily taxed, which weakens the fear of democracy, or the preference for autocracy, among the economic elites. This facilitates both the emergence and survival of democracy. Acemoglu and Robinson (2006, chap. 9) model a similar dimension of the structure of the economy – the capital-to-land ratio – and find that as this ratio increases (e.g., with industrialization), the costs

[10] Yi Feng and Paul Zak (1999) make the similar argument that increasing *wealth* makes more people take political action in favor of democracy (*cf.* Zak and Feng 2003). Persson and Tabellini (2009), in turn, present a theory where per capita income positively affects democratization and democratic survival by influencing how ordinary people internalize the true economic benefit of being in a democracy (which is assumed to be positive), which in turn makes them more likely to rebel against dictatorship and defend democracy against coups.

of repression and coups increase, the tax rates under democracy decline, and the size and affluence of the middle class increases, which in turn means that the likelihood of democratization and democratic survival increases. This is thus their "modernization story," similar to but narrower than Boix's (2003) notion of asset specificity.[11]

Obviously all of these five partially overlapping propositions invoke phenomena that are difficult to observe empirically in a large sample of countries. Nevertheless, the first two of them have been partially addressed already. There is, to begin with, no support in my data for the contention that income inequality drives democratization (or de-democratization), nor that this would explain the modernization effect.[12] To the extent that popular mobilization proxies for the vitality of civil society – an assumption that of course could be questioned (see, e.g., Kopecký and Mudde 2003) – I may further reject the second proposition. The cultural proposition I have dealt with elsewhere (Hadenius and Teorell 2005a; Teorell and Hadenius 2006; *cf.* Welzel and Inglehart 2006). Suffice to say here that the survey data hitherto gathered to assess this thesis is too scattered across both time and space to allow for any robust conclusions.

What remains then are the fourth and fifth propositions, both of which at least partly are incorporated as components in my composite modernization index. What happens if I disaggregate this index and these components are pitted against each other in a single model? Although one should expect no clear-cut results from such an exercise considering their high level of inter-correlation, the fourth proposition should lead me to expect that education trumps the other modernization indicators when it comes to explaining downturns. The fifth is proxied by several components, but should (apart from education) lead me to expect industrialization as the primary force hindering de-democratization.

[11] Baizhu Chen and Yi Feng (1999) instead suggest a model where economic development leads to democracy through the choice of redistribution policy. This idea is similar to Przeworski (2005) and Benhabib and Przeworski (2005), although the latter two only pay attention to why democracies survive at high levels of per capita income.

[12] True, the nature of the class structure could tap into other dimensions than economic inequality. Since I lack systematic cross-country data on class structure, I can, however, not test this idea more directly. Moreover, Renske Doorenspleet (2005) finds no significant relationship between transitions to democracy and measures of the size of the middle vs. working class in a country.

Table 3.4 *Explaining the Modernization Effect (downturns)*

	Model				
	(1)	(2)	(3)	(4)	(5)
Industrialization	−.001				
	(.002)				
Education	−.000				
	(.001)				
Urbanization	−.001				
	(.001)				
Health conditions	−.005				
	(.030)				
Media proliferation	.042**	.065***	.046***		
	(.017)	(.013)	(.010)		
Log(GDP/capita)	.016				
	(.022)				
Socioeconomic modernization				.061***	.033***
				(.015)	(.012)
No. of successful coups			−1.68***		−1.72***
			(.105)		(.095)
No. of observations	2,485	2,884	2,884	3,792	3,792
No. of countries	143	150	150	165	165

* significant at the .10-level, ** significant at the .05-level, *** significant at the .01-level.

Note: Entries are unstandardized regression coefficients with panel-corrected standard errors in parentheses. All models use downturns in the level of democracy as the dependent variable, and also include two lags of the level of democracy and the determinants in Table 2.1, 3.1, 4.1 and 5.1 as controls. All explanatory variables in the table except the no. of successful coups have been lagged one year.

As model (1) of Table 3.4 makes clear, however, neither of these expectations is borne out in the data.[13] As can be seen, neither the level of education, nor industrialization, urbanization or even national income affects the tendency to avoid downturns, when all other

[13] I have in this model made two groupings of the nine modernization indicators making up the overall index (see Appendix A), in order to introduce some order to the interpretations. First, the two health indicators (life expectancy and infant mortality) and second, the three indicators of media proliferation (the number of TVs, radios and newspapers per capita) are made into two separate factor indices.

modernization indicators are simultaneously being controlled for. But one indicator does exert a significant impact, even under these extremely tough controls: the level of media proliferation. Of course, the degree of multicollinearity (the extent to which the independent variables covary) is extreme. But it is as extreme for the media proliferation component as for the other modernization indicators. It is thus a noteworthy finding that this component comes out as the sole significant determinant.

This is a truly unexpected finding, to the best of my knowledge not anticipated in any of the literature purporting to explain the modernization effect.[14] Why would it be the case that media proliferation helps obstruct democratic backsliding? Although this is not the time and place to delve into such a theory-building effort, two observations on the special nature of the media are in place. First, there is some evidence that television, in particular, is the most forceful check and balance underpinning democracy. This evidence comes from systematic analysis of the so-called "vladivideos," that is, the recorded corrupt transactions by Vladimir Montesinos, Peru's secret-police chief under President Alberto Fujimori in the mid-1990s. These transactions reveal that the typical bribe paid to a television-channel owner was much larger than that paid to an opposition politician or to a judge. If the size of the bribe price indicates how much Montesinos was willing to pay to buy off those who could have checked his and Fujimori's authoritarian rule, television was in other words democracy's staunchest guardian (MacMillan and Zoido 2004).

Second, as opposed to industrialization or education, the hypothesized effects of which are not dependent on the current regime, media proliferation should be *expected* to have a democratizing impact that increases with an already achieved level of democracy. Media proliferation does not lead to democratization in an authoritarian context because widespread media outlets could be a forceful tool in the hands of an authoritarian regime if media freedom is not protected (Norris 2008, p. 189). As media freedom increases, however, the potential for widely disbursed communications technologies to safeguard democracy is unleashed. In other words, media proliferation can hardly

[14] In Lipset's (1959) original argument, measures of media proliferation were simply entered as proxies for national wealth, without any further theoretical justification.

be expected to foster democratization, but, if free from state control, it should be able to hinder de-democratization.

Unfortunately, this theory of an interaction between media freedom and proliferation is not easily amenable to empirical testing. I would instead like to add another piece of empirical evidence to help address this puzzle in the future. More specifically, how does a country backslide into lower levels of democracy? Although there are alternatives, including electoral misappropriation by the ruling party, one prominent path should be that of the coup d'état. If media proliferation helps in staving off backsliding by preventing government coups (either from happening or from succeeding), one should expect to see a reduction of its effect on downturns once successful coups are being controlled for. This is exactly what I observe in models (2) and (3) of Table 3.4. The impact of media proliferation, which is here entered alone as my most prominent modernization indicator, drops from .065 to .046 when successful coups are controlled for. This makes for a reduction of some 30 percent of its effect.

Two caveats should be borne in mind when interpreting this result. First, media proliferation significantly affects downturns even regardless of coups, which means that there are other important pathways to be explored. Second, I am not in a position to claim that I have "explained" 30 percent of the effect of media proliferation this way. The reason is that the impact of coups on downturns is truly tautological. To say that democracies fall when successful coups are instigated is not to claim much.

What this finding does indicate, however, is that a fruitful avenue for further research on this topic would be to explore the ways in which media proliferation may defer coup attempts, or make them less likely to succeed. It has for example been observed that one of the first objectives of a military seizure is to grasp control of the key broadcasting installations, such as national TV and radio stations (see, e.g., Nordlinger 1977, p. 103). To the extent that media proliferation proxies for a broad array of media outlets, such seizure may be more difficult to carry out. Alternatively, "scandal-hungry journalists" may be "swift to scent out any new coup conspiracy" (Randall 1993, p. 644). To develop and test such assertions, a fruitful avenue for future research could thus be to study failed or aborted coups under conditions of high media proliferation.

Of course, as a final word, one should perhaps not take the prominence of media proliferation among the modernization indicators too literally. To the extent that one wishes to continue treating socioeconomic modernization as one coherent syndrome, however, a similar logic for further research suggests itself. As models (4) and (5) of Table 3.4 show, the effect of this general index also decreases substantially once successful coups are controlled for. In effect, almost half the impact of socioeconomic modernization on downturns is due to its ability to deter or derail coups. To explore why this might be the case is definitely worth further inquiry.

Economic crises and authoritarian vulnerability

My mechanism-oriented account of why economic crises trigger democratic upturns is based on the case studies of Haggard and Kaufmann (1995). As already noted in Chapter 1, an explicit ambition of their theoretical model is to bridge the structure and agency divide by linking actors' preferences and action to exogenous economic conditions. The key presumption is that authoritarian regimes, while lacking the kind of diffuse legitimacy which may be bestowed by competitive elections, still rest on "authoritarian bargains" with specific support groups. More precisely, they mention three such pivotal sets of actors: "private-sector business groups," "middle-class and popular-sector organizations," and "military and political elites who control the state and the main instruments of coercion." Declining economic conditions and corresponding pressures for policy adjustment potentially disrupt the authoritarian bargains forged with all three, thus creating a more hospitable environment for democratization (1995, p. 29).

First, tough stabilization programs are likely to threaten several bases on which private-sector business groups tend to cooperate with the regime, such as the protection of private property, state-led development policies that favor certain sectors, or more particularistic favors and rents. When the authoritarian government's ability to deliver in these areas is weakened due to economic crisis, the chances are that business groups increasingly perceive democracy as a preferable alternative. As a result, they are more likely to defect from the authoritarian bargain.

Second, authoritarian regimes often deflect opposition from popular sector groups through public employment, public works projects and consumer subsidies. Again, as an economic crisis hollows out state resources, the government's ability to sustain these material rewards weakens. The primary weapon of disaffected popular sector groups is then the mobilization of protest. These protests, especially large-scale strikes and mass demonstrations, become a dual weapon against the incumbent regime, by both fueling deteriorating economic performance itself, and by turning economic grievances into political demands for regime change.

Third, and perhaps most importantly, economic crisis exacerbates divisions within the authoritarian regime itself. Haggard and Kaufman (1995) explicitly follow O'Donnell and Schmitter (1986) and Przeworski (1991) in arguing that "the most proximate cause for the exit of authoritarian regimes can almost always be found in splits within the elite." They add, however, that a downturn of the economy tends to widen the gulf between hardliners and softliners. To begin with, the military, which tends to be well represented among the hardliners, is an exclusive popular sector group itself, offering its allegiance only in return for material favors. The regime's weakened capacity to deliver these favors when tough adjustment programs are required may drive a deeper wedge between the hardliner military establishment and softliner groups among regime elites. Moreover, the combination of the first two components of Haggard and Kaufman's theory may themselves boost the strategic importance of regime divisions:

> [F]rom the perspective of the authoritarian leadership, the defection of private-sector groups and the widening of popular-sector protest increase both the cost of coercion and the risk that it will prove ineffective. It is precisely under such conditions that the splits we have noted within the regime begin to have strategic importance for the transition process. "Softliners" begin to calculate that the corporate interests of the ruling elite are best guarded by conciliation, rather than further repression. (1995, pp. 29–32)

In other words, economic crisis makes private-sector defection, popular protest and elite divisions interact to make democratization more likely.

Since the second of these three mechanisms, that of popular protest, is a determinant in itself to which I will return in Chapter 5, it will not be considered here. Having found that economic crisis propels democratic upturns even when the level of protest is being held constant, I want in this section only to find the mechanisms that explain the effect of economic crises other than through this particular pathway.

The case studies Haggard and Kaufman provide in order to substantiate their theory are based on the transitions to democracy in Peru in 1980,

Bolivia in 1982, Argentina in 1983, Brazil and Uruguay in 1985, and the Philippines in 1986 (1995). Three of these fit my concept of pathway cases very well, one relatively well, whereas two cases do not fit at all. The two non-fitting cases are Peru in 1980 and Brazil in 1985, both of which only experienced *inflationary*, but no real recessionary crises. Since inflation is not systematically related to democratization in my analyses, I do not consider these cases further.

Figure 3.1 displays how the four remaining cases are located in the partial regression plot of growth and democratic upturns. The plot itself is simply a multivariate analog to the well-known scatter diagram. What it shows is the relationship between growth (lagged one year) and upturns after taking all other determinants into account. The negative regression slope corresponds exactly to the short-term impact of –.540 that growth according to Table 3.1 exerts on upturns. Within this context, Argentina in 1983, Uruguay in 1985 and the Philippines in 1986 all fit very well to the concept of pathway cases. As indicated within brackets, they are ranked 10th, 11th and 12th among all 3,795 country years in terms of the pathway criterion.[15] Bolivia is somewhat more problematic with a pathway rank of 40 in 1982, but if I shift to the year of 1981 its pathway rank is 31.[16] Taken as a whole, then, I believe

[15] Figure 3.1 also highlights some other features of my pathway criterion. The first is that most pathway cases are fairly extreme outliers in the sense that there is a large amount of change in their level of democracy that is unaccounted for even considering their degree of economic crisis (i.e., they have large residuals). As argued in Appendix D, I see no reason why this should disqualify them as pathway cases for assessing the mechanisms responsible for this particular determinant. Second, by Gerring and Seawright's (2007) account, most pathway cases experience little or no change in their level of democracy. The top-ranked pathway case according to their criterion, for example, is Gabon in 1975, positioned right on the regression line to the very left of the figure (not labeled). Gabon in 1975, however, experienced zero change on the democracy scale, and thus would provide very weak evidence of potential mechanisms linking economic performance to democratization.

[16] This shift may seem somewhat surprising given that it was not until in 1982 that the military in Bolivia eased repression and finally surrendered power to the congress elected two years earlier (Collier 1999, p. 148). The explanation comes from an oddity in the timing of the Freedom House scores, which lack a separate coding for the particular year of 1982. Instead, the 1981 scores incorporate the events up until August 1982, which (according to Freedom House's judgment) appears to cover the most substantial regime changes. Since Bolivia was more severely hit by recessionary crisis in 1980 than in 1981, this peculiarity in timing means that the year of 1981 appears to fit better than 1982.

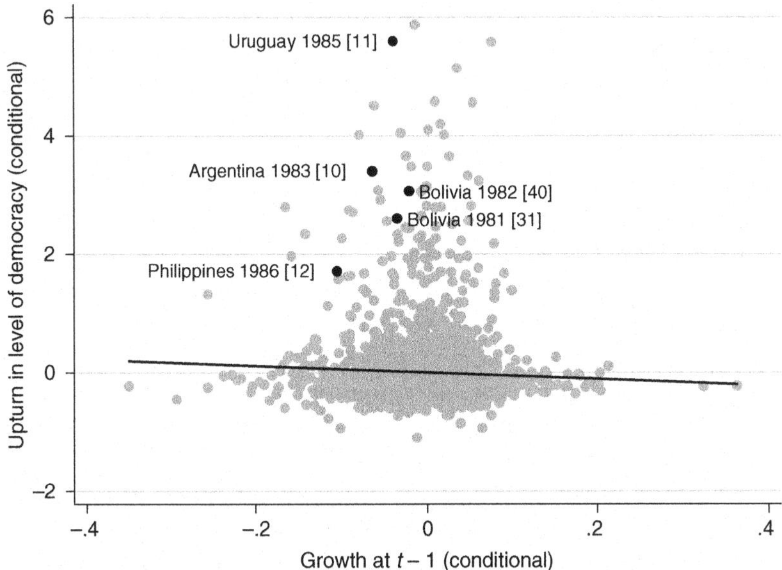

Figure 3.1 Case Studies of the Impact of Economic Crises on Upturns
Note: The graph is a partial regression (or added-variable) plot of the conditional relationship between economic growth, measured in fractions and lagged one year, and upturns (n =3,795). The figures within brackets are the rank order of each case in terms of the pathway criterion.

the case of Bolivia in the early 1980s fits the pathway criterion sufficiently well for my purposes.

The origins of the economic crises of these four countries in the early 1980s were a combination of past domestic policy mistakes and the international debt crisis. With the withdrawal of external lending, governments turned to the inflation tax to finance their fiscal and current-accounts deficits. After considerable hesitation adjustment measures were taken, such as devaluations and trade or exchange controls. The postponement of necessary policies, however, made their consequences even more disruptive (Haggard and Kaufman 1995, pp. 45–53).

The resulting defection of business elites was triggered by somewhat different grievances among the cases in question, depending on the nature of the original authoritarian bargain. In Bolivia and the Philippines, write Haggard and Kaufman, "business opposition crystallized against networks of favoritism that excluded significant private-sector interests" (1995, p. 56). The intricacies of the Bolivian transition from a military dictatorship headed by General Banzer to the restoration of democracy in 1977–82, wrought by coups, counter-coups and elections, cannot be assessed in detail here (see, e.g., Whitehead 1986; Collier 1999, pp. 143–49). Suffice to say that the Banzer regime was generally considered good for business. However, the advent of the extremely corrupt transitory military administration headed by García Meza in 1980–81 in particular led the major private-sector organization, the Bolivian Federation of Private Entrepreneurs (CEPB), to change stance. The business elite became convinced that the military had a "statist bent" and could not handle the economic crisis, and that the public sector was "becoming parasitic." Thus the CEPB already in August 1981 called for the restoration of the Congress and president elected prior to the Meza government (Haggard and Kaufman 1995, p. 57).

In the Philippines, the authoritarian regime was headed by Ferdinand Marcos, who as the then-elected president had seized power through a self-coup in 1972 by declaring martial law. As in Bolivia, private-sector elites in the Philippines had by and large endorsed martial law, but already in the early 1980s this support was beginning to crack under the pressure of economic decline. Several prominent members of the Makati Business Club, the main vehicle for the Philippine's non-crony private sector, started to speak out against the cronyism and corruption of Marcos' regime. Private-sector defection was, however, most importantly triggered by the assassination of Benigno Aquino, Marcos' long-time political opponent and himself from a prominent business-class family, in August 1983. After this event "the private sector played a crucial role in forging a centrist anti-Marcos coalition that included opposition politicians, academics, the Church, and the middle classes" (Haggard and Kaufman 1995, p. 56), which – as we shall see in Chapter 5 – eventually helped ensure the democratization of 1986–87.

In Argentina and Uruguay, usually considered as prominent examples of what O'Donnell (1979) termed "bureaucratic-authoritarian" regimes, the crisis dynamics unraveled somewhat differently. Here the grievance of private-sector groups was not primarily due to the erratic nature of corruption and cronyism, but rather to the inadequacies of technocratic control over economic decision making. Following the devaluations and tightened macroeconomic policies, serious strains between government and business began to surface. Argentina's major industrial association, The Industrial Union of Argentina, thus came out as outspoken critics of the military government after the bankruptcies of several industrial and financial firms in 1981 and 1982. In Uruguay, more or less the entire private business environment had already been alienated by the regime in the early 1980s. In Haggard and Kaufman's own words:

> With economic problems mounting, business elites began to reevaluate the costs and benefits of the technocratic decision-making style that characterized authoritarian rule . . . The private sector's gradual disaffection did not reflect a democratic epiphany, but a pragmatic response to changing circumstances. With authoritarian governments increasingly unable to deliver their side of the bargain, "voice" began to appear increasingly important to business groups. (1995, pp. 58–60)

The way in which all these four authoritarian regimes ended, finally, was significantly affected by how declining economic conditions widened intra-regime divisions. In the Latin American cases, these splits mostly occurred along the lines of hardliners and softliners within the military establishment itself. In Argentina and Bolivia, this led to a contracted process of coups and counter-coups, in the Argentinean case not ending until the disastrous Malvinas invasion had failed in 1982. In Uruguay, the transition was more peaceful as the military government gradually negotiated itself out of power, and the military establishment managed to remain more cohesive. The negotiations were, however, clearly affected by the economic difficulties, which weakened the hands of the diehards and promoted the acceptance of democracy among softliners. In the Philippines the declining economy deepened the rift between the civilian-led regime under Marcos and the military establishment, in the end leading to attempted mutiny in the wake of Marcos' attempt to steal the snap 1986 election (1995, pp. 66–71).

In sum, my statistical findings and Haggard and Kaufman's narratives of the four pathway cases combine as telling evidence that economic crisis is a truly causal determinant of democratization. That said, Haggard and Kaufman's account will not be the last theory on the consequences of economic crises for democratization. Nor can their case studies be considered the final word on the causal mechanisms linking these phenomena. Most importantly, the role of private-sector defection is of course conditioned on the existence of a private sector, which delimits the scope of this particular mechanism to the set of non-socialist economies (*cf.* 1995, pp. 371–74). The theory thus needs to be broadened to include other forms of authoritarian bargains with other support groups, and case study evidence from a broader array of economies needs to be mustered.

Another unresolved issue is why, assuming that Haggard and Kaufman's theory is correct, only recessionary and not inflationary crises act as significant determinants of democratization in my analyses. Related to this, one could ask whether it is the economic crisis itself or the particular policy response to crisis that is most critical. Timing is also of critical import. Although I for the sake of simplicity have imposed a uniform one-year lag in my statistical analyses of the effect of economic crisis on democracy, the case studies reveal a much more complicated pattern. In most instances, the economic crises were ongoing for several years before they precipitated regime change, but the time it took also varied by country. Future statistical work on the democratizing effects of economic crises must be made more sensitive to this issue.

Conclusion

In this chapter I have found that socioeconomic modernization affected the third wave of democratization by hindering backsliding toward authoritarianism. The most pertinent component of this underlying syndrome was media proliferation, which helps deter or derail coups. Recessionary crises, by contrast, triggered democratization, according to the case study evidence by provoking private-sector defection and intra-regime splits. Oil dependence instead blocked democratization, whereas freedom from state incursion in the economy hindered authoritarian reversals. Income inequality, however, did not exert any significant impact on the prospects for democratization during the third wave.

The power of economic prosperity is thus a double-edged sword. Whereas natural resource abundance and short-term economic growth keep democracy at bay, prior democratic achievements are better sustained at higher levels of socioeconomic modernization.

4 *The impetus from abroad: international determinants*

Politics has of course never been carried out in fully closed domestic arenas. Yet most observers agree that globalization during recent decades has been an important trend in the system of international relations. Countries are to begin with economically interdependent, and increasingly so. The expansion of international broadcast media, and the growing importance of intergovernmental organizations, also implies that national systems of government are becoming increasingly interdependent politically. Global ideas diffuse across country borders. Decision-making power in previously domestic affairs is being transferred to new government bodies in the international arena. Last, but not least, countries intervene intentionally in the domestic politics of one another.

There are thus various reasons to believe that international determinants played a key role in the third wave of democratization. But did they? In this chapter, I address this question after reviewing the extant literature on international determinants of democratization. My results speak in favor of there being three non-domestic forces at work: international trade, neighbor diffusion and pressure from regional international organizations. By again consulting both statistical and case study evidence, I then aim to uncover the mechanisms responsible for these results.

The literature on international determinants

There is a large and growing literature on factors impeding or enhancing democratization at the international level. An old school of thought in this regard comprises the so-called world system position and dependency theorists (for an overview see Bollen 1983, pp. 469–71; Hadenius 1992, pp. 91–98). They claimed that international capitalist exchange involving trade and investments favored the wealthy international "core" at the expense of the poor "periphery," which was exploited. In order to maintain this system of exploitation democratic rule in peripheral countries needs to be stifled, according to dependency theorists, since authoritarian leaders are supposedly more receptive to the interests of international economic centers.

However, most of the early cross-sectional tests of the dependency predictions produced weak or inconsistent support (Bollen 1983; Bollen and Jackman 1985; Gasiorowski 1988; Gonick and Rosh 1988). In a more recent account – although couched in the language of "globalization," presently more in vogue – Li and Reuveny (2003; 2009) have tested some of the old predictions in a cross-sectional time-series setting. Interestingly, their results by and large confirm dependency theory. According to their findings, both the volume of trade and portfolio investment inflows negatively affect democratization. And while foreign direct investment inflows – their third indicator of globalization – had a positive impact, it has weakened over time. Li and Reuveny conclude by stating that "the economic aspects of integration into the world economy are beginning to cause a decline in national democratic governance" (2003, p. 53).

That trade volume impacts negatively on democracy was also recently found by Roberto Rigobon and Dani Rodrik (2005). Li and Reuveny (2003), however, found a positive effect of another facet of international dependence: the spread of democratic ideas across countries, or what is usually referred to as democratic diffusion. To systematically assess such external diffusion or demonstration effects with large-*n* data is a fairly novel enterprise in this field. Yet hitherto the evidence has by and large confirmed expectations. Diffusion has been shown to affect democratization both at the most proximate level of neighbor states, at the level of world regions, and at the global level (Starr 1991; O'Loughlin *et al.* 1998; Kopstein and Reilly 2000; Starr and Lindborg 2003; Brinks and Coppedge 2006; Gleditsch and Ward 2006).

In a recent book, Pevehouse (2005) suggests another potential non-domestic determinant of democratization: regional international organizations. With a mixture of case study and statistical evidence, Pevehouse purports to show that democratic regional organizations can pressurize authoritarian member states to undertake democratic reforms, socialize military and economic elites into accepting democratic procedures, and bind newly elected elites in fledgling democracies to these reforms once committed. In this way, membership in democratic regional organizations, according to Pevehouse (2005), both precipitates movements toward democracy and enhances democratic survival.

Finally, a more drastic form of international determinant that has climbed onto the international agenda, particularly since the US-led invasions of Afghanistan and Iraq, is direct foreign intervention. States attempting to improve the level of democracy in another country may, for example, impose economic sanctions or stage a foreign military intervention. Recent comparative case and large-*n* studies, however, cast some doubt over the general efficiency of these strategies, noting that such impositions from abroad sometimes work and sometimes fail (Bueno de Mesquita and Downs 2006; Pickering and Peceny 2006; Grimm 2008; Hufbauer *et al.* 2009, pp. 67–69, 158–59; *cf.* Pickering and Kisangani 2006).

Most of these studies of international determinants have, however, not assessed the impact of globalization, diffusion, regional organizations and foreign interventions net of all other domestic influences of democratization. As should be evident, what for example appears to be a diffusion linkage between two countries could disappear once possible confounding factors simultaneously affecting democracy in both countries are taken into account. Basically the same goes for economic dependence, shared membership in regional international organizations, economic sanctions or foreign military intervention. I shall now try to remedy this by assessing international effects in the context of more fully specified models.

Empirical results

Turning then to Table 4.1, my results partly confirm the finding by Li and Reuveny (2003) and Rigobon and Rodrik (2005) that trade volume impeded democratization during the third wave. For this time period there was a statistically significant and negative, although substantively not very large, impact on upturns, implying that a 100 percent increase in a country's trade volume (relative to its GDP) led to an estimated .076 decrease in its propensity to democratize the following year. At face value this finding seems to confirm the old prediction by dependency theory that largely trade-dependent countries are hindered from democratizing, although this is an interpretation I shall return to later in this chapter. The effect is fairly robust to alternative specifications, but not quite to the same extent as the other determinants are. Most importantly, I find no effect of trade when only the within-country variation is retained, and the impact is sensitive to the choice of democracy measure. Moreover, in the fully imputed global sample the coefficient, while similar in magnitude, is only marginally significant (see Appendix C).

Table 4.1 *International Determinants*

	Short-run			
	General	Upturns	Downturns	Long-run
Trade volume	-.086*	-.076**	-.011	-1.08*
	(.051)	(.036)	(.026)	(.604)
Democratization among neighbors	.116***	.077***	.039**	1.45***
	(.031)	(.024)	(.019)	(.488)
Prior level of democracy among neighbors	.008	-.003	.011**	.097
	(.007)	(.005)	(.005)	(.089)
No neighbors	-.017	-.086**	.070	-.208
	(.069)	(.044)	(.044)	(.867)
Regional level of democracy	.019**	.008	.012*	.242**
	(.010)	(.007)	(.006)	(.118)
Global level of democracy	.010	.002	.009	.126
	(.017)	(.014)	(.011)	(.208)
Democratization of regional organization	.030	.029	.001	.373
	(.028)	(.021)	(.018)	(.367)
Prior level of democracy of regional organization	.028**	.035***	-.007	.348**
	(.013)	(.007)	(.009)	(.143)
No regional organization	.214**	.203***	.011	2.67**
	(.095)	(.062)	(.056)	(1.07)

* significant at the .10-level, ** significant at the .05-level, *** significant at the .01-level.
No. of observations = 3,795; no. of countries = 165; mean years observed per country = 23.0.
Note: Entries are unstandardized regression coefficients with panel-corrected standard errors in parentheses. All models also include two lags of the dependent variable and the determinants in Table 2.1, 3.1 and 5.1 as controls. Trade volume and democratization among neighbors and of regional organization have been lagged one year, whereas the remaining variables are lagged two years.

As shown in Table 4.2, for a more restricted sample of countries (due to limited data availability), larger integration into the world economy in terms of international capital flows according to my estimates did not impact on democratization during the third wave. Apart from being inconsistent with dependency theory, this contradicts Li and Reuveny's (2003; 2009) findings for both foreign direct investment and portfolio flows.

Turning back to Table 4.1, my next set of international determinants aim at capturing geographical diffusion effects – the spread of democracy

Table 4.2 *International Capital Flows*

	Short-run			
	General	Upturns	Downturns	Long-run
Foreign direct investment	-.046	-.088	.042	-.615
	(.093)	(.070)	(.047)	(1.27)
Portfolio investment	.143	.177	-.034	1.92
	(.154)	(.122)	(.075)	(2.10)

* significant at the .10-level, ** significant at the .05-level, *** significant at the .01-level. No. of observations = 2,577; no. of countries = 152; mean years observed per country = 17.0.

Note: Entries are unstandardized regression coefficients with panel-corrected standard errors in parentheses. All models also include two lags of the dependent variable and the determinants in Table 2.1, 3.1, 4.1 and 5.1 as controls. All explanatory variables in the table have been lagged one year.

or autocracy from one country to another. The measurement strategy here follows the larger literature by including the average level of democracy at three spatial levels: globally, among countries belonging to the same world region, and among neighboring countries. Of the three spatial levels included, only the most geographically proximate appears to have had an effect. If the mean level of democracy among neighboring countries was shifted upward one unit between time t–2 and t–1, the net expected change in democracy at time t was .116. The long-run equilibrium level of democracy was accordingly increased by 1.45 on the 0–10 democracy scale. This implies a fairly tight long-run adjustment of the levels of democracy among neighboring states. As the relative magnitudes of the impact on upturns versus downturns indicate, moreover, this neighbor diffusion effect is primarily driven by countries moving in the upwards direction. The effect on upturns is robust to most alternative specifications (see Appendix C),[1] whereas the impact on downturns depends on some relatively extreme influential observations.[2]

1 For reasons unclear to me, neighbor diffusion is not a statistically significant determinant of upturns when only the Freedom House measure of civil liberties is used as the dependent variable, and only marginally significant on Freedom House political rights. More research is needed to explain why the diffusion effect is thus primarily driven by the Polity measure of democracy.

2 These observations are Gambia in 1994, Ghana in 1981 and Thailand in 1976. If any of these three cases are omitted from the analysis, neighbor diffusion is no longer a statistically significant determinant of downturns.

At first glance, Table 4.1 appears to indicate that diffusion effects also occurred at the level of world regions, but this result falters once two extremely influential outliers are excluded.[3] In other words, during the third wave there seem to have been no diffusion effects at work (net of other influences) either at the regional or global level. In this regard my results differ from the existing literature on diffusion effects, the probable reason being my more fully specified explanatory model.

Next, I test Pevehouse's (2005) argument on the importance of regional organizations. I follow his own measurement strategy, which implies that the level of democracy for a specific military, economic or political intra-regional organization is defined as the average degree of democracy among the countries belonging to the same regional organization. For countries belonging to more than one regional organization, only the score for the most democratic regional organization is included. The results confirm one key prediction from Pevehouse's theory: During the third wave membership in relatively democratic regional organizations precipitated upturns in the level of democracy of a country – a result that turns out to be extremely robust to alternative specifications (see Appendix C).[4] As should be clear, it was the current level of democracy of a regional organization that mattered, not the change. I may further conclude that the statistical pattern is not driven by countries joining democratic regional organizations, since the same results apply when controlling for the number of regional organizations to which a country belongs, as well as change in that number (results not shown). The key finding is thus that countries *belonging* to a regional organization in which all member countries were fully democratic (earning a score of 10) on average increased their democracy scores by .28 as compared to countries belonging to regional organizations where all member states were fully authoritarian (i.e., with a score of 0), implying a long-term upward shift in level of democracy by 3.48.

[3] These outliers are Turkey in 1980 and Fiji in 1987, where military coups brought down democracy to a level more in tune with their respective regional averages at the time. Once these two outliers are excluded, regional diffusion exerts no significant impact on democratization.

[4] The result is insensitive to the exclusion of four relatively influential outliers: Turkey in 1983, Guyana in 1975, Guinea-Bissau in 1994 and Portugal in 1974. I also get similar results when using the mean of the level of democracy among the regional organizations to which a country belongs rather than the maximum.

Table 4.3 *Foreign Interventions*

	Short-run			
	General	Upturns	Downturns	Long-run
Economic sanctions	–.068	.146	–.213**	–.720
	(.143)	(.099)	(.104)	(1.53)
No. of observations	2,630	2,630	2,630	2,630
No. of countries	158	158	158	158
International military intervention	.119	.408*	–.289	1.19
	(.330)	(.238)	(.210)	(3.28)
No. of observations	2,181	2,181	2,181	2,181
No. of countries	124	124	124	124
Foreign intervention index	–.045	.197**	–.242**	–.481
	(.136)	(.096)	(.101)	(1.45)
No. of observations	3,035	3,035	3,035	3,035
No. of countries	159	159	159	159

* significant at the .10-level, ** significant at the .05-level, *** significant at the .01-level.
Note: Entries are unstandardized regression coefficients with panel-corrected standard errors in parentheses. All models also include two lags of the dependent variable and the determinants in Table 2.1, 3.1, 4.1 and 5.1 as controls. All explanatory variables in the table have been lagged one year.

I find no support, however, for the flip side of Pevehouse's argument: that regional organizations also help democracies survive. In terms of my empirical strategy, that is, I find no effect of regional organizations on downturns.

Turning, finally, to the impact of foreign intervention, I perform three simple tests in Table 4.3 on a more restricted sample of countries. Economic sanctions mostly occur in the form of cut-offs of finance, aid and/or trade (see Hufbauer *et al.* 2009). As the uppermost panel indicates, such sanctions during the third wave had a statistically significant but negative impact on downturns. This implies that economic sanctions imposed by democratic countries on average led to *more* backsliding toward authoritarianism. Hostile military interventions here involve actions where troops on the ground move into the territory of another country in order to oppose the target government or support rebel groups (Pickering and Peceny 2006). In the middle panel, I find that military intervention hostile to the incumbent regime had a marginally significant but positive impact on upturns. In neither case, however, were there any general average effects on democratization, which is explained by the fact that the effects of both types of foreign interventions are reversely signed for upturns as compared to downturns.

This more general finding comes out even more clearly in the lowermost panel, where I collapse the measures of economic sanctions and military interventions into one "index," simply indicating whether *any* form of intervention occurred. This substantially increases the number of interventions included, and also allows me to cover a longer time span (in effect, from 1974 to 2001). As can be seen, this index exerts a significant and positive impact on upturns, and a significant but negative impact on downturns. There is no general effect, however, neither in the short- nor in the long-run. In line with the previous literature, I thus find that foreign interventions imposed by democratic countries are a mixed blessing. They are almost as likely to improve as to deteriorate the conditions of democracy in the target country.

In sum, I find three robust international determinants of democratization during the third wave: trade volume, with a negative impact, as well as neighbor diffusion and membership in democratic regional organizations, both with a positive impact. I now turn to an exploration of what mechanisms may explain the three.

Trade dependency and stalled democratization

As already noted, that countries dependent on the external world in terms of trade should be less likely to democratize is an idea dating back to dependency and world system theories in the 1970s. Although most of these writings concentrated on growth and global inequality, they also yielded predictions on the prospects for democracy. Most importantly, these scholars assumed that the world could be divided into a set of wealthy and powerful democracies at the "core," and a set of poor and marginalized countries at the "periphery." Most simply put, the notion was that the economic and political elites in these two sets of countries worked in tandem to suppress and limit the suffrage of the general populace in the periphery. In terms of trade, the argument goes, the core countries penetrate the peripheral countries economically, and an authoritarian government in these countries is necessary to sustain this exploitation (see, e.g., Bollen 1983; Hadenius 1992, pp. 91–98).

In Table 4.4, I test whether the negative impact of trade volume on upturns could be explained in terms of with *whom* one trades. Since I

Table 4.4 *Explaining the Effect of Trade Volume (upturns)*

	Model			
	(1)	(2)	(3)	(4)
Trade volume	−.087	−.111*	−.081	−.106*
	(.054)	(.057)	(.054)	(.057)
Trade with US, UK and France		.104		.101
		(.070)		(.069)
Trade with China and USSR/Russia			−.140	−.117
			(.206)	(.204)

* significant at the .10-level, ** significant at the .05-level, *** significant at the .01-level.
No. of observations = 2,961; no. of countries = 153; mean years observed per country = 19.3.

Note: Entries are unstandardized regression coefficients with panel-corrected standard errors in parentheses. All models use upturns in the level of democracy as the dependent variable, and also include two lags of the level of democracy and the determinants in Table 2.1, 3.1, 4.1 and 5.1 as controls. All explanatory variables in the table have been lagged one year.

have only information on the latter for a subset of countries and years (data is from Gleditsch 2002), I start in model (1) by rerunning the model with all determinants on this more restricted sample. As can be seen, the negative coefficient for trade on this sample is of approximately equal size, even slightly stronger (as compared to Table 4.1), but not statistically significant. Although this is unfortunate, it does not completely obviate the logic of testing whether the effect decreases when potential mechanisms are being controlled for. In model (2), I thus test the expectation from dependency theory that the negative effect of trade is due to trade with the "core" economies of the world. Although one could quibble about what countries more exactly form this core, few would deny that the United States, Great Britain and France are among them. When controlling for the share of trade with these particular countries, however, the negative coefficient on general trade volume is unaffected (it even increases somewhat). Equally important, trading with these core economies in itself does not hurt democracy. This finding goes directly against the grain of dependency theory.

By an alternative version of this theory, however, it could be that what matters is being dependent on trade with a powerful authoritarian state whose security interests favor imposing autocracy in the partner countries as well. Two suggestions for such "regional hegemons" that directly come to mind are of course China and the USSR/Russia. Controlling for bilateral trade volume with these two countries in model (3) again produces insignificant results, however, and does not diminish the negative effect of trade volume. Nor are the results different if I control for trade with both the capitalist core and hegemonic authoritarian countries in model (4). In sum, the negative trade effect is a finding in want of a theoretical explanation.

What explains neighbor diffusion?

The growing literature on democratic diffusion has suggested several causal mechanisms through which the process of neighbor diffusion may occur. Two of the most plausible rival explanations are that neighbor diffusion may occur through imposition or emulation. In the first case, countries that move toward democracy themselves try to promote democratization among their neighbors (Brinks and Coppedge 2006, p. 467; Gleditsch and Ward 2006, p. 919). Their reasons for doing so may vary, but one likely possibility is that they would do so in order to enhance internal security. If democracies are less likely to fight each other, as democratic peace theory would have it, then fledgling democracies have a security interest in helping the democratic opposition topple incumbent regimes among its neighbors (Pevehouse 2005, p. 18). In the case of emulation, by contrast, the driving force of diffusion comes from within the neighboring countries themselves. By emulating the successful example of the neighbor that first installs democracy, by discovering "that it can be done" and learning "how it can be done" (Huntington 1991, p. 101), the democratic opposition may raise its chances of succeeding in overthrowing its own autocratic incumbent. Also the incumbent elites may be affected through emulation, since "reluctant leaders in autocracies may be more willing to initiate difficult reforms if the experiences of other states suggest that the costs and consequences of reforms may not be as bad as they had feared" (Gledistch and Ward 2006, p. 920). The two mechanisms of imposition and emulation are of course not mutually exclusive. In the words of Beissinger, it may not "simply be a matter of the pull of example," but "also in part a matter of the push ... by those who have already succeeded" (2007, p. 266).

Unfortunately, the data at my disposal does not allow me to fully disentangle these two mechanisms of diffusion. Indirectly, however, I may invoke evidence brought to bear on both of them. To begin with, I

Table 4.5 *Explaining the Neighbor Diffusion Effect (upturns)*

	Model			
	(1)	(2)	(3)	(4)
Democratization among neighbors	.081***	.077***	.089***	.088***
	(.025)	(.024)	(.027)	(.027)
Democratization of regional		.029	.027	.030
organization		(.021)	(.021)	(.022)
Inflation among neighbors			−.001	
			(.004)	
Growth among neighbors			−.272	
			(.290)	
Demonstrations among neighbors				−.249
				(1.005)
Riots among neighbors				.243
				(1.004)
Strikes among neighbors				.046
				(.033)
No. of observations	3,795	3,795	3,706	3,719
No. of countries	165	165	162	163

* significant at the .10-level, ** significant at the .05-level, *** significant at the .01-level.
Note: Entries are unstandardized regression coefficients with panel-corrected standard errors in parentheses. All models use upturns in the level of democracy as the dependent variable, and also include two lags of the level of democracy and the determinants in Table 2.1, 3.1, 4.1 and 5.1 as controls. The neighbor democratization and democratization of regional organization variables have been lagged one year, whereas the remaining variables in the table are lagged two years.

have already in Table 4.1 controlled for one plausibly powerful mechanism of imposition: the influence of regional organizations. Since regional organizations, by their nature, bring together countries located in close geographical proximity, the process of neighbor imposition may of course work through the channels of a regional organization. What then is the effect of neighbor diffusion when this mechanism is not included in the model? Model (1) of Table 4.5 provides the answer. Without controlling for regional organizations, the effect of neighbor democratization is .081. The reduction of this effect to .077 in model (2) is, however, miniscule. I thus find no support for this particular process of neighbor imposition, namely that it would work through the channels of a common regional organization.

In models (3) and (4), I try instead to proxy for some of the possible processes through which neighbor emulation may occur. Imagine a hypothetical country A, surrounded by countries B, C and D. The underlying idea is to control for events in the neighboring countries B, C and D that may first have triggered democratization in these countries and then caused democratization through emulation in A. To the extent that I may uncover such events, the direct effect of democratization in B, C and D on democratization in A should dissipate. In model (3), following this line of thought, I include indicators of economic crises among neighboring countries. To the extent that authoritarian regimes were toppled by economic crisis, as my results in the previous chapter tend to support, one might plausibly believe that the spread of economic crisis to neighboring countries masquerades as neighbor diffusion. This is, however, not the case. The positive effect of neighbor democratization on upturns is unaffected by the extent of economic crisis in neighboring countries, whereas the latter has no independent effect in itself.

In model (4), finally, I perform a similar exercise, but by introducing indicators of popular mobilization among neighbors. Recent work on the so-called "colored revolutions" that swept through Serbia, Georgia, Ukraine and Kyrgyzstan in the first years of the twenty-first century has uncovered important diffusion processes at work through the spread of collective protest (see, e.g. Beissinger 2007; Tucker 2007). If these mechanisms travel back in time, and to other geographical places, perhaps what drove neighbor diffusion during the third wave was the spread of popular protest from one country to the other? Again, however, expectations falter when countered with empirical evidence. As model (4) shows, there is no reduction in the effect of neighbor democratization. And popular mobilization among neighboring countries does not affect democratization, net of other influences.

Further work thus needs to be done in order to pinpoint the causal mechanisms through which neighbor diffusion works. A key contribution in this regard would be to bring in more systematic case study evidence to assess whether the rough proxies for neighbor diffusion really pick up real-world processes on the ground. An indication that this might not be quite so is that most of the effect of this variable, according to my estimates, seems to have taken place in a part of the world with, to the best of my knowledge, comparatively little case evidence of neighbor imposition or emulation: Sub-Saharan Africa. There is, for example, substantial anecdotal evidence to the effect that experiences in the near abroad affected the mindset of pro-democratic forces in the sequential fall of communist regimes in Eastern Europe. In the words of Timothy Garton Ash, who was a local observer at most of these dramatic transitions, with strong personal connections to the democratic opposition: "Everyone knew, from their neighbours' experiences, that it could be done. More than that, their neighbours had given them a few ideas about how it should be done" (1990, p. 127). It has also been stated that Latin American democratization during the third wave was largely a process of regional diffusion (Mainwaring and Pérez-Liñán 2005a; 2005b).

Whereas the neighbor diffusion effect is highly robust to the exclusion of Eastern European or Latin American regimes (or any other of the world regions), however, it falters completely if I exclude Sub-Saharan African countries from the estimation sample. Similarly, among the twenty most fitting cases according to the pathway criterion, only one is located in Eastern Europe (Armenia in 1998), and six in Latin America, whereas ten are Sub-Saharan African countries (most prominently the Central African Republic in 1993, and Zambia and Angola in 1991). A critical test for the neighbor diffusion hypothesis in the future, at least in the form it is now being proxied for in statistical studies, would thus be to assess the events more closely in these particular cases.

Do regional organizations foster democratization?

I will now perform such an assessment, but for the third and final international determinant: membership in democratic regional organizations. The argument for neighbor diffusion – that the measure of the influence of regional organization is very approximate in nature – applies equally well here. Recall that, following Pevehouse (2005), I measure the level of democracy of a regional organization as the mean level of democracy among its member states, and then for each country insert the level of democracy of the most democratic regional organization to which that particular country belongs (without taking the level of democracy in the country itself into account). The fact that I in Table 4.1 find a statistically significant effect of the level of this variable on upturns, net of all other determinants, is of course not necessarily evidence of a causal relationship. It could simply reflect the fact that countries belonging to the same regional organizations democratize in tandem (albeit with some time lag), or that they tend to approach the same long-run equilibrium level of democracy due to other exogenous reasons that have not been controlled for. Case study evidence is thus needed to test whether this measurement strategy really picks up a real-world impact of regional organization. And, at least indirectly, case study evidence for such an effect could affect our belief in the neighbor diffusion variable as well.

Pevehouse hypothesizes three distinct causal mechanisms through which membership in a democratic regional organization may further democratization in a country. The first he simply calls *pressure*. Through open verbal condemnation and threats of sanctions or other punishments, such as membership suspension, a regional organization may hurt or at least threaten to hurt the economy of an authoritarian regime, and even help to delegitimize it domestically: "If allies and institutional partners treat the regime as a pariah state, this can impact on public and elite perceptions within the state. These pressures can help to weaken an authoritarian regime's grip on power" (2005, pp. 17, 19).

The second mechanism is termed the *acquiescence* effect. Much as Haggard and Kaufman (1995), Pevehouse assumes that an authoritarian regime depends on the support of certain critical elite groups that may veto an attempted move toward democracy. Involvement in a democratically committed regional organization, the theory goes, may dampen fears of democracy among these elite groups and thereby help them acquiesce to the transition. Pevehouse provides two more specific examples of such groups, and thus of how this mechanism may operate. The first is credible commitment to liberal-economic protection of property-right infringements through membership in regional economic and/or trade organizations. This particular acquiescence is thus mostly crucial for the private-sector economic elite, whose preferences for democracy may be "locked in" through the ties to a regional organization. The second example is socialization of the military by cooperating with other more democratic countries in regional security organizations or military alliances. By interacting with military elites from these other countries, the military may be persuaded that "the role of the military is not that of an internal police force involved in domestic politics, but rather to protect the state from external enemies" (2005, pp. 20–25).

Finally, regional organizations may promote democratization by *legitimizing* interim governments, that is, caretaker governments in power between the breakdown of autocracy and before the holding of founding elections. Membership in democratic regional organizations

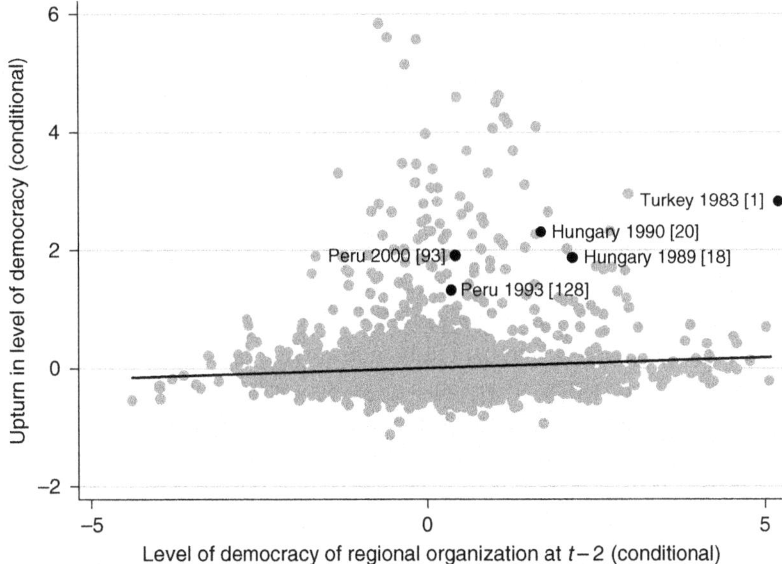

Figure 4.1 Case Studies of the Impact of Regional Organizations on Upturns
Note: The graph is a partial regression (or added-variable) plot of the conditional relationship between the level of democracy of a country's most democratic regional organization, lagged two years, and upturns (n = 3,795). The figures within brackets are the rank order of each case in terms of the pathway criterion.

may help these fragile governments to credibly signal their commitment to complete the move to democracy (2005, pp. 25–27).

The three case studies for which Pevehouse traces evidence of these causal mechanisms are highlighted in Figure 4.1. The redemocratization of Turkey in 1983 turns out to be the best fitting of all 3,795 cases in terms of the pathway criterion. The transition to democracy in Hungary in the late 1980s also fits relatively well, with the "liberalization" of 1989 ranked 18th and the move to more "full democracy" in 1990 ranked 20th. The Peruvian cases, however, do not fit as well, being ranked 93rd and 128th, respectively. I shall return to an interpretation of this below and now instead turn to the case study evidence for each of these three countries.

Turkey

The military intervention in Turkey on September 12, 1980 was the third time the military had unseated a civilian government since the inauguration of multiparty politics in 1950. Under the auspices of the National Security Council, chaired by General Evren, the military dissolved the government and Parliament, banned all political activities, monitored the press and installed martial law. Arrests and harsh repression of tens of thousands of political activists and journalists followed. The return to multiparty competition was initiated in 1982 through the drafting of a new constitution, approved in a nationwide referendum, and completed in November 1983, when the one party not headed by a military was able to win a majority of seats in national elections (Evin 1994, pp. 23–26; Dagi 1996, pp. 125–26; Pevehouse 2005, p. 140).

Although General Evren already at his first press conference after the takeover promised to reinstall a new democratically elected civilian government in due course (Dagi 1996, p. 125), Pevehouse argues that the actions of primarily two regional organizations in the area helped to shape the timetable of this transition back toward democracy. The first of these was the European Economic Community (EEC), with which Turkey had signed an association agreement in 1970. The EEC mostly put economic pressure on the military regime in Turkey by first increasing its financial assistance to Turkey in 1981, and then withdrawing that aid conditional on improvements in human rights and the return of democracy (Pevehouse 2005, p. 146; Dagi 1996, pp. 129–30, 137–38).

Turkey not being a member state of the EEC, however, the relevance of this case evidence for explaining the statistical relationship between regional organizations and democracy could be questioned. In effect, the EEC never enters my (or Pevehouse's) data for the Turkish case. Instead, there are three political, economic or military regional organizations of which Turkey was a member in 1981 (two years before the significant upturn in 1983): the Council of Europe (COE), NATO and the Organization for Security and Cooperation in Europe (OSCE). Fortunately, the COE is the second organization for which Pevehouse (2005) is able to trace case study evidence for Turkey.[5] The COE was able to put psychological pressure on the military regime by exploiting

[5] Strictly speaking, the COE is not *the* regional organization whose democracy score enters my (and thus Pevehouse's) data, since Turkey's most democratic regional organization was NATO. The difference in democracy level between NATO and the OSCE in 1981 is miniscule, however (being 9.58 for the OSCE and 9.76 for NATO), and, as argued before, the effect of regional organizations is robust to the replacement of the maximum by the mean level of democracy among all regional organizations.

the great symbolic importance membership in the council had for Turkey. Already in September 1980, the Parliamentary Assembly of the COE condemned the events in Turkey and called for an immediate return to democracy. The issue of suspending Turkey's membership was also discussed on several occasions in the years to come, although that threat was never realized (Dagi 1996, pp. 131–34). The COE sent multiple fact-finding missions to Turkey to investigate allegations of human rights abuses, the most crucial of which arrived in late 1981, only a month after the military government had completed its stranglehold on the opposition by banning all political parties. Turkey tried to reject this visit by a 25-member delegation but was pressured to admit it. Only a week before the delegation's arrival, moreover, General Evren announced an approximate date for new general elections, a move that at least partly was motivated by an anxiety regarding how the report from the delegation would affect Turkey's future status in the Council (Dagi 1996, pp. 137–38; Pevehouse 2005, p. 147).

Pressure from the Council of Europe thus constitutes the major causal mechanism present in the Turkish case. True, membership in NATO could have provided room for an acquiescence effect, but NATO appeared to have been very soft on the Turkish military regime in the early 1980s. Although there are some allegations of it in the literature, even Pevehouse (2005, p. 147) concedes that "NATO's contribution to the redemocratization of Turkey flowed from its socialization of officers in the Turkish military is fairly weak."

Hungary

The critical democratizing reforms in Hungary were initiated in early 1989, when the Communist Party, which had been in power since after the end of World War II, legalized independent political parties. Round-table talks in September/October that same year ended in an agreement to hold genuine multiparty elections, as well as in several other constitutional amendments that were approved by a national referendum in November. Free and fair parliamentary elections were held in the spring of 1990, which resulted in the formation of a coalition government comprising opposition political parties under Prime Minister Antall (Pevehouse 2005, pp. 116–17; also see Gill 2000, pp. 196–97; Saxonberg 2001, pp. 8–9).

The case study evidence for an effect of regional organizations in Hungary is, however, somewhat strained. Apart from the problem that

Pevehouse (2005) mostly discusses the impact of regional organizations to which Hungary was not a member in 1989–90 (the EEC and NATO), or one that it did not join until 1990 (the COE), there is in this case also a more general temporal disjunction. Namely that most of the activities *any* regional organization directed toward Hungary took place *after* 1990. The most important effects, according to Pevehouse, were exerted by the EEC and the COE. Already in July 1989 the EEC had initiated an economic restructuring program, including both grants and loans, geared toward Hungary and Poland (implying a causal mechanism of direct economic benefits, not anticipated by Pevehouse's theoretical framework). The COE, after granting membership to Hungary in November 1990, also provided technical assistance, and together with the EEC helped legitimize the Antall government and to signal its commitment to continued reforms (Pevehouse 2005, pp. 121–26). By that time, however, Hungary had already completed its move from 4.1 in 1988 to 9.16 in 1990, according to the democracy scale used throughout this book.[6] Its later progression to the highest score of 10.0, achieved only in 2004, was gradual and does not drive my result on the impact of regional organizations on democratization.

In 1987–88 (applying the two-year lag from my statistical model), Hungary was a member of three regional organizations: the Council of Mutual Economic Assistance, the Warsaw Pact and the OSCE. Of these three, the OSCE is of course the most democratic (with a democracy score of around 7.80, excluding Hungary), and thus the one that should play the democracy-enhancing role posited by Pevehouse (2005) in order to explain the statistical impact of regional organizations on upturns. However, most of the influence the OSCE appears to have exerted again occurs after 1990. Pevehouse primarily discusses the OSCE's importance for an acquiescence effect, which allegedly would have helped to socialize the Hungarian military into accepting civilian supremacy. Although NATO's role in this regard probably overshadows the OSCE through the Partnership for Peace agreement (launched in 1994!), the OSCE also provided retraining of Hungarian military leaders in order to encourage Western-style civil-military relations

[6] As a matter of fact, Hungary "completed" its "transition to democracy" in 1990 also according to the operational criterion Pevehouse himself uses to establish this, that is, receiving a polity score of at least +6.

(2005, p. 119). There is, however, no evidence that this occurred as early as in the late 1980s, nor that the military ever posed a threat to the transition to democracy in Hungary. If anything, the acquiescence of the Hungarian military might have played a role in discouraging a later coup, but that would be part of a mechanism linking regional organizations to the absence of downturns (a relationship my statistical analysis does not support).

What the OSCE might have provided that fits the timing of Hungary as a pathway case is more direct pressure on the Communist regime. Although there is some evidence suggesting that the 1975 Helsinki Final Act (on which the OSCE is based) promoted a general climate of support for oppositional movements, particularly in Poland and Czechoslovakia (2005, p. 118; Whitehead 1997, pp. 44–47), there is no direct support for this in the Hungarian case. And while there seems to be a temporal proximity between the OSCE's adoption of the Vienna Concluding Document in January 1989, where it made "great strides forward in the sensitive area of human rights" (Hyde-Price 1994, p. 237), and the legalization of opposition parties in Hungary in the February, I have not been able to find any confirmation of a direct link between these two events (nor has Pevehouse). In sum, then, the Hungarian case provides only limited support for a democratizing effect of the one democratic regional organization it belonged to in the late 1980s. There is more to suggest that the EEC played a critical role by extending economic assistance conditional on a completed transition to democracy, but, then again, that is not evidence in favor of the importance of organizational *membership*.

Peru

Ten years after the reestablishment of democracy in Peru in 1980, the political outsider Alberto Fujimori was elected president with an overwhelming majority. After increased tensions with the legislative and judiciary branches of government, Fujimore instituted a "self-coup" (*autogolpe*) on his own government by dissolving congress and suspending the judiciary on April, 5, 1992 (Pevehouse 2005, pp. 128–29). Pevehouse follows two events – one in 1993, the other in 2000 – which he deems critical to the return of democracy to Peru. I shall follow this subdivision in order to check the alleged importance of regional organizations for democratization in the Peruvian case.

In both events, the Organization of American States (OAS) was the external progenitor exerting pressure on Peru.[7] In 1991 the OAS member states approved the Santiago Declaration (Resolution 1080), which mandated that the OAS must convene an immediate emergency meeting in the event of an interruption of democracy in any member state. This resolution was immediately invoked in the wake of Fujimori's autogolpe, leading the OAS to a swift condemnation of his actions and calling an emergency meeting in the Bahamas in May. After a series of coordinated visits by OAS ambassadors, Fujimori decided to attend. Amidst allegations of the threat of sanctions, Fujimori addressed the OAS assembly concerning his actions, and promised a more swift return of democracy than he had initially anticipated. Instead of holding a plebiscite to legitimize his rule, which Fujimori had initially planned, this led to rescheduled elections to a new congress, which would also serve as a constitutional assembly drafting a new constitution, held in November 1992 (Pevehouse 2005, pp. 128–29). After a year of deliberation, the constituent assembly approved a new draft constitution that passed by a small margin in a national referendum in October 1993 (Mauceri 1997, p. 902; Cameron 1998, p. 225).

Was this a democratic achievement accomplished by the OAS, as Pevehouse argues? There are reasons to be skeptical about that interpretation. In fact, what Fujimori seems to have accomplished was mostly to untie his hands and dictate a solution to a crisis his own autogolpe had spawned (Levitt 2006, p. 104). In the words of one astute observer:

> Fujimori's forces controlled the entire process of rewriting the constitution and restoring Congress, from start to finish ... Fujimori and allies manipulated the process for their own ends with little serious external resistance. In fact, by sending election monitoring teams to observe the November vote, the OAS and the US inadvertently gave their seal of approval to an electoral

[7] In 1991 Peru was a member of four regional military, economic or political organizations: the Latin American Integration Association (LAIA), the Agency for the Prohibition of Nuclear Weapons in Latin America, the Latin American Economic System, and the OAS. Although the OAS was strictly speaking the next most democratic of these organizations (the most democratic being LAIA), the difference between them is inconsequential (the democracy score was 7.8 for the OAS, 8.0 for the LAIA, excluding Peru itself). In 1998, when Peru had also joined the Asia-Pacific Economic Organization, the OAS was the most democratic of Peru's regional organizations.

> process that, on the outside, appeared fair and transparent but that had been designed to exclude Peru's mainstream political parties. The Fujimori government emerged more powerful and consolidated than prior to the coup. (Legler 2003, p. 63)

It can thus hardly be argued that the OAS should be complimented for "restoring democracy" in Peru in 1993.

Given that the 1993 event in any case does not fit the pathway criterion very well, we might instead turn to the events culminating in Fujimori's downfall in 2000. The actions of the OAS this time no doubt appear more critical. Beginning in the spring, the OAS monitored the presidential elections in which Fujimori defeated the opposition's frontrunner Toledo, but without gaining the required majority of votes. After increased suspicions of electoral fraud, the OAS mission left Peru, denouncing the run-off elections to be held in May as illegitimate. This made Toledo withdraw his candidacy, and Fujimori could safely win the contest. As a response to these events, however, the OAS submitted a high-level mission to Peru with the purpose of "strengthening democracy." This mission came to play a key role in the Peruvian case by establishing a round-table which brought together government, opposition as well as civil society representatives. True, the event that in the end triggered Fujimori's downfall was the disclosure on September 14 of a videotape which showed the leader of the government intelligence service, Vladimir Montesinos, bribing an opposition member of congress. In the dramatic events that followed, however, the round-table "served as an institutional forum through which domestic and international forces could pressure Fujimori during the crisis." The round-table pressured the president to announce new elections to be held in 2001, and blocked military interventions in the process. When in November Fujimori resigned and fled the country, unable to escape from the massive corruption scandal that unraveled, the round-table eased the transition to an interim government (Pevehouse 2005, pp. 135–37; also see Cooper and Legler 2001; McClintock 2001; Legler 2003).

Summary

To sum up, the case study evidence in support of an effect of democratic regional organizations on upturns is fraught with problems. A first thing to note is that Pevehouse's (2005) *theoretical* argument draws heavily on psychological phenomena. Perceived threats, socialization and legitimization are all highly cognitive mechanisms. The case study evidence, however, rarely touches this fine-grained level of analysis. With respect to the COE's role in Turkey, the potential influence of the OSCE in Hungary and the OAS in Peru, open pressure is the one of Pevehouse's mechanisms that is most well documented. Yet there is precious little insight into how this pressure was experienced from the perspective of the actors themselves.

Second, as I have stressed in both the Turkish and Hungarian cases, there is a mismatch between the particular regional organization that enters my statistical analyses and the ones for which Pevehouse provides case study evidence. Given that his strategy for gauging the level of democracy among regional organizations should be seen as a proxy rather than as a direct measure, this may seem less problematic at a general level. After all, the fact that *some* regional organizations actually exerted important influences in the cases that fit the pathway criterion could be interpreted as indirect evidence that the measurement strategy works. Yet one would prefer this strategy not only to work, but also to work for the right reasons. Moreover, in the Hungarian case the problem is not just about what regional organizations did the work, but when they did it (most of the evidence indicates that this occurred *after* the transition to democracy).

Third, and related to this, Pevehouse's case study evidence cannot fully dispel the suspicion that the one regional organization that really has had power to influence domestic processes during the third wave of democratization is the EEC (later the EU). Perhaps there is no general effect of democratic regional organizations, but what really works is perhaps the promise of future membership in this extremely rare case of an unusually powerful organization. True, the role of the OAS in Peru in 2000 is an important exception to this, but not even this case fits the pathway criterion very well. And perhaps the role of the OAS in Peru is a very unique exception? A recent review of the democracy-enhancing role of the OAS in Latin America states that "Peru is perhaps the closest thing to a successful case of OAS intervention," and more generally that the importance of the OAS for democracy promotion seems to be in decline in the early twenty-first century (Boniface 2007, pp. 42–43, 57).

The case study evidence in favor of a democratizing effect of regional organizations is thus mixed. There seems to have been an effect with respect to the Council of Europe in Turkey in 1983, and the Organization of American States with respect to Peru in 2000. The support for a similar mechanism operating in Hungary from the Organization for Security and Cooperation in Europe, and the OAS in Peru in 1993, is, however, more strained.

Conclusion

I have in this chapter found statistical evidence indicating that trade volume impeded democratization during the third wave, but why this would be the case remains unclear. Moreover, neighbor diffusion is robustly related to democratization, but again without any observable causal mechanisms discovered, and mostly in a region (Sub-Saharan Africa) where it has rarely been documented. Membership in democratic regional organizations also appears to promote democratization, but the case study evidence in support of this contention is mixed. Foreign intervention, finally, sometimes works, sometimes not. In sum, the impetus from abroad at first seems obvious. But on closer inspection its inner workings appear elusive.

5 *The force from below: popular mobilization*

Democratization never just happens. Someone has to take action to install, or protect, democratic institutions. In the most immediate sense these actions are usually taken by political elites: that is, by key decision makers in the governmental organizations of the state. It has often been noted, however, that another forceful actor, the populace or "demos" itself, sometimes enters the scene, pushing for or resisting reforms. To what extent did this force from below affect the third wave of democratization? In this chapter I first review the literature and empirical evidence to this effect, and then, in order to uncover the causal mechanisms at work, I turn to case studies of three critical incidences of democratization wrought through peaceful demonstrations.

The literature and empirical results

In the founding texts of the strategic approach, as noted in Chapter 1, democracy appeared to have been brought about in the context of demobilized masses (O'Donnell and Schmitter 1986). This view, which was primarily based on experiences from Southern Europe and Latin America, was, however, challenged empirically in later accounts of the same world regions (Bermeo 1997; Collier 1999). Moreover, the contrast seems even sharper in relation to the subsequent collapse of authoritarian regimes in Asia, Eastern Europe and Sub-Saharan Africa. In these instances collective action undertaken by the mass public appears to have been a widely occurring phenomenon, with alleged democracy-enhancing effects (Bratton and van de Walle 1997, pp. 83–4; Geddes 1999, p. 120; McFaul 2002, pp. 222–23; Bunce 2003, pp. 171–78; Schock 2005). Evidence from the "colored revolutions" in Eastern Europe and Central Asia points in the same direction (Beissinger 2007; Tucker 2007). Anecdotal evidence also suggests that democratization in both Western Europe and Latin America in the early twentieth century followed in the wake of social unrest and popular mass action (Acemoglu and Robinson 2006, pp. 67–68, 71–73; also, see Tilly 2004).

From a theoretical perspective, this is what we should expect if the "social forces" approach to explaining democratization were to prove correct, although this literature has never been very specific on causal mechanisms (Slater 2009). Strike activity should thus be one form of popular mobilization predicted to impact on democratization, particularly within the strand of this tradition that emphasizes the importance of organized labor (Rueschemeyer *et al.* 1992; Collier 1999). But an effect of more general forms of protest activity undertaken by other groups in society, including both violent clashes and peaceful demonstrations, could also be conjectured (Foweraker and Landman 1997; Gill 2000; Wood 2000; 2001; Schock 2005). Although less attention has been paid to the subject lately, there also seems to be a growing awareness of an older tradition claiming that popular mobilization may not be unreservedly beneficial for democracy. Bermeo (2003a), for one, takes note of the critical importance of labor mobilization and strike activity in undoing democracy in Latin America during the 1970s (also see Armony 2004).

In light of these observations there are surprisingly few large-*n* studies of the possible effect that popular mobilization may exert on democratization. To the best of my knowledge only two other global studies relate to the effect of popular mobilization (Lipset *et al.* 1993; Przeworski *et al.* 2000), but neither of them makes this assessment in dynamic models explaining regime change. I thus concur with Coppedge's (2003, p. 125) verdict that "the true impact of political mobilization . . . remains an open question."

To resolve this question, I turn to Table 5.1. Confirming the expectations of the social forces tradition, large numbers of peaceful antigovernment demonstrations facilitated upturns toward democracy during the third wave. It should be kept in mind that this variable, much as all the other time-varying determinants tested, is lagged one year. What I observe is thus *not* an upsurge of popular protest that is an integral part of the democratization process itself. What is being captured is instead the impact of popular mobilization in one year on the propensity to democratize the *following year*, all else being equal, which lends stronger support to a causal interpretation of its impact. This estimated short-run increase in the rate of democratization was .038 per demonstration, whereas the long-run equilibrium level of democracy increased by .475 per demonstration. The result is completely insensitive to the all

Table 5.1 *Popular Mobilization*

	Short-run			
	General	Upturns	Downturns	Long-run
Peaceful demonstrations	.038***	.039***	–.001	.475***
	(.009)	(.007)	(.006)	(.142)
Riots	–.010	–.004	–.007	–.129
	(.010)	(.007)	(.007)	(.124)
Strikes	–.043*	–.019	–.024	–.541
	(.026)	(.019)	(.016)	(.332)

* significant at the .10-level, ** significant at the .05-level, *** significant at the .01-level. No. of observations = 3,795; no. of countries = 165; mean years observed per country = 23.0.

Note: Entries are unstandardized regression coefficients with panel-corrected standard errors in parentheses. All models also include two lags of the dependent variable and the determinants in Tables 2.1, 3.1 and 4.1 as controls. All explanatory variables in the table have been lagged one year.

robustness checks applied in the Appendix C.[1] This confirms, on systematic evidence, that during the third wave popular mobilization played a more influential role for the outcome than "transition paradigm" theorists initially acknowledged.

However, I do not observe homogenous effects of all forms of popular mobilization. Riots (i.e., violent clashes involving the use of physical force) did not exert any impact on democratization. Although the general effect is negative and marginally significant, nor did strikes (aimed at national government policies or authority). Thus, although the effect of demonstrations is consistent with the more general "social forces" approach to explaining democratization, I find no systematic evidence in favor of a special role played by labor through the organization of strike activity (*cf.* Foweraker and Landman 1997; Collier 1999). Moreover, *pace* Bermeo's (2003a) insightful analysis of the Latin American experience of the 1970s, no forms of popular mobilization appear to work as triggers of downturns toward autocracy.

[1] The result is also insensitive to the exclusion of two relatively extreme influential outliers: Bolivia in 1980 and Argentina in 1983. Even more convincingly, the result holds when the square root of the number of demonstrations is used instead.

Is the peacefulness of anti-government demonstrations critical, or are we simply observing a form of popular contention that operates on a sufficiently large scale to undo authoritarian regimes? The fact that violent riots have no effect speaks in favor of the former interpretation, but the lack of an effect from peaceful strike activity, in favor of the latter. Another test of which interpretation is correct would be to apply a direct measure of violent popular contention, namely domestic armed conflict. In effect, there are theoretical ideas, and even some sketchy empirical evidence, of a *positive* link between the incidence of civil war and democratization. One suggestion is that the parties to a civil conflict could choose to invite the people as arbitrator: to hold an election and pass their power to a democratically elected government as a mechanism for conflict resolution (Wantchekon and Neeman 2002; Wantchekon 2004; Sollenberg 2008; *cf.* Wood 2000; 2001). In accordance with this proposition is Leonard Wantchekon's (2004, p. 17) observation that nearly 40 percent of all civil wars that took place between 1945 and 1993 resulted in an improvement in the level of democracy. Similarly, Bermeo (2003b, p. 159), by a rough estimate, states that at least half of the democracies founded after 1945 that still exist "emerged either in the aftermath of a war or as a means of bringing an ongoing war to an end." While these studies suggest a positive impact of civil war *termination*, a different mechanism suggested is that armed conflict in and of itself helps solve collective action problems in attempts (or threatened attempts) to overthrow an authoritarian regime (Acemoglu and Robinson 2006). This would thus suggest a positive impact of even the *outbreak* of civil war.

In Table 5.2, I test the democratizing impact of domestic warfare, here being defined as conflicts between the government and internal opposition groups incurring at least twenty-five battle-related deaths (Gleditsch *et al.* 2002). As the results show, while there was a negative impact, particularly on downturns, of having an ongoing civil conflict of this type in the past two years, there was no significant impact of either war termination or outbreak in the previous year. In other words, neither the Acemoglu and Robinson (2006), nor the Wantchekon (2004) conjectures are supported for the third wave period. This, in turn, lends support to the contention that the effect of demonstrations not only stems from the fact that they are a form of popular mobilization, but also from the fact that they are peaceful.

Table 5.2 *Domestic Armed Conflict*

	Short-run			
	General	Upturns	Downturns	Long-run
Civil conflict:				
Ongoing at *t*–2	–.083*	–.016	–.068**	–.996*
	(.048)	(.033)	(.031)	(.583)
Outbreak at *t*–1	.100	.087	.012	1.19
	(.091)	(.061)	(.062)	(1.10)
Termination at *t*–1	–.053	–.028	–.024	–.627
	(.108)	(.075)	(.065)	(1.30)

* significant at the .10-level, ** significant at the .05-level, *** significant at the .01-level.
No. of observations = 3,450; no. of countries = 155; mean years observed per country = 22.3.
Note: Entries are unstandardized regression coefficients with panel-corrected standard errors in parentheses. All models use yearly change in the level of democracy as the dependent variable, including two lags of the level of democracy and the determinants in Tables 2.1, 3.1, 4.1 and 5.1 as controls.

Why are peaceful demonstrations conducive to democratization?

But why? Why do popular demonstrations foster democratization, and why is it critical that they are peaceful? The most promising attempt to tackle these grand questions, together with relevant case study evidence, can be found in the work of Kurt Shock on "unarmed insurrections."[2] According to Schock (2005, pp. 40–44), the main explanation lies in what Lee Smithey and Lester Kurtz (1999) call the "paradox of repression": that an unarmed challenge may be sustained and even promoted in the face of brutal state force directed against it. There are several reasons why this dynamic may occur. Non-violent protest requires no special technology or equipment, nor is it critically dependent on the physical fitness of its implementers. It thus has "the potential to allow

[2] Thompson (2004) documents case study evidence from fifteen "democratic revolutions" in Asia and Eastern Europe. The main thrust of his argument, however, lies in detailed descriptions of events, the conditions under which uprisings occur and their characteristics. As opposed to Schock (2005), no coherent account of why popular mobilization helps topple authoritarian regimes is developed.

the maximum degree of active participation in the struggle by the highest proportion of the population" (Schock 2005, p. 40). Moreover, harsh repression against peaceful demonstrators may have a mobilizing effect by spreading a sense of victimization, or even martyrdom, of innocent people. It may further or even spawn elite divisions by questioning the legitimacy of the regime, and it risks leading to mutinies or defections within the military and security forces, when they are ordered to shoot at innocent people. Finally, unarmed protest raises the probability of third-party involvement, such as by transnational social movements, international organizations and foreign governments, by highlighting the fact that the incumbent regime rests on physical force rather then voluntary acquiescence. This in turn may further mobilize activists to join the unarmed cause.

In all these respects, violent methods sharply differ. Armed rebellion requires weaponry and "has historically been limited to young, physically fit, ideologically indoctrinated or mercenary males" (Schock 2005, p. 40). Thus, the share of the population that may join an armed insurgency is comparatively limited. Using violence against the regime, moreover, is to fight the government on its own turf, where the challengers are likely the inferior party. It also justifies the state's use of repression in the name of "law and order" and "national security." Finally, violence may alienate potential supporters in the population, solidify the regime elites by creating a common enemy, and polarize third parties (Schock 2005, p. 44).

Although the contrast is less sharp, all these dynamics also help explain the difference between situations where peaceful mobilization occurs and where it does not. By provoking large numbers of people, by exacerbating elite divisions and mobilizing third parties against the regime, a democratizing outcome is made more likely in the wake of peaceful demonstrations.

But why then does the authoritarian regime sometimes give in to the demands of challengers, sometimes not? Schock (2005, pp. 49–52, 143–44), on the one hand, stresses internal features of the challenging movement – such as being decentralized but still coordinated within an umbrella organization – that may facilitate its resilience in the face of repression. Given that this resilience has kicked in, on the other hand, the critical feature is whether the resistance can "tap into the state's dependence relations." Although the conceptual language differs, here Schock basically adheres to Haggard and Kaufman's notion of "authoritarian bargains" discussed in Chapter 3:

In any society, the state directly depends on segments of its own populace to rule. If any of these segments, such as military personnel, police officers, administrators, or workers in energy supply, transportation, communications, commerce, or other key sectors, refuse or threaten to refuse to carry out their duties, the state's power is significantly undermined. (2005, p. 53)

To these domestic support groups, Schock (2005) adds the potential "indirect dependence relations" that the regime may sustain with third-party forces on the international scene. In both instances the key assumption is that an authoritarian state explicitly or implicitly draws its support from some groups or sets of actors, and that the withdrawal of that support undermines regime survival and opens the prospects of democratization.

Again it seems fair to assume that this mechanism is less likely to occur in the absence of popular mobilization. In sum, then, Schock (2005) argues that "unarmed insurrections," incorporating a large set of non-violent activities (among which I only measure the occurrence of peaceful demonstrations), may lead to democratization by sustaining the challenge in the face of repression, thereby spawning elite divisions and mobilizing third-party support, and by disrupting the material and other support bases of the regime.

The case studies that provide Schock with supportive evidence in favor of these propositions are the political transformations of the Philippines in the 1980s, South Africa in the late 1980s and early 1990s, as well as the transition toward democracy in Nepal and Thailand in the early 1990s. As shown in Figure 5.1, three of these cases fit fairly well to the pathway criterion: The Philippine transition, which occurred over a couple of years, ranks 13th in 1984, 19th in 1986 and 11th in 1987.[3] South Africa in 1990 is ranked 14th and Nepal in 1991 22nd among all 3,795 country years in my estimation sample. The case that does not fit is Thailand in 1992, where the transition back to democracy was so swift as to occur in the same year as the people mobilized against the military dictatorship installed in the previous

[3] Although Marcos was forced to step down in February, 1986, surrendering power to a transitional government headed by Corazon Aquino, there were no clean elections or a ratified constitution until 1987. Moreover, already in 1984 a critical election was held where the opposition for the first time ran on a united ticket (see, e.g., Thompson 1995). In accordance with this, both Freedom House and Polity score the Philippine transition as occurring gradually over these consecutive years (with the largest shift occurring in 1986–87).

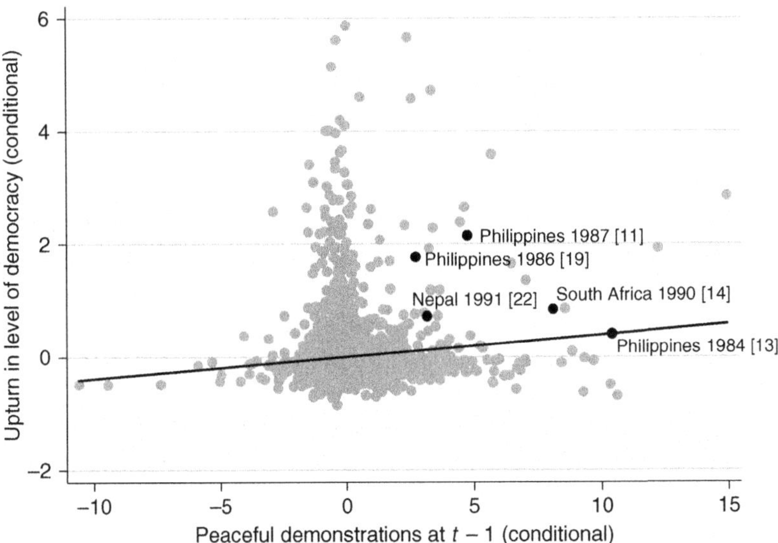

Figure 5.1 Case studies of the impact of peaceful demonstrations on upturns
Note: The graph is a partial regression (or added-variable) plot of the conditional relationship between the number of peaceful demonstrations, lagged one year, and upturns (n = 3,795). The figures within brackets are the rank order of each case in terms of the pathway criterion.

year. Since I impose a one-year lag in my estimates of the effect of popular mobilization, I will thus not incorporate Thailand among the supportive case study evidence that follows.

The Philippines

As already mentioned in Chapter 3, the event that first triggered massive popular mobilization in the Philippines was the assassination of Marcos' main political rival, Benigno Aquino, upon his homecoming from US exile in August 1983. "In the days following the assassination," writes Schock (2005, p. 73), "hundreds of thousands of people filed by Aquino's open coffin, and an estimated two million people from all socioeconomic strata gathered to witness Aquino's funeral procession." From October that same year, weekly anti-Marcos demonstrations were staged in the Makati business district, but also freedom marches, so-called "parliaments of the streets," occurred irregularly, involving labor, peasant, student and teacher associations, as well as women's, human rights groups and gatherings of the urban poor. Another organizational specialty was taken up in January 1984, so-called *welgang bayan*, or "people's strikes," based on a general workers' strike but more comprehensive, "as all stores are closed, all public transportation is stopped, and community members construct barricades to stop the operation of private vehicles" (Schock 2005, p. 75). Such large-scale strikes were organized on several occasions throughout 1984, and on a particularly momentous scale in May and June, 1985 (Schock 2005, pp. 76, 83). By November that year, popular protest had deprived Marcos of almost all legitimacy. In an attempt to shore up his rule, he decided to call snap presidential elections for February 7, 1986 (originally scheduled to be held in 1987).

This decision proved to be the last nail in the Marcos regime's coffin. Backed up by the powerful Catholic Church and an independent electoral watchdog organization called NAMFREL, the opposition's main candidate, Corazon Aquino, managed to claim victory at the polls. Since the official and state-controlled electoral commission claimed Marcos the winner, the task to adjudicate in the conflict was passed to the similarly controlled parliament. On February 16, as the parliament certified Marcos' fraudulent victory, Aquino led a rally of approximately two million people, proclaiming victory for herself and condemning Marcos. She also announced a renewed non-violent disobedience campaign to be launched on February 26, the day after Marcos' planned inauguration, involving a general strike and a boycott of all crony-controlled banks, media outlets as well as a refusal to pay utility bills.

This campaign was preempted, however, by an abortive military coup attempt by two ministers from Marcos' own administration – the generals Enrile and Ramos. When their plotted coup was revealed on February 22, they barricaded themselves in two military camps just outside of Manila and announced their defection from the Marcos government and their support of Aquino. Manila's Archbishop Sin, who had spoken out against the regime since the establishment of martial law in 1972, now urged people to support the mutiny, drawing tens of thousands of supporters to surround the camps and protect the military rebels with their bodies. This effectively blocked Marcos' attempt to crush the mutiny by military means. By February 25, hundreds of thousands of civilians were gathered outside the military camps, at the same time as Aquino set up a parallel government to denounce Marcos' rule. By this time the US administration under President Reagan, a close friend of Marcos, officially withdrew its support for Marcos' rule. The following day he fled the country (Schock 2005, pp. 77–79).

All essential parts of Schock's theory of how popular mobilization may topple authoritarian regimes were in place in the Philippine case. The protest activities evidently mobilized large numbers of people, and from most segments of society. They exacerbated elite divisions, particularly the split between crony and non-crony business elites, and within the military (as the unraveling of the Enrile–Ramos mutiny made clear). Finally, they tapped deeply into the state's dependence relations, both within and outside the country. The strikes and boycotts undermined the already recessionary economy, destabilized the business climate and in the end caused massive capital flight. Not the least important, the protest activities eventually triggered the withdrawal of US support for Marcos (Schock 2005, pp. 88–90).

South Africa

South Africa had since independence in 1910 been ruled on the principles of racial segregation, later consolidated under the *apartheid* system, denying political rights and civil liberties for the black majority population. A series of popular struggles throughout the 1980s, first ignited by the mass shootings in Soweto in 1976, however, finally brought this authoritarian regime to its end. Three umbrella organizations are generally considered as having provided leadership for the uprisings: the United Democratic Front (UDF), launched in 1983 to oppose a new constitutional proposal by the government; the Congress of South African Trade Unions (COSATU), formed in 1985 in response to a state of emergency leading to heightened repression of labor; and, of course, the African National Congress (ANC), founded in 1912 but banned in 1960, which thus mostly provided an underground support base in events unraveling up until repression was lifted in 1990 (Schock 2005, pp. 57–59, 64, 67–68).

The South African resistance movements drew upon a wide range of non-violent (and, as we shall see, some violent) actions to oppose the regime. Two waves of protest may be identified. The first, unsuccessful in the short term, culminated in two states of emergency in 1985 and 1986. The second, occurring in 1989, is the one that lends South Africa the status of a pathway case in my analyses. During the first wave, the UDF organized, apart from large-scale demonstrations, a series of boycotts on housing rents, services, schools and local business outlets, while COSATU, apart from labor strikes, organized "stayaways," in which workers and students "would stay at home in support of a variety of economic and political demands" (Schock 2005, pp. 61, 65). When the first state of emergency in 1985 only fuelled the uprising and also led to bloodshed and riots, a second, nationwide and more effective state of emergency was installed in 1986. This brought an end to the demonstrations, but not to the stayaways and the rent and consumer boycotts (Schock 2005, pp. 62–63; Price 1991, pp. 266–67). Although the UDF was banned in 1988, its detained activists organized a hunger strike including more than 600 prisoners in February, 1989, eventually leading to their release (Schock 2005, p. 63). This sparked the second wave of protest throughout the country, called the "new Defiance Campaign," "collectively encompassing hundreds of thousands of demonstrators, and effectively neutralising the state of emergency" (Zunes 1999, p. 159).

Together with a general strike in August that same year, "essentially shutting down commerce in Pretoria, Johannesburg, Durban and East London, and severely crippling industry in the Western Cape" (Zunes 1999, p. 156), this marked the beginning of the end of the authoritarian regime. After P. W. Botha had stepped down due to a stroke, F. W. de Klerk was first elected new party leader of the incumbent National Party in February 1989, and then national president in September (Wood 2000, p. 180). In early February 1990, de Klerk declared that the state of emergency was to be lifted, the ANC and UDF unbanned, and political prisoners, among them Nelson Mandela, to be released. This formed the start of a protracted negotiation between the ANC and the government, eventually leading to free and fair elections with universal suffrage in 1994 (Schock 2005, pp. 56, 68).

The year in which South Africa enters my statistical results as a pathway case, that is in 1990, is thus not the year of a completed transition to democracy, but the year of partial political opening (i.e., "liberalization," in terms of the old transition paradigm parlance). It is thus noteworthy for the gradualist strategy toward measuring democracy I employ that Schock's mechanisms are still in full sway in the South African case.

The popular uprising in South Africa clearly mobilized large segments of the population, for the most part by being able to sustain protest activities in the midst of harsh repression, and generated substantial third-party support, both from white South Africans and from abroad, most notably Great Britain and the US. It also precipitated elite divisions, most importantly the divide between the hardliner "securocrats" and the softliner "internationalist reformers" within the government (Schock 2005, pp. 68, 89). The former group, closely associated with P. W. Botha, comprised personnel within the major security agencies and emerged as the most powerful government body after the second state of emergency in 1986. On the other side of the division were officials associated with economic policy and foreign relations, both of whom started to see negotiations and more radical democratic reform as the only way out of the government's predicament. The election of F. W. de Klerk, who stood on the latter's side, thus "marked the ascendancy of the internationalist-reformers over the securocrats" (Price 1991, pp. 252, 275–76). Finally, popular mobilization undermined the South African state's legitimacy and resources, most directly by exploiting the apartheid system's dependence on black labor, but also indirectly by reinvigorating international support for economic sanctions (Schock 2005, pp. 85–87).[4]

Nepal

As compared to both its Philippine and South African counterparts, the transition toward democracy in Nepal was a swifter affair. After a short democratic interlude in the late 1950s, Nepal was governed as an absolutist monarchy from 1960, although under the trappings of the so-called *panchyat* system, with consultative bodies at various levels that, however, were completely controlled from the royal palace (Schock 2005, pp. 121–22). The trajectory of the pro-democracy movement in the country took a new direction from the late 1980s, when the Nepali Congress Party, which prevailed as an underground organization despite being banned under the constitution, forged an alliance with the several communist parties of the country. Beginning on February 18, 1990, this movement of forces staged an organized unarmed rebellion against the monarchy and its *panchyat* system.

[4] As Elisabeth Wood (2000, chap. 6–7) has persuasively shown on the basis of extensive interview data, this also caused the withdrawal of regime support from the South African economic business elite, which instead started to push the incumbent Nationalist Party rulers to initiate democratic reform.

The first peaceful demonstration gathered some ten thousand people in central Kathmandu, but also in several other cities around the country, and was met with harsh police brutality, including arrests, deaths and injuries. A general strike was called the following day, again leading to clashes between unarmed demonstrators and police forces. On February 25, a second wave of demonstrations swept across the country, "ushering in a period of terror unprecedented in recent Nepalese history." Approximately one thousand protestors were arrested, some of whom were subsequently tortured, and the government used specially trained thugs to attack the demonstrators (Schock 2005, p. 124).

After these events, according to one observer, "the level of participation began to dwindle," but the pro-democracy movement then turned to other more covert protest measures instead (Parajulee 2000, p. 87). Most notable among them were strikes, since it is harder for the regime to punish people for what they do *not* do than for what they do, and so-called "blackouts," whereby all lights were turned off between 7.00 and 7.30 p.m., "signaling solidarity and widespread support for the movement" (Schock 2005, p. 124). Through these and other inventive measures, the pro-democracy movement managed to regain momentum in a new series of large-scale protest demonstrations by early April.

In the midst of "continuous strikes and demonstrations," King Birendra on April 6 attempted to appease the masses by sacking the prime minister and promising limited reform (Parajulee 2000, p. 90). In response, people poured into the streets of Kathmandu and most other major cities in the largest demonstration ever to have occurred in the country, involving hundreds of thousands of people. While there was shooting and occasional violence, demonstrators mostly stayed peaceful. Shortly before midnight that same day the king issued a proclamation, broadcast over Radio Nepal, to lift the ban on political parties (Schock 2005, p. 125). Within days the king began negotiating with the opposition, leading to the formation of a new interim government, the dissolution of the *panchyat* system, and the establishment of a constitutional amendment system (Parajulee 2000, pp. 93–94). A new constitution that circumscribed monarchical powers under a parliamentary system was promulgated in November, followed by parliamentary elections that were generally considered free and fair in 1991 (Schock 2005, p. 125; Parajulee 2000, pp. 105–16).

All components of the mechanism linking popular mobilization to democratization are again present in the Nepalese case. The pro-democracy forces were clearly able to sustain their campaign in the face of repression, and "anti-government sentiment was only intensified by the violent repression of unarmed demonstrators" (Schock 2005, p. 140). The popular uprising also drove a wedge between more liberal reformist and the hardline conservative factions within the regime. The foreign minister, belonging to the former group, resigned from the cabinet – in part due to the violent repression used by the regime – by late March, and a cabinet reshuffle in early April was implemented to purge the government of softliner ministers. Also members of the National Panchyat (the party-less parliament) condemned the use of violence, pointing to yet another rupture within the elite (Parajulee 2000, p. 89). In Schock's own words, "[m]ass political action and elite defection formed a combination that was potent in the toppling of the regime – to the extent that the regime was overturned despite the fact that the military remained loyal throughout the crisis" (2005, p. 140).

Not least important, the unarmed popular insurrection undercut the regime's critical dependence relations. On the domestic scene, this occurred most prominently by the withdrawal of support from government employees, such as lawyers, doctors, nurses and university professors (Schock 2005, p. 136; Parajulee 2000, pp. 83–88). Internationally, the pro-democracy movement consciously exploited Nepal's dependence on foreign development aid. As the violent repression of unarmed citizens represented grave human rights violations, the popular uprising mobilized third-party support from transnational NGOs such as Amnesty International and Asia Watch. Eventually the US, Germany and Switzerland "publicly condemned the repression of the government, threatened to withdraw aid, and privately pressured the government to negotiate with the pro-democracy movement" (Schock 2005, p. 137).[5]

[5] In a sample survey of a broad range of pro-democracy activists and government representatives in Nepal, Parajulee (2000, chap. 6) documents the widely held belief that donor countries, particularly the US and Germany, as well as international human rights organizations and the international media, played a significant role in the success of the Nepalese transition to democracy. Although the "Indian connection," mostly through India's imposition of sanctions against Nepal in 1989, was also an international factor of importance (Parajulee 2000, chap. 5), that external influence took place before the popular uprising started, and thus cannot account for its success (*cf.* Schock 2005, pp. 136–37).

Summary

Schock's theory and case study evidence obviously does not answer all questions related to why and how popular mobilization affects democratization. An important puzzle that arises from my statistical findings is why only demonstrations, not strikes, appear to have a significant impact. As the cases of the Philippines, South Africa and Nepal all clearly document, strike activity was a crucial part of the popular insurgency, particularly when it came to severing the authoritarian regimes' dependence relations. Schock (2005, pp. 38–40) does not distinguish between demonstration and strike activity, but views both as an integral part of the non-violent action repertoire. Why then do the number of demonstrations in my results affect democratic upturns irrespective of the amount of strike activity? And why does strike activity appear inconsequential?

As noted in Chapter 3, one of Haggard and Kaufman's (1995) key pathways through which economic crises affect democratization is by the mobilization of popular protest. This suggestion is actually also in keeping with how their case studies line up in my statistical findings. The three economic crisis cases depicted in Chapter 3 (that is, apart from the Philippines: Bolivia, Argentina and Uruguay), as well as the cases of Peru in 1978 and Brazil in 1985, are all among the top twenty-five pathway cases for my effect of peaceful demonstrations on upturns. As Haggard and Kaufman persuasively argue, poor economic performance in these cases helped trigger the mobilization of protest against the regime, first based on economic grievances but along the way turning the protest agenda toward broader civil liberties and political rights issues (1995, pp. 60–64). However, they never distinguish explicitly between strikes and demonstrations, and hence cannot help explain why strikes in my data are not related to democratization.

Except for the Philippines the Haggard and Kaufman cases are also included in Collier's (1999, p. 23) list of "recent democratization" cases, where she deemed "pro-democratic labor action" consequential for the outcome. Adding two of the cases on her list, Portugal in 1976 and Spain in 1978, with the corresponding pathway ranks of 6 and 12, respectively, there seems to be even more prima facie case study evidence that popular mobilization is causally linked to democratization. Again, however, Collier restricts her attention to *labor* mobilization, finding strikes to be "the cutting edge" of popular mobilization's effect on democracy (1999, p. 185). This again speaks to the need for an account of the mechanisms linking popular protest to democratization that explains why participation in labor strikes is not systematically related to democratization.[6]

Another remaining puzzle concerns the role played by violence. As noted above, Schock (2005) explicitly aims at explaining why the non-violent character of these uprisings matters, and my statistical finding with respect to both riots and civil conflicts tends to confirm this claim. But among the three cases under study, only the Nepalese was free from popular violence. In the Philippines the armed wing of the Communist Party had been waging a revolutionary guerilla war against the regime since the early 1970s, and in South Africa the ANC had been committed to armed rebellion for decades. Was it really then the unarmed insurrection that toppled the authoritarian regime in these cases, or could the parallel armed rebellion have contributed with a possible "radical flank effect"?

Schock argues that the armed strategy of the Philippine rebels effectively inhibited widespread support for their existence, and that it, by contrast, encouraged US support for the Marcos regime (2005, pp. 71, 90). The unarmed insurrection on both accounts differed, since it mobilized momentous support from within the country while eventually deterring external regime support from the US. In the South African case, moreover, the ANC never formed a real military threat to the state (2005, p. 66).[7] Nevertheless, Schock (2005, pp. 158–60) concedes that it cannot be ruled out that the armed insurgents in the Philippines and South Africa did play a supportive role in the toppling of the authoritarian regime, although they apparently were unable to beat the regime in military terms.

[6] Apart from poor data quality, which is of course always a possible culprit, timing could be at least part of the answer. Both the Philippine and the South African cases would seem to suggest that labor mobilization partly precedes the broader demonstration activities. This pattern is also what Joe Foweraker and Todd Landman (1997, chap. 5) found in their more detailed mobilization data from Spain, Chile, Brazil and Mexico. In accordance with this hypothesis, if I lag the strike variable two years instead of one, so that it in the data precedes the demonstrations variable, its coefficient turns positive (although still not significant).

[7] It is also noteworthy that according to the civil conflict measure I apply (see Appendix A), armed resistance *ended* in South Africa in 1989, that is, the year before the political opening.

A final puzzle concerns timing. Apart from the Nepalese case, the cases under study were sustained mobilization campaigns occurring over several years: in the Philippines for around 30 months, in South Africa for over a decade. What explains these differences? And how can future statistical work on this topic make their findings more sensitive to country-specific lag specifications?

Having mentioned these remaining puzzles, the combination of my statistical findings with the causal mechanisms accounted for by Schock's case study evidence lend support to a truly causal interpretation of the relationship between peaceful demonstrations and democratization.

Conclusion

To sum up, I have in this chapter found empirical evidence to the effect that peaceful demonstrations were a positive trigger of democratization during the third wave. Case study evidence supports the notion that this occurred by increasing the likelihood of divisions between hardliners and softliners within the regime elite, by incorporating larger segments of society in a more sustained protest through the paradox of repression, and by tapping into the state's economic and other dependency relations. I have, however, found no systematic support for a link between riots, strikes or domestic armed conflict and democratization. There is a strong force from below, when peaceful.

6 *Exogenous shocks and authoritarian regime types: institutional contingency*

One of the latest turns in the field of comparative democratization has been an increased attention paid to different types of authoritarianism. There is a growing literature on the dynamics of different forms of autocracies, including the "hybrid" regimes located in the gray zone between democracy and autocracy (Geddes 1999; 2003; Diamond 2002; Levitsky and Way 2002; Schedler 2002a; 2002b; 2006). In this chapter I shall contribute to this body of knowledge by testing the extent to which different authoritarian regimes have different propensities to democratize, both in and of themselves and in response to exogenous shocks. Since different institutional traits are what distinguish different regime types, I shall thus explore the institutional contingency of democratization. As opposed to most previous studies, however, I shall not be concerned with the institutional configurations distinguishing between democracies, such as forms of government and the electoral system (see, e.g., Persson and Tabellini 2003; Cheibub 2007) or other power-sharing institutions (Norris 2008). Instead I focus on the consequences of authoritarian institutions, mostly argued to be a neglected subject in the field (Snyder and Mahoney 1999).

In contrast to the theoretical eclecticism of previous chapters, I shall in this chapter take a more deductive approach. My theoretical point of departure will be Geddes' (1999; 2003) seminal treatment of the logic of military, one-party and personalist dictatorships.[1] Extending the argument into some other authoritarian regime types omitted by Geddes, I first derive expectations regarding how types of authoritarian regimes affect democratization, and how they respond to exogenous shocks. I then present my estimation strategy, followed by the findings.

[1] A more recent theoretical framework for understanding authoritarian regimes that I will not address in this chapter is Gandhi and Przeworski's (2006; 2007; also, see Gandhi 2008), the most important reason being that they mainly claim to *explain* the emergence of different institutional setups under autocracy, not the latter's *effect* on democratization.

I conclude by stating the implications for theory and discussing some remaining puzzles.

Types of authoritarian regimes and democratization

As I have argued together with Axel Hadenius elsewhere (Hadenius and Teorell 2007), Geddes' (1999) neat tripartite division of types of authoritarianism into military, single-party and personalist regimes (as well as amalgams thereof) appears incomplete and in some senses too simplistic. To begin with, Geddes excludes two important types of authoritarianism: monarchies (Herb 1999) and the multiparty autocracies, often also referred to as "competitive authoritarian" (Levitsky and Way 2002) or "electoral authoritarian" (Schedler 2002b; 2006) regimes. Second, Geddes does not distinguish between truly one-party regimes (where no opposition is allowed) and "dominant" or "hegemonic" party regimes (where a single party rules yet leaves some room for opposition). Finally, I concur with Brooker in arguing that personalism is not a regime type in itself, but "only a secondary or supplementary feature of a regime" (2000, p. 37). In other words, any kind of regime – military, one-party, monarchy or other – may display more or less concentration of power in the hands of a single leader.

In keeping with these points of criticism, I will here rely on the typology of authoritarian regime types in Hadenius and Teorell (2007), which apart from one-party and military regimes distinguishes between monarchies and multiparty autocracies, and which within the latter group takes into account the degree of domination of the largest party, as well as treating personalism as a continuous trait more or less present within all regime types. What expectations may I then derive with respect to these refined regime categories?

Key to the understanding of military regimes, according to Geddes (1999; 2003), is the insight that officers favor survival and unity of the military as institutions over anything else, including the goal of remaining in office. As a result, factions within the military are locked in a coordination game where both intervening in and staying out of politics form self-sustainable equilibria as long as internal unity is upheld. This makes military regimes highly vulnerable to internal splits: since there is "life after democracy" for the military as an institution, officers prefer to liberalize the regime and withdraw to the barracks when factional splits over policy or leadership succession become threatening. Military regimes thus have a built-in mechanism that makes them more amenable to democratization. Moreover, exogenous shocks that may create internal rivalries should have a discernible impact on military regimes' tendency to democratize.

This scenario contrasts most clearly with the logic of single-party regimes, where party cadres according to Geddes (1999, 2003) simply prefer holding on to office. Rival factions within the ruling party have no incentive to break off from the regime, since the game they play vis-à-vis the majority faction has a single equilibrium: that all factions remain united and in office. This makes single-party regimes impervious to the threat of factional splits, and hence both less likely to democratize and more resistant to exogenous shocks.

A similar difference in expectations between military and one-party regimes may be derived from Bruce Bueno de Mesquita *et al.*'s (2003) "selectorate theory." According to this theory two generic features determine the nature of a regime: the size of its "winning coalition" – the group of people whose support is essential if the incumbent is to remain in power – and its "selectorate" – the pool of persons with the characteristics institutionally required to be part of the winning coalition. In one-party systems, party membership is generally exclusive, although the formal criteria for membership eligibility could be very generous. In other words, one-party systems generally have very small winning coalitions compared to their selectorates (Bueno de Mesquita *et al.* 2003, pp. 52–53, 70). According to the selectorate theory, this means that the incumbent dictator can rely on a strong sense of loyalty among his or her supporters, since there is a large probability of being excluded from the present winning coalition in the event that the incumbent is overthrown in the future. Hence, defection from the regime becomes very risky (Bueno de Mesquita *et al.* 2003, pp. 65–68). In military regimes, by contrast, although the winning coalition may still be very small, so is the size of the selectorate, which usually comprises just the officer corps within the armed forces (Bueno de Mesquita *et al.* 2003, pp. 51–52, 71). By implication, the loyalty among members of a *junta* is considerably weaker, since there is a larger probability of being able to form an alternative coalition to oust the incumbent. Defections thus become likelier. By assuming that defections propel democratization, and that exogenous shocks are an important trigger of defection, military regimes should thus be more likely to democratize, particularly when facing exogenous crises.

From these accounts I may elicit two clear theoretical expectations:

H1a: Military regimes are more likely than one-party regimes to democratize.

H1b: Military regimes are more likely than one-party regimes to democratize as a response to exogenous shocks.

In Geddes' own account this latter expectation is most explicitly spelled out with respect to the effect of economic performance: "Military governments are more vulnerable to economic downturns than are other authoritarianisms because poor economic performance is likely to precipitate or worsen splits in the officer corps. On average, military governments can survive only moderate amounts of economic bad news, whereas single-party governments are remarkably resilient in the face of disastrous economic performance" (1999, p. 135). The same logic could, however, easily be extended to other kinds of exogenous shocks, such as popular protest and international pressure to reform.[2]

In order to arrive at expectations for monarchies, I can no longer rely directly on Geddes' (1999; 2003) theory, since monarchies are not among her regime types. True, one might first be tempted to infer that monarchies should operate with a logic similar to that of "personalist dictatorships" (in Geddes' terminology). Monarchies, unlike most personalist dictatorships, however, have established rules for leadership succession. As Michael Herb (1999) shows in his intriguing account of the monarchies in the Middle East, these rules may even prevent excessive "personalism" by relying on royal family consensus in picking the leadership successor, and by distributing the highest state offices among multiple family members who thereby hold their own power resources as a check on the absolutist whims of the ruler.

[2] Ronald Wintrobe, however, arrives at exactly the opposite prediction for "tinpot" regimes, of which military regimes are a subspecies (Wintrobe 1990). There are two instruments of power in Wintrobe's theory: repressing one's opponents and distributing rents in return for loyalty. In tinpot regimes, Wintrobe argues, these are inversely related: since the dictator only claims the minimum amount of power needed to remain in office, he may lower the amount of repression as the level of loyalty increases, and vice versa. Since economic improvements tend to increase popular loyalty to the regime, they should be expected to be followed by decreases in repression in tinpot regimes. The following prediction is that military regimes should be *less* likely to democratize as a response to economic downturns. As will be clear below, this prediction is not borne out by my data.

Perhaps somewhat unexpectedly, I would instead like to point to two mechanisms that should make monarchies work more like military dictatorships. The first is the similarity in the size of their support bases. As pointed out by Bueno de Mesquita *et al.* (2003, pp. 51, 70–71), monarchies are similar to military regimes not only in having small winning coalitions, but also in terms of having a small selectorate: in monarchies the selectorate basically comprises the royal family. As a result, we should expect more factionalism and defections from monarchies, similar to military regimes. One-party systems, by contrast, should be more skilful at co-opting pressure to reform from potential opposition forces.

Second, as the experience of constitutional monarchy in the West has taught us, there may actually be "life after democracy" for the monarchy as an institution (much as for the military). The fact that ceremonial powers, popularity and prestige may be bestowed upon the king even after giving up the exclusive right to rule should facilitate piecemeal democratic reform. This point of fact is again borne out well by Herb:

> It is the peculiar virtue of monarchism – for gradual liberalization – that kings do not claim their offices by virtue of popular mandate . . . Kings are born to power, not elected to it. Monarchs can allow free elections and allow the people a voice in the conduct of the government without surrendering their thrones, or all of the power that goes with them. Other sorts of modern authoritarian rulers, by contrast, claim a popular mandate to rule; elections that express the will of the people threaten their power. (1999, p. 263)

For these reasons, I expect monarchies to perform similarly to military regimes. This leads to the following two hypotheses:

H2a: Monarchies are more likely than one-party regimes to democratize.
H2b: Monarchies are more likely than one-party regimes to democratize as a response to exogenous shocks.

Turning to multiparty autocracies, finally, prevalent deductive theories of authoritarian regimes are again of limited use. Geddes (1999; 2003) does not treat multiparty autocracies as a separate regime type, and Bueno de Mesquita *et al.* (2003, p. 53) tend to discuss them in tandem with the one-party systems, sometimes using the word "rigged electoral system" for the latter. By implication, the predictions from these theories as regards multiparty autocracies are unclear.

Drawing on a larger literature, I may, however, point at two reasons for expecting multiparty autocracies to differ from one-party regimes.

First, we may expect multiparty autocracies to be attentive to pressures for democratization for the very same reason that elites in well-established democracies are expected to be attentive to reform demands: they want to cling on to power and hence try to satisfy the preferences of their voters (see, e.g., Drazen 2000, pp. 77–90). However, since the connection between voters' preferences and electoral outcomes is mediated by electoral irregularities, and hence should be much weaker in multiparty autocracies (Schedler 2006, p. 8), this responsiveness should of course be of a more diluted nature as compared to well-established democratic settings.

The second mechanism predicting the same outcome more fully acknowledges the authoritarian nature of these regimes. According to this logic the internal dynamics of multiparty autocracies works as a "nested game" in which incumbents and the opposition simultaneously "measure their forces in the electoral arena" and "battle over the basic rules that shape the electoral arena" (Schedler 2002a, p. 110). The electoral contest (for votes) in multiparty autocracies is largely structured by winning a reputation for effective goods delivery, a contest in which the ruling party, by controlling state resources, of course has the upper hand (Lust-Okar 2006; Magaloni 2006; Greene 2007). The meta-contest (over rules) mostly concerns issues of electoral governance, such as the establishment of an independent electoral commission and procedures for adjudicating post-electoral disputes (Eisenstadt 2004; Magaloni 2006), and reform of the electoral system, which is usually rigged in the ruling party's favor (Diaz-Cayeros and Magaloni 2001; Posusney 2002; Mozaffar and Vengroff 2002; Lust-Okar and Jamal 2002).

The tug-of-war between the ruling party and the opposition in these dual arenas makes multiparty autocracies an unstable equilibrium. Whereas the ruling party pulls the levers toward authoritarian control, the opposition pushes the system toward more democratization (Schedler 2002a). Two factors, however, make the opposition the more likely ultimate winner in this contest. To begin with, as argued by Joy Langston (2006) and Beatrice Magaloni (2006; 2008), the chance to compete in elections under an alternative party banner increases the likelihood of defections from the ruling coalition when compared to single-party regimes. The greater the expected benefits from such defections, the shakier becomes Geddes' (1999; 2003) one-party equilibrium, where all rival factions stay put. In other words, multiparty autocracies are more likely than one-party regimes to suffer from splits within the ruling elite, a condition that has long been argued to favor democratization (O'Donnell and Schmitter 1986).

When exogenous shocks in addition threaten the electoral support of the ruling party, this scenario becomes even likelier. Economic downturns or sanctions imposed from abroad may hollow out the regime's resources to buy off the electorate (Magaloni 2006, *cf.* Greene 2007). Popular mobilization by the opposition fuels intra-elite divisions (Eisenstadt 2004). Most importantly, *peaceful* protest tends to drive in a wedge even deeper between the hardliners and softliners, whose divergence over policy even to begin with tends to circle around divergent preferences for repression (Schock 2005).

Second, the alternative route open for ruling party elites in multiparty autocracies – to compete under an alternative party banner – is of course risky, since a vote for a minor opposition party by the voters could be perceived as wasted (Magaloni 2006). In order to stand a real chance of competing with the ruling party, the opposition parties thus have much to gain from uniting. The coalescence of the opposition is in turn considered critical to the chances of democratic regime change (Bratton and van de Walle 1997; Howard and Roessler 2006). This is thus the second factor making multiparty autocracies more likely to democratize: that they make opposition unification more likely.

According to van de Walle (2006), these twin dynamics – splits from the ruling party and opposition unification – may be self-reinforcing by turning into a "tipping game" in which strategic calculations on the returns of defection by regime incumbents affect the likelihood of opposition cohesion, and vice versa. This also entails that the behavior of actors within multiparty autocracies is largely determined by their "perceptions about the viability of the regime" (van de Walle 2006, p. 86). Such perceptions should also be affected by exogenous shocks such as economic downturns, popular mobilization and pressure from abroad.

As compared to one-party regimes, then, where minority factions are locked into a stable equilibrium of remaining loyal to the regime, multiparty autocracies should be more sensitive to pressures for democratization. This leads to the following two expectations:

H3a: Multiparty autocracies are more likely than one-party regimes to democratize.

H3b: Multiparty autocracies are more likely than one-party regimes to democratize as a response to exogenous shocks.

From this difference *in kind* between one-party and multiparty autocracies, moreover, should also follow a difference *in degree*. Namely that the more multiparty autocracies are dominated by a single party, the more they should behave similarly to one-party regimes. Thus, I may also derive a fourth set of implications from my theory of authoritarian regime types:

H4a: Within the group of multiparty autocracies, the tendency to democratize should decrease with the relative size of the largest party.

H4b: Within the group of multiparty autocracies, the tendency to democratize as a response to exogenous shocks should decrease with the relative size of the largest party.

Estimation strategy

The hypotheses developed above will in this chapter be tested while controlling for the full set of determinants assessed previously. This implies an estimation sample that will at best consist of 3,647 valid observations on 165 countries in the world from 1972 to 2005.[3] My dependent variable will as before be measured as the annual change in the average Freedom House and Polity scores (both converted to a scale of 0–10). I contend that this way of specifying the dependent variable is in keeping with theoretical expectations. What the models of authoritarian regime types developed above predict is authoritarian regime responses of various sorts, including minor shifts in the rules of the game, *not* only the ways in which these regimes extricate themselves and turn into "democracies."

There are also methodological reasons for my choice of a graded dependent variable, as argued in Chapter 1, since I avoid imposing a more or less arbitrary threshold value at which regimes are considered "democratic." Paradoxically, however, I cannot steer clear of this obstacle with respect to the key independent variable: the typology of authoritarian regime types. As this is a typology of *authoritarian* regimes, I need to distinguish this broad authoritarian family from its democratic counterpart. This is of particular importance with respect to

[3] The reason that I lose one year as compared to previous analyses is that the data on authoritarian regimes collected in Hadenius and Teorell (2007) stops in the year of 2005.

the multiparty autocracies, since the only characteristic that makes these regimes different from "democracies" (as a regime type in its own) is a threshold located somewhere along a graded democracy scale. In order to minimize arbitrariness in where to establish this threshold, in Hadenius and Teorell (2007) we estimate the mean cut-off point separating democracy from autocracy in five well-known categorical measures of democracy: those of Przeworski *et al.* (2000), Mainwaring *et al.* (2001), and Reich (2002), together with Freedom House's and Polity's own categorical thresholds for democracy. Along the 0–10 graded democracy scale, this estimated threshold is located at 7.5.

I then rely on the classification in Hadenius and Teorell (2007) of regimes falling below this cut-off point into monarchies, military, one-party and multiparty autocracies.[4] Although amalgams of these regime types exist – most notably multiparty monarchies, military multiparty and military one-party regimes – I have in this chapter chosen to concentrate on pure types for simplicity. In viewing monarchical and military institutions in these amalgams as more fundamental than the structure of the party system, I have in effect treated all monarchical amalgams as monarchies, and all military amalgams as military regimes. The distribution of the ensuing classification of regime types, including regimes passing the 7.5 threshold criterion and accordingly labeled "democracies," is depicted in Figure 6.1. As can be seen, in the estimation sample for which I have data on other determinants, the most common authoritarian regime type is the multiparty autocracy, constituting 21 percent of the country year observations, followed by the military regime at 16 percent. Apart from a small residual category of "other" authoritarian regimes, making up less than 2 percent of the estimation sample, the least common authoritarian regime types during this time period were the monarchies (7 percent) and the one-party regimes (6 percent).[5]

[4] For details on coding rules and sources for these classifications, see Hadenius and Teorell (2007) and the codebook on my website: www.svet.lu.se/documents/JTE_autoregimecodebook2.pdf. There is a fifth basic type of authoritarian regime in the typology called a *no-party* regime, the distinguishing feature of which is that elections are held to the highest office of state but only individual candidates, not political parties, are allowed to participate. Due to missing data, however, there are no such regimes in my estimation sample.

[5] This distribution of course conceals some important trends, the most important being the rise of democracies and multiparty autocracies, and the fall of military and one-party regimes over time (see Hadenius and Teorell 2007).

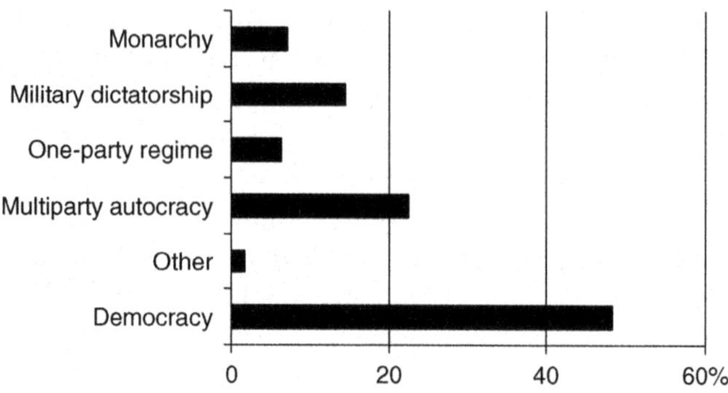

Figure 6.1 The Distribution of Regime Types, 1972–2005
Note: The figure depicts the share of country years classified into each regime category within the estimation sample of 3,657 country years.

Following the strategy laid out in previous chapters, I will control for previous levels of democracy and, when testing the effects of regime types, lag the regime variables one year.[6] In addition, I control for "democracies" as a regime type on their own, both to guard against sample selection bias and in order to pry into the workings of these regimes compared to the multiparty autocracies. In order to test H4a and H4b I also include the degree of single-party domination, measured as the fractional size of the largest party in parliament within multiparty regimes and democracies. I will also control an ancillary regime characteristic: the degree of "personalism," measured as the mean executive turnover computed across each entire regime spell (again, see Hadenius and Teorell 2007).

[6] There is, however, a potential pitfall involved in this procedure with respect to regime types that needs to be addressed. Since the mean level of democracy varies to a great extent across regime types (see Hadenius and Teorell 2007), there is a risk that what the regime dummies may be picking up is simply the transitory effect of countries moving into or out of specific regime categories. What I want to pick up, however, is any effect going beyond this, in a sense that of "staying" within a particular regime type. In order to accomplish this, when I test the effect of regime types lagged one year in Table 6.2 below I also control for a series of dummy variables denoting whether a country in the current year moves into or out of each regime category. More specifically, there are eleven such transition dummies, two each per regime type minus one used as a reference category. For ease of exposition, I do not display the coefficients for these transition dummies in the table.

I operationalize the concept of "exogenous shocks" by focusing on three generic types of events explicitly discussed by Geddes (1999, p. 131): popular protest, economic crisis and foreign intervention (for details on measurement, see the Appendix A). I measure the first in terms of the number of peaceful demonstrations and the second in terms of the growth rate, both of which have in previous chapters been shown to affect democratization. Following Geddes (2002), my measure of foreign intervention is the "foreign intervention index" introduced in Chapter 4, and indicates whether the country in question was subject to a hostile military intervention and/or economic sanctions imposed by a democratic country.

All three measures fulfill a statistical condition for being interpreted as "shocks" to a national system of government: they vary more within countries over time than across countries at a singular point in time.[7] At the same time there is a need to take note of a strategic problem that may infringe upon my ability to correctly estimate the consequences of these shocks. This problem most clearly presents itself with respect to popular mobilization and foreign intervention, both of which are acts performed by presumably purposeful actors. To the extent that these real-world actors think strategically, they may be expected to weigh the costs against the expected benefits before deciding to take action against a certain regime. This might pose two problems to my data. The first is that what might matter is not the actions actually undertaken, but the *threat* of such actions. This is basically how popular rebellion is supposed to work in the game-theoretic theories of democratization suggested by Boix (2003) and Acemoglu and Robinson (2006), but it has also been suggested with respect to the decision to impose economic sanctions on a foreign country (Lacy and Niou 2004). Since I only observe acts of popular mobilization and foreign intervention that have actually occurred, I might thus underestimate the importance of these phenomena in real-world politics.

Second, to the extent that the actors involved themselves experience differences between regime types that are similar to the ones hypothesized in this chapter, they may factor in these perceptions before deciding to take action. This would mean, for example, that both popular

[7] More specifically, the ratios of the within- over the cross-country standard deviation for these three variables are 1.87 (demonstrations), 2.08 (growth) and 3.50 (foreign interventions).

Table 6.1 *Distribution of Exogenous Shocks across Regime Types*

	Peaceful demonstrations	Abs (growth)	Foreign intervention index
Monarchy	.098	.046	.005 (1)
Military	.655	.044	.043 (21)
One-party	.401	.052	.018 (4)
Multiparty	.814	.038	.027 (18)
Democracy	.609	.034	.011 (16)
Other	1.28	.051	.120 (5)
No. of observations	3,658	3,658	3,035

Note: Entries are mean values of the respective indices across regime types, except the figure in parentheses for the external pressure index, which denotes the absolute number of hostile military interventions and/or economic sanctions undertaken. Only observations in the estimations samples of Table 6.3 below are included.

mobilization and foreign intervention are instruments of pressure that are more rarely used against one-party regimes, since these regimes are perceived to be less vulnerable. The descriptive information in Table 6.1 in effect lends some support to this notion of strategic anticipation. The figures may be interpreted as the frequency with which each exogenous shock occurs across different regime types. It is clear that both peaceful demonstrations and foreign intervention are much more commonly undertaken against military and multiparty autocracies compared to one-party regimes. Economic performance shocks, on the other hand, which do not contain the same strategic element, appear to hit all regime types with approximately the same frequency (as indicated in the "Abs (growth)" column).[8]

This could imply that those actions of popular mobilization and foreign intervention that are actually undertaken against one-party regimes are a censored sample, as it were, only including events with an unusually high expected probability of success. As a result, the differences in effects across regime types may be underestimated. In the case of foreign interventions this problem is exacerbated by the fact that so few of these events occur. All in all there are only four

[8] In order to treat economic upturns and downturns similarly, I have in Table 6.1 taken the absolute value of the annual growth rate.

instances of foreign interventions undertaken against one-party regimes in my estimation sample, and only *one* directed toward monarchies. It should thus be made clear from the outset that we cannot expect very precise estimates of how the consequences of foreign interventions vary across regime types.

Holding these caveats in mind, my approach to modeling the effects of exogenous shocks will be to incorporate (multiplicative) interaction terms between each exogenous shock and the regime dummies.[9] These interaction terms capture the difference in the effect of a given shock variable and the omitted regime category. Since my theoretical conjectures concern contrasts with the one-party regimes, I use them throughout as the omitted regime category. In order to accommodate for the possibility that exogenous shock variables may be expected to have a varying impact depending on the level of democracy in the country where they take place, I also include an interaction effect between each exogenous shock variable, respectively, and the level of democracy at t–1.[10] Finally, I test H4b by adding yet another interaction effect: between exogenous shocks and the degree of party domination (i.e., the size of the largest party). This hypothesis would be supported if we find the same relative (and statistically significant) difference in the effects of exogenous shocks between more or less one-party dominated multiparty regimes as we find between multiparty and one-party regimes.

Empirical results

In Table 6.2, I test the general propensity of different regime types to democratize, when controlling for all previously tested determinants, but regardless of their exposure to shocks. The setup is equivalent to the one used in previous chapters, with results presented separately for the general effect on democratization, the effect on upturns and downturns separately, and the long-term effects. With one-party regimes being the

9 Since the transition dummies, which are required to capture the lagged effect of regime types appropriately (see n. 6, p. 126), in themselves consume large amounts of temporal variation in the dependent variable, I will, however, refrain from lagging the regime types when testing for contingent effects. The shocks thus occur at t–1, but are here assumed to be experienced only at time t, that is, when the regime categories are being measured.

10 This is thus the alternative strategy to estimate different effects on movements away from or toward democracy mentioned in Appendix C.

Table 6.2 *Types of Authoritarian Regimes*

	Short-run			
	General	Upturns	Downturns	Long-run
Regime type:				
Monarchy	−.050	−.019	−.031	−.393
	(.051)	(.039)	(.038)	(.399)
Military dictatorship	.038	.077**	−.039	.299
	(.039)	(.037)	(.031)	(.304)
Multiparty autocracy	.186**	.167***	.019	1.46***
	(.078)	(.064)	(.044)	(.511)
Democracy	.547***	.294***	.253***	4.29***
	(.116)	(.088)	(.061)	(.537)
Other	.091	.201**	−.110	.712
	(.101)	(.088)	(.071)	(.790)
Mean executive turnover	.150**	.182***	−.033	1.18**
	(.064)	(.049)	(.039)	(.503)
Size of largest party	.112	.028	.084**	.882
	(.070)	(.058)	(.035)	(.573)

* significant at the .10-level, ** significant at the .05-level, *** significant at the .01-level. No. of observations = 3,647; no. of countries = 165; mean years observed per country = 22.1.

Note: Entries are unstandardized regression coefficients with panel-corrected standard errors in parentheses. All models also include two lags of the dependent variable, the determinants in Tables 2.1, 3.1, 4.1 and 5.1, and the regime transition dummies, as controls. One-party regimes are treated as the reference category for regime type. All variables in the table have been lagged one year.

reference category, coefficients for the other regime types capture the difference in democratizing propensity between this particular type and the one-party regimes. As can be seen, there is some support for hypothesis H1a: military dictatorships are more prone to democratize than one-party regimes. This difference in democratizing propensity is statistically significant when only upturns are considered, but it does not hold for downturns. In other words, whereas military dictatorships are more prone than one-party regimes to move upwards on the democracy scale, they have no larger propensity to uphold the levels of democracy already achieved. Moreover, the democratizing propensity of monarchies is in no case significantly different from that of one-party regimes. H2a is thus not supported.

The largest substantial difference among regime types is the one between multiparty autocracies and single-party regimes. On average, multiparty autocracies increase their democracy scores by .186 more than one-party regimes, holding all other determinants constant. This amounts to a difference in the long-term equilibrium level of democracy of 1.46. This difference between multiparty autocracies and single-party regimes is clearly dominated by the effect on upturns.[11] Thus, multiparty autocracies are more likely than one-party regimes to improve their level of democracy, but share the same propensity to sustain their democratic achievements. The relative size of the largest party *within* multiparty autocracies, however, only significantly impacts on downturns, and *positively* so. Among the multiparty autocracies, there is thus a tendency that single-party domination impedes de-democratization, which is not what my theory would predict. In other words, whereas there is clear support for H3a, there is no support for H4a.

There is thus an inherent propensity to democratize among multiparty autocracies, as compared to closed single-party systems. This result is insensitive to all but one robustness test performed in Appendix C.[12] As a further indication of robustness, this is also what Brownlee (2009) finds, although based on a different scheme for authoritarian regime classification. Moreover, I find that mean executive turnover, an auxiliary regime characteristic intended to capture (the inverse of) the degree of personalism, is positively related to democratization. In other words, personalized regimes are less likely to democratize, as should be expected, but the propensity among multiparty autocracies to lean toward democratization holds regardless of this tendency. It should also be noted that since I control for the previous level of democracy, and only measure the authoritarian regime types at time *t*–1, endogeneity cannot explain the propensity of multiparty autocracies to democratize, as suggested by Jennifer Gandhi and Ellen Lust-Okar (2009, p. 416).

I now turn to the question of whether the institutional varieties among autocracies also predict different propensities to democratize as a response to exogenous shocks. The results for each shock, still using one-party regimes as the reference category, are in Table 6.3 presented

[11] This effect is also robust to the exclusion of two relatively influential outliers: Uruguay in 1985 and Lebanon in 2005.

[12] The one exception is that the effect does not hold for the Freedom House civil liberties score.

Table 6.3 *The Contingent Effect of Exogenous Shocks*

Exogenous shock:	Peaceful demonstrations		Growth		Foreign intervention index	
	(1)	(2)	(3)	(4)	(5)	(6)
Regime type:						
Monarchy	–.029	–.023	–.014	–.011	–.099	–.098
	(.064)	(.064)	(.063)	(.064)	(.073)	(.074)
Military dictatorship	–.064	–.062	–.064	–.061	–.031	–.030
	(.058)	(.058)	(.056)	(.056)	(.057)	(.057)
Multiparty autocracy	.769***	.736***	.898***	.956***	.940***	.936***
	(.120)	(.118)	(.117)	(.119)	(.137)	(.137)
Democracy	1.57***	1.55***	1.87***	1.92***	1.87***	1.87***
	(.174)	(.172)	(.166)	(.168)	(.202)	(.202)
Other	.485***	.487***	.541***	.541***	.490***	.490***
	(.131)	(.131)	(.122)	(.122)	(.139)	(.139)
Shock	.064***	.061***	–2.02***	–2.08***	.452	.458
	(.017)	(.017)	(.604)	(.602)	(.337)	(.337)
Shock × level of democracy	–.034***	–.033***	1.06***	1.08***	–.381***	–.387***
	(.004)	(.005)	(.207)	(.203)	(.068)	(.070)
Regime type interactions:						
Monarchy × shock	–.095	–.097	–1.13	–1.13	2.06***	2.08***
	(.078)	(.078)	(.714)	(.719)	(.743)	(.743)
Military × shock	.034	.031	.991	.990	–.066	–.057
	(.026)	(.026)	(.805)	(.803)	(.422)	(.425)

Multiparty × shock	.146***	.207***	–2.93***	–5.91***	1.45***	1.78**
	(.027)	(.030)	(1.06)	(1.36)	(.501)	(.839)
Democracy × shock	.242***	.290***	–7.89***	–1.77***	2.72***	3.01***
	(.038)	(.038)	(1.64)	(1.81)	(.634)	(.919)
Other × shock	.083**	.079**	–2.92*	–2.94*	.830*	.842*
	(.036)	(.036)	(1.59)	(1.59)	(.471)	(.473)
Mean executive turnover	.492***	.492***	.495***	.501***	.473***	.471***
	(.081)	(.081)	(.083)	(.083)	(.083)	(.083)
Size of largest party	–.189**	–.128	–.206**	–.295***	–.257**	–.251**
	(.093)	(.092)	(.093)	(.100)	(.117)	(.116)
Shock × size of largest party		–.119***		4.99***		–.564
		(.039)		(1.44)		(1.21)
No. of observations	3,638	3,638	3,638	3,638	3,035	3,035
No. of countries	165	165	165	165	159	159

* significant at the .10-level, ** significant at the .05-level, *** significant at the .01-level.

Note: Entries are unstandardized regression coefficients with panel-corrected standard errors in parentheses. All models include two lags of the level of democracy and the determinants in Tables 2.1, 3.1, 4.1 and 5.1 as controls. All exogenous shock variables have been lagged one year.

in two columns each, with and without controlling for the conditional effect of largest party size among multiparty autocracies. Thus, starting with popular mobilization, model (1) shows that the effect of peaceful demonstrations among one-party regimes with zero level democracy (at t–1) is .064 and statistically significant. This effect decreases, however, as a country moves up the democracy scale, as the significant but negative interaction effect with the the level of democracy at t–1 indicates. Once this conditional effect has been controlled for, there is one difference across authoritarian regime types that stands out, again between one-party and multiparty regimes, showing that the latter – in line with theoretical expectations (H3b) – are more sensitive to peaceful demonstrations than the former.[13] There is, however, no statistically significant difference between one-party regimes on the one hand, and military dictatorships or monarchies on the other, in their propensity to be affected by peaceful demonstrations. In other words, neither H1b nor H2b is supported.

The intricate interplay between initial level of democracy, regime type and the effects of peaceful demonstrations is illustrated in Figure 6.2. Due to the negative interaction effect with level of democracy at t–1, the slopes for all regime types reach their maximum in the most authoritarian regime and then regress toward more negative values as the previous level of democracy increases. At all levels, however, the rate of democratization in multiparty autocracies is significantly more positively affected as compared to one-party regimes. Whereas the line for monarchies is consistently below that for one-party regimes, which is slightly below that for military dictatorships, the differences among these regime types never prove statistically significant.[14]

Turning back to Table 6.3, model (3) reports very similar results with respect to economic performance. As can be seen, the effect of growth in fully authoritarian one-party regimes is negative, consistent with the finding in Chapter 3 that economic crises in authoritarian regimes

[13] This finding is robust to the exclusion of four relatively influential confirming outliers (Turkey in 1980, China in 1989, Uruguay in 1985 and Indonesia in 1999), as well as one influential disconfirming outlier (Hungary in 1989).

[14] Among regimes at the right-most end of this figure, it would at first sight appear as if one-party regimes are more vulnerable to peaceful demonstrations. This is, however, an artifact of extrapolation beyond the empirical reach of my data, since there actually exist no one-party regime years at a higher level than 4.08 (at t–1).

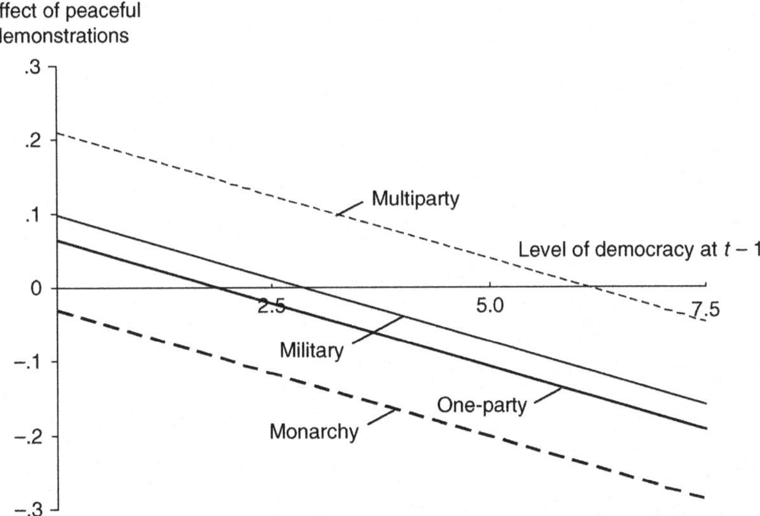

Figure 6.2 Contingent Effects of Peaceful Demonstrations
Note: The figure depicts the predicted increase in the rate of democratization following a unit change in the number of peaceful demonstrations, conditional on the level of democracy at *t*–1 and the authoritarian regime type ($n = 3{,}638$). All estimates are from model (1) of Table 6.3.

trigger democratization. The positive and statistically significant interaction effect between growth and the level of democracy at *t*–1 means that growth produces more democratization, the higher the initial level of democracy. More important for present purposes, according to expectations (H3b) there is a sizeable and statistically significant difference between the effect of economic performance among one-party and multiparty regimes, the latter being more vulnerable to economic crises than the former.

Again I make use of a graphical display in order to convey the intricacies of these dynamic patterns. As shown in Figure 6.3, authoritarian regime types respond differently to shocks in economic growth. For one-party regimes, the effect at zero level of democracy is –2.02 and statistically significant. With rising levels of democracy, this effect increases, meaning that for most one-party regimes (having an average previous level of democracy at 1.6) economic performance never has any statistically significant effect on democratization. At similar levels of democracy, however, the situation with multiparty autocracies is

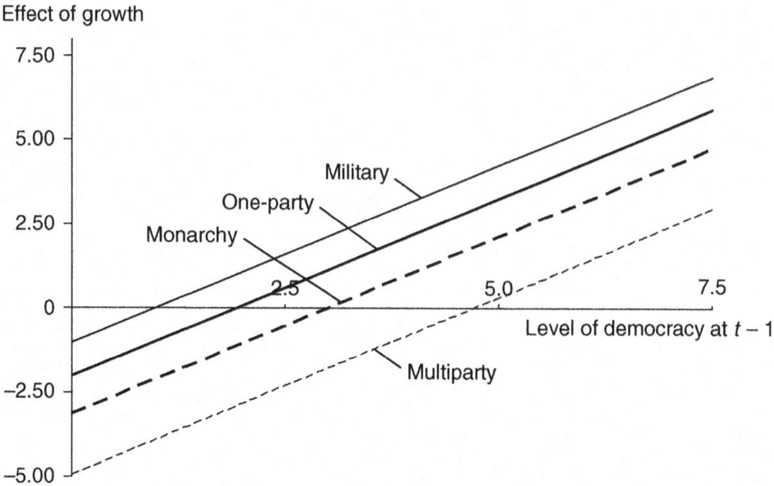

Figure 6.3 Contingent Effects of Growth
Note: The figure depicts the predicted increase in the rate of democratization following a 100 percentage change in the growth rate, conditional on the level of democracy at t–1 and the authoritarian regime type (n = 3,638). All estimates are from model (3) of Table 6.3.

starkly different: growth here has a negative impact, implying that economic crisis stimulates democratization. Monarchies and military regimes are located below and above the one-party regimes, respectively, although the difference among them is not statistically significant (not supporting H1b or H2b).

Turning to the results for foreign interventions in model (5) of Table 6.3, there is no significant baseline effect among one-party regimes at zero level of democracy. Together with the significant but reversely signed interaction effect with level of democracy, however, this finding is actually in line with the result from Chapter 4, indicating that foreign interventions have no average effect on democratization. While there appears to be a positive interaction effect for monarchies (which would have supported H2b), this effect hinges on the single monarchy affected by a foreign intervention in my estimation sample: Jordan, which in 1991 – the year after the Gulf War economic blockade – made a small improvement in its democracy score. This is thus obviously not a robust finding. Again, however, I find that foreign interventions do have a significantly stronger effect in multiparty autocracies than in one-party regimes, lending additional support for H3b. This is a noteworthy result in light of the data limitations constraining my tests for foreign intervention noted upon previously.[15] It deserves to be repeated, however, that there are only four cases of foreign interventions directed toward one-party regimes in my estimation sample (as indicated by Table 6.1 above).[16] There is thus no solid empirical evidence underlying this result.

Finally, I turn to the conditional effect of size of the largest party within multiparty regimes, that is, to testing proposition H4b. The expectation, to recap, is that each exogenous shock should have an effect on democratization that is conditional on the extent to which one single party "dominates" a multiparty autocracy. As can be seen, this expectation is in Table 6.3 borne out for both peaceful demonstrations (model 2) and economic growth (model 4), but not for foreign interventions (model 6). Thus, although multiparty systems are more prone than one-party regimes to democratize as a response to demonstrations, this propensity decreases with the size of the largest party in parliament. As an illustration, the democratizing effect of a unit increase in the popular mobilization index in an average multiparty autocracy, at 4.96 in the level of democracy (at t–1) and where the largest party controls 60 percent of the parliamentary seats, is .032, compared to .009 in a system where the largest party makes up 80 percent of the seats (where the latter effect is not statistically significant). Similarly, the positive interaction between size of the largest party and growth in model (4) indicates that multiparty regimes more dominated by a single party are more resilient to exogenous shocks in their economic performance. For two of the three shocks tested, I thus find support for H4b.

Conclusion

Let me now summarize the findings for the tests of my four composite hypotheses on how different authoritarian regimes affect democratization differently. With respect to H1a, there is a significant difference in the democratizing propensity of military regimes per se as compared with

[15] This effect is also robust to the exclusion of one extremely influential outlier: Thailand in 1976.

[16] These cases are economic sanctions against China in 1989 and 1991, against Malawi in 1992, and a foreign military intervention against Zambia in 1977.

single-party rule, although this only applies for increases in the democracy scores (i.e., upturns). I have, however, in no instance found that military regimes are more prone to democratize than one-party regimes as a response to exogenous shocks. Thus, H1b is rejected outright. What explains this failed expectation is open for interpretation. Geddes' (1999; 2003) theoretical account of the differences in internal dynamics between one-party and military regimes could still be correct as far as the propensity for internal splits within the regime is concerned; or, as in Mesquita *et al.*'s (2003) selectorate theory, in terms of the strength of the loyalty norm. But these splits are then not necessarily propelled by exogenous shocks, at least not the ones probed empirically here.

To disentangle these interpretations more systematically would be a worthy subject for further inquiry in future case studies. As a matter of fact, two of the strongest pathway cases for the effect of military regimes on upturns in Table 6.2 are the democratic transition in Chile 1989 and in Turkey in 1983 (being ranked 1st and 8th in terms of the pathway criterion). In Haggard and Kaufman's (1995, chap. 3) case study accounts both the Pinochet and the Evren military regimes are depicted as "withdrawing in good times." Both regimes had survived economic performance crises several years before, and although the Chilean transition was not devoid of popular mobilization, the cycle of protest had peaked several years before the transition (see, e.g., Foweraker and Landman 1997, chap. 5). Chile and Turkey would thus be excellent cases for studying why military regimes may be more prone to democratizing than one-party regimes despite the absence of exogenous shocks.[17]

I find no significantly stronger propensity to democratize among monarchies as compared to single-party regimes. Moreover, monarchies – much as military regimes – are not more prone than one-party regimes to democratize when facing exogenous shocks (with the exception of foreign interventions and the case of Jordan in 1991). In other words, H2a and H2b are rejected. Scarcity of data probably explains

[17] Haggard and Kaufman argue that what distinguished Chile and Turkey (together with South Korea) from other military dictatorships was their stronger fusion of military and political authority, greater specialization of military roles, and simply their length of time in power. In various ways, then, these regimes had a more institutionalized basis of power, with a stronger capacity to contain internal divisions (1995, p. 42). If this argument is correct, it might necessitate a more nuanced subdivision of various regime characteristics *within* the category of military dictatorships.

part of these somewhat erratic results for monarchies. In all, I only have 259 observations from 14 monarchies in my estimation sample, which of course reflects the fact that these regimes have become relatively rare in the modern world. In order to assess the democratizing potential among monarchies more comprehensively in the future, longer historical time series would thus be needed.

H3a and H3b are the most well supported hypotheses in my data. Multiparty autocracies democratize to a larger extent than one-party regimes both in and of themselves and in response to both popular protest and short-term economic performance. This result even extends to foreign interventions, but the latter effect hinges on very few observations for one-party regimes. Moreover, *among* multiparty autocracies the tendency is similar: the more a multiparty regime is dominated by one "hegemonic" party, the less they democratize as a response to peaceful demonstrations and growth (lending support for H4b, although not for H4a).

This finding appears to run counter to skepticism of authoritarian elections. Jason Brownlee (2007, p. 10), for example, holds that elections are "symptoms, not causes" of regime change. Lust-Okar (2006, p. 468), moreover, argues that "elections are more likely to help sustain the authoritarian regime than they are to promote democracy," and Gandhi (2008, p. 188) that multiparty elections in autocracies "will not pave the way toward democracy" (also see Carothers 2002, pp. 8, 15). Since multiparty autocracies differ from other authoritarian regime types by the semi-competitive nature of their elections, my results would instead appear to be more in line with, for example, Staffan Lindberg's (2006) institutional learning theory of democratization.[18]

More theoretical and empirical work is, however, needed to disentangle the more specific mechanisms through which this effect occurs. Geddes (1999, 2003) and Bueno de Mesquita *et al.*'s (2003) theoretical models, as mentioned, provide little help in this regard, since they do not even distinguish between one-party and multiparty autocracies. In the theoretical section above, I instead developed two possible ways of understanding these regimes, one based on democratic "responsiveness" to voters, the other on authoritarian "defections." I have no way of distinguishing these two models directly in the data. It bears noting,

[18] In a newly published piece I also find more direct evidence in favor of Lindberg's (2006) proposition, at least as far as long series of multiparty elections and non-electoral facets of democracy are concerned (Teorell and Hadenius 2009).

however, that the nominal category of "democracies" (i.e., regimes that have passed the estimated 7.5 threshold on the democracy scale) in Table 6.2 display an even stronger propensity to democratize than do multiparty autocracies. In Table 6.3, moreover, a consistent pattern is that democracies respond to peaceful demonstrations, economic downturns and foreign interventions similarly to multiparty autocracies, only that response is consistently stronger. Multiparty autocracies thus appear to behave like bleak versions of their more fully "democratic" counterparts.

Had this not been the case, I could with some certainty have dismissed the "responsiveness to voters" mechanism, since that mechanism according to theory is the one operating in fully "democratic" countries. Nevertheless, I am not in a position to reject the "defections" mechanism either. It could be that competition for votes only starts operating as a constraint on office holders once a certain threshold of competition has been reached. Below this threshold, the strategic struggle between regime and opposition could account for the expected behavior. In other words, my findings are consistent with both mechanisms. Moreover, these two mechanisms are by no means incompatible. The threat of defections is a likely incentive for regime incumbents to be more responsive to demands for reform. Depending on the balance of power among incumbent and opposition forces, such reforms may in turn spur rather than prevent further defections by making a victory for the opposition more likely. There is thus a potential spiraling logic to the dynamics of multiparty autocracies.

7 *Conclusions*

The third wave of democratization that has swept the globe since the mid-1970s has brought profound change to millions of people around the world. Regardless of whether democracy leads to other valued outcomes such as growth, peace and prosperity, having a democratic system of government in and of itself is an improvement in the quality of life for most citizens. Democracies, by their very nature, to a lesser extent than autocracies harass and jail people for having political views opposing the government. Democracies, also by their very nature, to a lesser extent than autocracies outlaw political and civil society organizations for criticizing incumbent rulers. Political power in democracies is bestowed upon those that win free and fair elections, not according to hereditary succession, threats from the barrel of a gun, or simply from the lack of free choice at the ballot box. Since these are features of democracies that make them democracies, by definition, they are not independent outcomes. Nevertheless, they are in and of themselves highly preferred moral virtues.

How does democracy, thus being a preferable system of government, come about? What are the determinants of democratization? In this book I have tried to answer these questions through a combination of two types of empirical evidence: a large-*n* statistical analysis of 165 countries around the world in the period 1972–2006, measuring democratization as change in the average Freedom House ratings and Polity scores, and small-*n* case study work on nine episodes of democratization occurring in Argentina, Bolivia, Hungary, Nepal, Peru, the Philippines, South Africa, Turkey, and Uruguay. In this concluding chapter I will summarize my findings and discuss their implications.

Summary of findings

The major findings of this empirical investigation may be summarized as follows:

1. The share of Muslims in the population is negatively related to both increases and (although less robustly) decreases in democratization. That is, it both impeded upturns and triggered downturns during the third wave.
2. Economic crises, peaceful demonstrations, neighbor diffusion and democratic regional organizations were robustly related to positive increases in the level of democracy (upturns).
3. Conversely, geographically large countries, and countries whose economies are largely dependent on oil exports or foreign trade, were significantly less likely to experience increases in their level of democracy.
4. Socioeconomic modernization, measured broadly as the syndrome underlying industrialization, urbanization, education, improved living conditions, media proliferation and national income, was a robust impediment to decreases in the level of democracy (upturns). So was freedom from state incursion in the economy. In other words, during the third wave modernization and economic freedom prevented de-democratization.
5. Colonial origin, non-Muslim religious denominations, ethnolinguistic and religious fractionalization, natural resource abundance in terms of minerals, inflation, economic inequality, foreign direct investment and portfolio allocations, regional and global diffusion, foreign military intervention and economic sanctions, as well as riots, strikes and armed domestic warfare were *not* robustly related to democratization during the third wave.
6. Many large-*n* tests of explanatory mechanisms fail. The negative effect of geographical size is substitutable for population size, but is not due to insularity (island status). The negative effect of large trading volumes cannot be explained in terms of specific trading partners, such as the core capitalist economies (US, UK and France) or authoritarian hegemons in the international system (USSR/Russia and China). Moreover, democratizing countries do not affect democratization among their neighbors by the diffusion of economic crises or popular protest, or by employing pressure from within joint regional international organizations.
7. Some large-*n* tests, however, do shed some light on the explanatory mechanisms. Whereas the negative impact of a Muslim population cannot be accounted for by female subordination, this effect is

restricted to a particular part of the world: the Middle East and North Africa. The "Muslim gap" thus mostly appears to be an "Arab gap." Moreover, the effect of socioeconomic modernization is not due to income disparity, nor driven by human capital or the economic structure (e.g., industrialization), but by media proliferation. Richer countries were thus less likely to de-democratize, not so much because they were rich but because they provided broad access to media such as via radios, TVs and newspapers.

8. The cases of Bolivia in 1982, Argentina in 1983, Uruguay in 1985 and the Philippines in 1986 all experienced substantial increases in their level of democracy, and this increase was relatively well explained by the effect of having experienced a recessionary economic crisis. This implies that these cases fit the criterion of a "pathway case" for this particular determinant. Haggard and Kaufman's (1995) argument that economic crises drive democratization by prompting business-sector defection from the authoritarian bargain, public-sector mobilization and internal splits within regime elites is supported in these cases. It thus appears to be a well-founded mechanism to explain the democratizing effect of economic crises.
9. In the same sense, the cases of the Philippines in 1984–87, South Africa in 1990 and Nepal in 1991 are "pathway cases" for the effect of peaceful demonstrations. This supports the theory, derived from Schock (2005), that peaceful rather than violent popular uprisings promote democratization by mobilizing larger numbers of people, by again exacerbating intra-elite divisions, and by hurting the state's economic and other dependency relations, both within and outside the country.
10. Pevehouse's (2005) argument that democratic regional organizations may enhance democracy by pressuring their member states is corroborated with respect to the role of the Council of Europe in the pathway case of Turkey in 1983, and the Organization of American States in the (somewhat less well-fitting) pathway case of Peru in 2000. The support for a similar mechanism operating in the case of Hungary in 1989–90 from the Organization for Security and Cooperation in Europe, or in the case of the OAS in Peru in 1993, is, however, more strained. Moreover, Pevehouse's other two mechanisms – the acquiescence and legitimizing effects – are not supported.

11. Large-*n* analysis based on the classification of authoritarian regime types in Teorell and Hadenius (2007) shows that multiparty autocracies during the third wave were in and of themselves more prone to democratize than one-party dictatorships. This effect mostly applied to the likelihood that these regimes would move toward higher levels of democracy (upturns). Multiparty autocracies were also more prone to democratize in response to exogenous shocks such as economic crises, popular mobilization and (although less robustly) foreign intervention. This evidence is supportive of a theory that characterizes the inner workings of limited multiparty regimes as a two-level game between incumbent and oppositional parties (Schedler 2002a), and that stresses the importance of elections for exacerbating intra-elite regimes' splits and opposition coalescence (Langston 2006; Magaloni 2006; 2008; van de Walle 2006).
12. Finally, military regimes were by themselves also more prone to move toward democracy (upturns) than one-party regimes, but not in response to exogenous shocks. With one non-robust exception (the effect of foreign interventions), monarchies were statistically indistinguishable from one-party regimes, both with respect to their tendency to democratize in and of themselves and in response to shocks.

Explanatory performance

The list of determinants that according to my statistical evidence were robustly linked to democratization during the third wave are summarized in Figure 7.1. I now turn to the question of how well all these determinants, when taken together, explain the incidence of democratization. I will restrict attention to those determinants that are observed for my full estimation sample. In order to compare the explanatory performance in the short-run and the long-run, I make use of the same distinction in time horizons as previously. In order to assess short-term performance, I simply compare the predictions my model yields over a one-year period to the actual yearly change in the level of democracy. In order to assess long-term performance, I must instead compare the actual level of democracy in a given year with the level of democracy that would ensue if all variables were allowed to experience their full

	TRIGGERS (of)	IMPEDIMENTS (to)
Upturns	Economic crisis Neighbor diffusion Regional organizations Peaceful demonstrations Multiparty autocracy	Muslim population Size Fuels Trade volume
Downturns	Muslim population	Socioeconomic modernization Economic freedom

Figure 7.1 Summary of Robust Statistical Findings
Note: The statistical analyses also included the following determinants, which had no robust effect: colonial origin, non-Muslim religious denominations, ethnolinguistic and religious fractionalization, inflation, natural resource dependence in terms of minerals, economic inequality, international capital flows, regional and global diffusion, foreign interventions, riots, strikes and civil conflict.

long-run effects. One could think of this latter state as the long-run equilibrium level of democracy to which a country is attracted. The question of long-run explanatory performance then pertains to how far from this long-run equilibrium the level of democracy is in each country in any given year.[1]

I compute two fit indices in order to assess explanatory performance. The first is the ordinary explained variance, adjusted for the degrees of

[1] Some forerunners in using this statistical approach are worth mentioning. Barro computes the long-run forecasts of democracy for each country, but without reporting the long-run parameters (1999). Londregan and Poole (1996), by contrast, report the long-run effect parameters but without computing the equilibrium democracy levels. None of them assess the long-run predictive performance.

freedom.[2] The second estimate is the standard error of the regression (also known as the root mean squared error). It is simply the standard deviation of the residuals, that is, the unexplained part of the dependent variable. Being expressed in the same measurement units as the dependent variable, its minimum value is zero, indicating perfect fit, but unlike the R-squared it lacks a normed upper bound. In order to ease its interpretation, I compare it to the actual variance in the dependent variable,[3] and compute the so-called reduction in prediction error variance, which measures how much better we are at predicting the dependent variable by knowing the scores of our determinants (see Appendix B).

These two fit indices are presented in Table 7.1. It is easily verified that the predictive performance of the short-run model is low. The R-squared for the full model in the general short-run equation reaches 6.0 percent explained variance, or a 3.1 percent reduction of the prediction error. Interestingly, there is a large difference in explanatory performance of upturns versus downturns. Whereas the explained variance in upturns reaches some 9 percent explained variance at best, the corresponding figure for downturns is only just below 3 percent. Again these results are similar when seen from the perspective of reduction in prediction error. In other words, although the model fares rather poorly in both instances, it does a better job at explaining short-term movements upward on the democracy scale than at explaining movements downwards. The most likely reason for this difference is that I find a broader array of explanatory factors related to upturns, such as economic crises, neighbor diffusion, regional organizations and popular mobilization.

More importantly, however, by looking at explanatory power in the long-run the picture radically changes. In the full model the R-squared reaches its long-run maximum of 57.8 percent explained variance, or a reduction in prediction error of 35.0 percent. This means that the actual

[2] It should be noted that by putting yearly *change* of the democracy index on the lefthand side of my equations, I avoid inflating the R-squared by the static variance common to both the level of democracy and its lagged values (a common problem in panel regressions, which might otherwise report levels of explained variance well above 90 percent for no other than this simple reason).

[3] In the estimation sample of 3,795 observations the standard deviation of change in level of democracy is .711, of upturns .525, of downturns .450, and of the level of democracy 3.32.

Table 7.1 *Explanatory Performance*

	Short-run							
	General		Upturns		Downturns		Long-run	
	R^2	*RPE*	R^2	*RPE*	R^2	*RPE*	R^2	*RPE*
Purely autoregressive model	.024	.012	.048	.024	.000	.000	-	-
Full model	.060	.031	.093	.047	.029	.015	.578	.350
Without social determinants	.057	.029	.088	.045	.024	.012	.533	.317
Without economic determinants	.060	.030	.089	.046	.024	.012	.551	.330
Without international determinants	.050	.025	.081	.041	.027	.014	.468	.271
Without popular mobilization	.056	.028	.082	.042	.028	.014	.628	.390

No. of observations = 3,795; no. of countries = 165; mean years observed per country = 23.0.

Note: R^2 refers to the explained variance adjusted for degrees of freedom, *RPE* to the reduction in prediction error variance. The purely autoregressive model only includes the two lags of the dependent variable. The full model adds all determinants in Tables 2.1, 3.1, 4.1 and 5.1. The additional four models omit, one group at a time, the determinants in Table 2.1 (social determinants), 3.1 (economic determinants), 4.1 (international determinants) and 5.1 (popular mobilization).

level of democracy on average comes fairly close to the long-run equilibrium level determined by the explanatory variables.

The fact that these determinants perform rather poorly in explaining short-term democratization is well in line with the uncertainty and unpredictability so much stressed by O'Donnell and Schmitter (1986) and other adherents of the strategic approach or "transition paradigm." Since short-term changes in democracy cannot be predicted by even the most comprehensive statistical models, according to this argument, there must be room for action on the part of strategic elites or other key players in the countries under study. This also seems to support the argument proffered by Przeworski *et al.* (2000, p. 137) that transitions to democracy appear to occur by chance, although my results indicate that, albeit still at a low level, upturns are more easily explained than downturns. What may appear unpredictable and erratic in the short-run, however, turns out to be stable and predictable in the long-run. In other words, when projected against a longer time horizon democratic development is not as unpredictable as adherents of the voluntaristic or chance-oriented "strategic" views have asserted. On the contrary, in this time perspective the structural approach to democratization performs relatively well. As a matter of fact, O'Donnell and Schmitter were themselves well aware of this in that they did not deny "the long-run causal impact of 'structural' (including macroeconomic, world systemic, and social class) factors." Their assertions regarding the non-structural determinants of democratic transitions only concerned short-term dynamics (1986, pp. 4–5).

Is there a particular group of determinants accountable for this pattern? The lower four rows of Table 7.1 address this question according to the thematic grouping of variables I have upheld in previous chapters. In each row one of the groups of variables is omitted from the model. The ensuing fit indices then indicate the importance of this group for the overall explanatory performance (the lower the fit when a group is omitted, the larger its overall explanatory importance). There are some differences among the groups. Generally the international determinants appear as the most powerful predictors of democratization, but then one should keep in mind that they rely most heavily on proxies (for neighbor diffusion and regional organizations) that are fairly close to the dependent variable itself. Domestic economic and social factors would appear to matter the least, whereas – at least in the short-run equations – popular mobilization entertains a position somewhere in between. Overall, however, these differences are very small, reflecting the fact that all groups of variables share a substantial amount of variance even to begin with. With the one exception of popular mobilization's negligible importance for understanding long-run democratization, these results thus do not allow any firm conclusion as to what kind of determinants matter more than others. What they do allow me to conclude is that whereas my models explain little of the short-term dynamics, they fare considerably better in explaining regime change over the long haul.

Figure 7.2 highlights this finding even more sharply. I have here plotted the observed amount of change in the level of democracy from the first to the last year of observation against the predicted long-run equilibrium level of democracy from the first year of observation

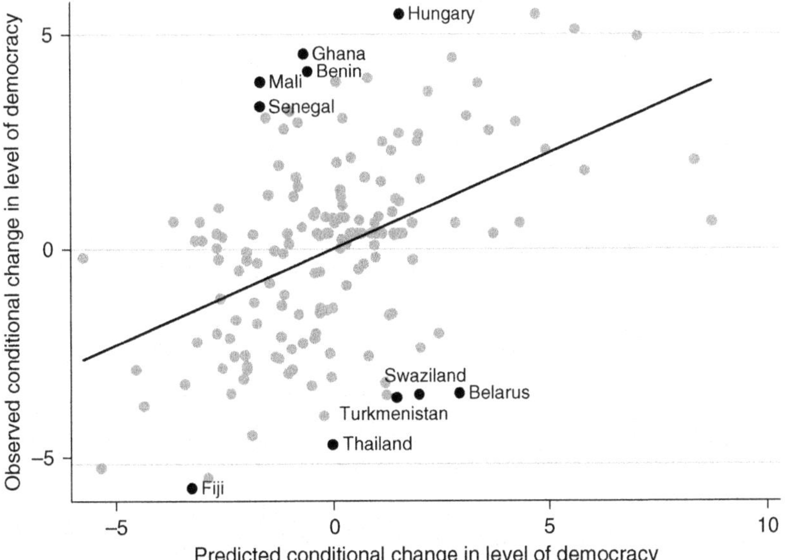

Figure 7.2 Observed vs. Predicted Long-Run Change in Democracy
Note: The graph is a partial regression (or added-variable) plot of the relationship between observed and predicted long-run change in the level of democracy between the first and last year of observation, after having taken the level of democracy at the first year of observation into account ($n = 163$). The slope coefficient is .430, and the partial correlation .443. The ten countries with largest residuals are highlighted.

for each country, after having taken the initial level of democracy into account.[4] Although the time frame thus varies by country, on average 22.4 years of observation are covered, and half of the countries in the estimation sample represent more than 28 years of change. Despite this, there is a fairly tight relationship between the observed and predicted amount of change. The partial correlation between the two is .443, and the adjusted R-squared for the full model, including the initial level of democracy, is 40.1 percent. Of course there are exceptions to this relatively good fit between longer-term predictions and change: I have

[4] The reason why only 163 countries are included in Figure 7.2, although I have 165 countries in my estimation sample, is that two countries only appear for a single year: Djibouti and Tajikistan. No long-term change for these countries may thus be computed.

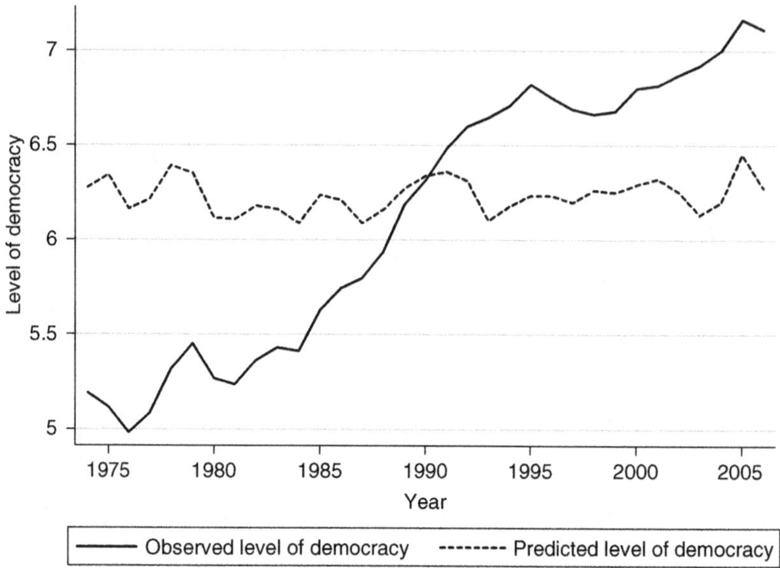

Figure 7.3 Observed vs. Predicted Trend in Level of Democracy
Note: The plot is based on the 3,795 country years in my estimation sample. The observed level is simply the mean of democracy; the predicted level is the expected value of democracy once all determinants are held constant at their mean value.

highlighted the ten most deviant cases. As can be seen, quite a few of them are African cases, including both overachievers (such as Ghana, Mali, Benin and Senegal) and underachievers (such as Swaziland). Democratization of Hungary was also relatively unexpected when judged from its structural prerequisites at the beginning of my observation period for that country, in 1974, whereas democracy according to long-run expectations in Belarus and Turkmenistan should have fared much better than it actually has. These exceptions notwithstanding, I may conclude that the overall relationship between long-run predictions and actual change is far better than the short-term explanatory performance.

A final way of illustrating this pattern is portrayed in Figure 7.3. Instead of comparing the country-level fit between observed and predicted long-run change in democracy, I here look at the extent to which the *aggregate trend* in democracy can be explained with reference to my determinants. The solid line thus simply reflects the third wave of democratization (albeit for the subsample of observations for which I have valid data on all explanatory factors). To what extent can this trend be accounted for by the determinants of democratization? To address this question, the dashed line shows the global trend that *would* have occurred in the last three decades if the determinants had all been held constant at their respective means (excluding, however, the lagged levels and global mean of democracy, since they could too easily predict aggregate trends). As can clearly be seen, in this counterfactual scenario there would have been no visible trend in the level of democracy. In other words, my determinants again display a remarkable ability to account for long-term developments.

Towards an integrated theory of democratization?

What are the theoretical implications of these findings? My results confirm the continued importance of all three intellectual traditions that have dominated the field of comparative democratization studies: the structural approach initiated by Lipset (1959), the strategic approach heralded by Rustow (1970) and O'Donnell and Schmitter (1986), and the social forces tradition originated by Moore (1966). Structural conditions do matter, particularly in the long-run; but so do elite actors, particularly in the short-run. Moreover, the mass of citizens themselves matter when able to organize peaceful insurrections against the regime.

As noted in Chapter 1, in recent years a fourth approach to explaining democratization, based on the formal game-theoretic models of economics, has emerged (Boix 2003; Acemoglu and Robinson 2006). The key theoretical virtue of this novel approach is that it integrates the previous three traditions by providing structural conditions explaining preferences and actions of ordinary citizens ("social forces"), in turn affecting the strategic choices made by political elites. The fact that my results confirm all the three previous and theoretically disparate explanations for democratization thus reinforces the fruitfulness of the economic approach for further theoretical integration in the future.

All economic models of democratization are, however, not equally well suited for this task. On my reading the most promising approach to such theoretical integration to date is the work of Boix (2003). Recall that Boix models regime transitions in a game-theoretic framework, where the rich may choose not to repress, in which case democracy ensues, or to repress at a certain cost, in response to which the poor may choose to revolt against the regime or acquiesce. Similar to Acemoglu and Robinson (2006), Boix assumes that actors are only concerned about their income, which due to the tax rate is larger for the rich under autocracy, and for the poor under democracy. As opposed to Acemoglu and Robinson's model with perfect information, however, the poor are uncertain about the likelihood that the rich will use repression.

A number of predictions ensuing from this model concur with my findings in this book. To begin with, popular mobilization should increase the likelihood of democratization by increasing the repression costs of the rich (Boix 2003, pp. 44–46); the underlying rationale for this prediction is also well in line with the "paradox of repression" as outlined in Chapter 5. Geographical smallness should also be positively linked to democratization since it increases capital mobility by decreasing the physical distance that has to be traversed in order to reach another country, and thus makes the rich better off under democracy (Boix 2003, pp. 41–44). Moreover, having an economy dominated by natural resource abundance such as oil, or being strongly controlled by the state, increases asset specificity. This hurts democracy by making the rich relatively better off under dictatorship (Boix 2003, pp. 42–43).

The poor's perception of the probability that the rich will employ repression, moreover, may help explain two of my findings. The first concerns the apparently erratic nature of short-run changes in the level of democracy as compared to the more predictable long-run equilibria. By prompting citizens to update their beliefs regarding the likelihood that different courses of action will have different consequences, short-term political events have more unpredictable consequences than the more slow-moving forces that shape income distribution or the degree of asset specificity. The second concerns diffusion effects: the presence of information uncertainty helps explain why events in neighboring countries may lead domestic actors to reestimate the chances of achieving their goals in light of the recent experience of similar actors abroad (Boix 2003, p. 29); in other words, information uncertainty is consistent with diffusion through emulation.

Obviously Boix's model cannot explain all my findings, nor are all of them consistent with his predictions. There is, for example, no autonomous role played in the model by economic downturns, nor is a feature such as pressure from a regional organization easily incorporated. Boix's model also lacks a viable causal mechanism accounting for the negative impact of the percentage of Muslims and trade dependence.[5] A more fundamental prediction that does not materialize in my data, as mentioned in Chapter 3, is the effect of economic inequality. Another is the finding that the socioeconomic modernization effect is not primarily driven by aspects of asset specificity.

A critical feature economic models will need to incorporate in the future, moreover, is the nature of the "authoritarian bargain," in Haggard and Kaufman's (1995) terminology, or the regime's "dependency relations," in Schock's (2005) words. Common to both notions is the assumption that authoritarian regimes are forged on the basis of certain support groups, and that they are mostly hurt either when these groups defect from the regime or when dissention spreads among them. By using overly abstract categories such as the "rich" or the "elite," most game-theoretic models to date have missed this crucial dimension. Since the nature of these support groups varies by regime type, one could envision different paths toward democracy from different authoritarian origins. Future economic approaches to explaining democratization thus should pay less attention to issues of redistribution and the importance of income inequality. Instead they need to disaggregate their understanding of authoritarianism in order to acknowledge the institutional underpinnings of different types of autocracies. Most importantly, the rich machinery of formal models developed for understanding electoral politics within democracies must be adapted for understanding the working of electoral politics in autocracies, as the promising attempts of Magaloni (2006) and Greene (2007) make clear.

The mechanisms suggested by Haggard and Kaufman (1995) and Schock (2005) also intersect in other important ways that could be endorsed by future integrative approaches. The most obvious connection is of course that popular mobilization is part of Haggard and Kaufman's (1995) economic crisis mechanism. Although this seems to suggest that economic downturns are an important trigger of popular discontent, we should not be blind to the possibility of a causal arrow running in the opposite direction. That is, when large segments of the population are mobilized against the regime, this may in turn hurt the

[5] Boix (2003, pp. 142–43) does mention, however, that the effect of trade should depend on whether skilled or unskilled labor is the abundant sector in the economy, but this mechanism only operates through its effect on income distribution.

economy. Another shared feature is that both economic downturns and popular mobilization affect democratization by way of widening internal regime splits between hardliners and softliners, as originally argued by O'Donnell and Schmitter (1986). There is, however, a difference in what drives the wedge into this fissure. Whereas the economic seed of dissention concerns material rewards, or conflict over what policy responses best secure these awards, the elite rupture that originates in popular contention is more moral in nature. At the end of the day, it concerns the rightfulness of a regime shooting at its own people.

The mechanisms uncovered in the case studies of this book also highlight the intricate interplay between domestic and international drivers of democratization. With respect to the effect of regional organizations, the flow of causality of course simply runs from the international system into domestic regime politics. But economic crises too have international determinants. This was clearly evident in the Latin American and Philippine cases explored, since their economic problems originated in the international debt crisis. By tracing the funnel of causality backwards in this way, one may even reach the conclusion that all determinants of the third wave of democratization were fundamentally international in nature (Drake 1998). This would, however, miss another key feature of this causal nexus, termed by Peter Gourevitch (1978; 2002) "the second image reversed": the consequences domestic forces have in turn for international relations. Nowhere is this more obvious than in the case of popular mobilization. In the Philippine case, the withdrawal of US support for Marcos was a direct response to the sustained series of protests leveled against his regime, and the aborted military coup that occurred in its wake. In South Africa, the unarmed insurrection changed international attitudes toward the apartheid regime and directly triggered the imposition of sanctions against it. In Nepal, likewise, international withdrawal of development aid was a consequence of the popular uprising. In other words, international and domestic determinants of democratization constantly shape each other. In Lawrence Whitehead's words: "Although there will always be some purely domestic and some exclusively international factors involved, most of the analysis will contain a tangle of both elements" (1996, p. 24).

Lessons for the future study of democratization

The comparative study of democratization has a long pedigree in the social sciences, transcending both the disciplinary boundaries separating sociology, economics and political sciences, and the methodological divide between "quantitative" and "qualitative" approaches. Apart from the need for theoretical integration, this study suggests a few methodological lessons for the future of this field.

To begin with, the wrangle over whether domestic or international forces most importantly shape democratization deserves further attention. Since most domestic determinants have international precursors as well as ramifications, there is much to be gained from being more careful in disentangling the two sides of the domestic/international divide in future efforts to explain democratization. Moreover, studies of democratic diffusion and the potential impact of international organizations must more carefully test the foundations of their approximate measurement strategies. More specifically, case study work needs to be employed in order to show that diffusion or international pressure really works on the ground in the cases for which it has been proxied statistically.

Moreover, large-*n* studies of democratization need to be made more sensitive to country-specific causal lags. This is not only a methodological but also a theoretical concern. In some countries deep economic recession, for example, can continue for years before hurting the regime, in others a swift economic downturn is all that is needed to tip the balance to the opposition's advantage. What explains these variations and how can they be accommodated for in statistical models of cross-sectional time-series data for a large sample of countries? On a related note, I have in this book only assessed explanatory performance in the very short- (yearly) and the very long-term perspective. How can the intermediate-term explanatory performance of models of democratization be assessed?

The next generation of large-*n* studies must also take more seriously the problem of missing data and, by implication, inadvertent sample selection bias. Recall that I have in this study only been able to include 165 of the total of 196 independent countries existing in the world at more than one time point during the observation period, 1972–2006. In addition I have relied on the multiple imputation algorithm developed by Gary King *et al.* (2001) in order to test the robustness of my findings for the thirty-one countries excluded due to missing data. Nonetheless, collecting real rather than imputed data for these countries would of course be preferable in the future. Other prioritized data considerations would be to collect yearly data on religious and ethnolinguistic denominations, to move beyond testing these determinants based on country constants, and to validate Banks' (2009) unique measurement series on popular mobilization events, which now only draws on rough media accounts (see Appendix A).

Small-*n* studies of democratization in the future would be advised to select their countries for study through more elaborate use of preexisting large-*n* data and results. Only thus can the combination of case study and statistical work amount to more than the sum of its parts. The criterion of "pathway cases," which I develop from Gerring and Seawright (2007), is tailored for this specific purpose. But of course other criteria for case selection from a population of large-*n* data will have to be envisioned in the future, for example including criteria for selecting matched cases for comparison, for selecting cases where the *absence* of an event such as democratization is the primary outcome to explain, or for selecting cases to test the *joint* effect of particular determinants.

Finally, despite that qualitative case studies generally have an edge over large-*n* studies when it comes to uncovering mental processes and cognitive phenomena, the existing body of case study work on democratization has not been able to make full use of this comparative advantage. More specifically, we need to know more about the ethnographic dimension of democratization: how it is experienced from the subjective perspective of the main actors themselves. This will be crucial for testing critical assumptions regarding the quality of information and the process of preference formation in the economic approach to explaining democratizing mentioned above. It will also be needed in order to test sweeping generalizations such as Tilly's that "democratization commonly occurred as a result of struggles during which . . . few if any of the participants were self-consciously trying to create democratic institutions" (2004, p. 9).

Lessons for democracy promotion

Since the end of the cold war, the international aid community has been giving increasing priority to the goal of promoting democracy in developing countries. Can this be done? If yes, how? What strategies should prove most efficient for promoting democracy abroad? With one notable exception (Finkel *et al.* 2007), the emerging literature on democracy promotion is predominantly based on case studies and individual project evaluations (Green and Kohl 2007). It should be immediately acknowledged that the present study is not specifically designed to assess the prospects of democracy promotion. Some important lessons for democracy promoters, however, follow from my findings.

First, as argued by Steven Finkel *et al.*, democracy promotion may be primarily thought of as an agent-empowering form of development assistance. "Targeted democracy assistance," Finkel *et al.* argue, "works to educate and empower voters, support political parties, labor unions, and women's advocacy networks, strengthen human rights groups, and otherwise build 'constituencies for reform'" (2007, p. 410). My finding that democratization in the short-run perspective is not determined by structural factors is compatible with considerable room for maneuver on the part of these domestic actors. By implication, democracy promotion may pay its dividends. A key feature to concentrate resources on in this regard would be the capacity of societal actors to mobilize non-violent protests against the incumbent regime. This strategy will prove particularly rewarding when there are intra-regime splits between hardliners and softliners to exploit, and when mobilizing tactics could be found that hurt the material and other support bases of the regime.

Support for multiparty elections should be another key policy priority, despite allegations to the contrary (see, e.g., Paris 2004; *cf.* Carothers 2007). According to my theory and findings, even flawed and fraudulent elections may set forces in motion that over time decrease the incumbent regime's grip on power, making conditions more favorable for the opposition. This is particularly the case when the regime faces exogenous shocks such as economic crises or peaceful popular mobilization.

I find no general tendency that foreign military intervention promotes democracy in the target country, and this applies to the imposition of economic sanctions as well. It thus seems likely that the use of force is not a strategy to recommend for democracy promoters.

Maximizing popular access to the mass media is a strategy to safeguard democratic progress that has been already achieved. This concerns access to radios, TVs as well as newspapers. When censorship has lifted and some freedom of the press has been attained, this works as an antidote to authoritarian coups d'état. According to my findings, however, promoting economic development in authoritarian regimes would not be an advisable democracy-promoting strategy. To begin with, democratization is stimulated by short-term economic crises, not growth. Secondly, long-term development does not affect the prospects for democratization, but the chances of sustaining democratic reforms that have already been enacted.

This suggests a possible trade-off, at least in the short-run, between the foreign policy goals of promoting economic growth on the one hand, and that of promoting democracy on the other. Large-*n* studies have not been able to demonstrate a robust positive democratizing effect of development aid (Bratton and van de Walle 1997; Goldsmith 2001; Knack 2004; Dunning 2006; *cf.* Wright 2009). My results suggest an explanation for why this might be the case. Although the part of foreign aid that is specifically targeted to democracy promotion may prove effective, the lion's share, which goes to development assistance, may hinder democratizing by fostering economic growth among authoritarian regimes.

Lessons for the future of democratization

Forecasting is admittedly not the strongest branch of social science. There are thus good reasons to be cautious when trying to predict the future of democracy in the world. To begin with, as this book has demonstrated, even the broadest and most inclusive statistical models perform dismally poorly in trying to predict the short-term development of democracy during the third wave. There are no reasons to doubt that this will also be the case for future developments. In addition, a prerequisite for being able to make any short-term predictions to begin with is that there exists reliable information on the future state of the predictors, that is, the determinants of democratization. This is again hardly the case. What will happen to the future world economy? In which countries will the opposition be able to overcome its collective action problems and stage a large-scale non-violent insurrection capable of hurting the incumbent regime? As long as they lack reliable answers to questions like these, social scientists have to refrain from short-term forecasts of democratization.

The long-term forecasts, however, should be more reliable. In Figure 7.4 I have plotted the observed level of democracy for countries against their *current* long-run equilibrium level of democracy predicted when all determinants are included. All 165 countries in my estimation sample are here included in their final year of observation. As can be seen, there is a strong linear relationship between predicted and observed levels

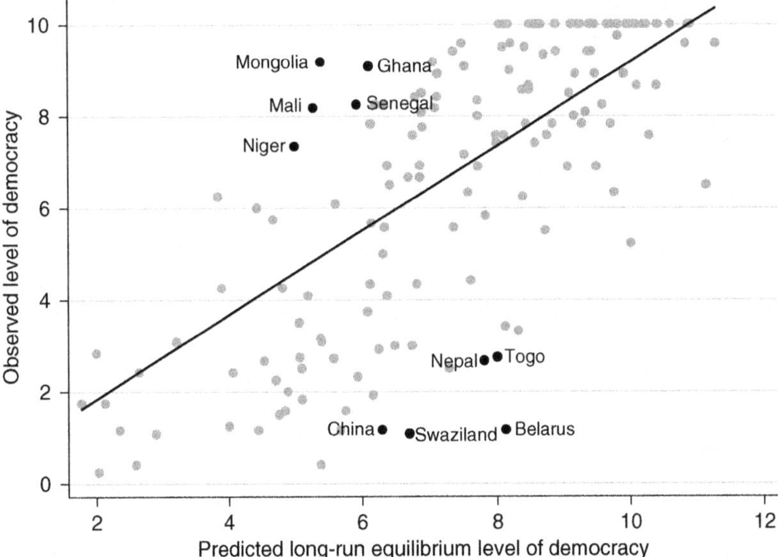

Figure 7.4 Observed vs. Long-Run Equilibrium Levels of Democracy
Note: The plot is based on the last year of observation for each of the 165 countries in my estimation sample. The slope coefficient is 1.06, and the correlation .76. The ten countries with largest residuals are highlighted.

of democracy. Most countries thus align fairly well with their long-run predictions. Equally interesting, however, are the countries that depart from this general relationship. They come in two guises: underachievers, which have reached much lower levels of democracy than predicted from their structural prerequisites, and overachievers, which have outperformed expectations. For reference I have highlighted the five most deviant cases in each group for which there was a long-run expectation in my final estimation year, that is, in 2006. Among the overachievers, we find the exceptional cases of Mongolia, but also the African success stories of Mali, Senegal and Ghana. These countries are thus "deviant democracies": "countries that have seemingly beaten the odds and democratized within an unfavorable structural setting" (Doorenspleet and Kopecký 2008, p. 698). From their history we may learn what conditions, beyond the reach of our structural models, helped them in "upping the odds" and achieving unexpectedly high levels of democracy (Doorenspleet and Mudde 2008). This, however, also means their futures are insecure. The long-run equilibrium level of democracy in these countries exerts a pull toward increasing authoritarianism.

In the group of underachievers, on the other hand, we find the notable examples of Belarus, Swaziland, Togo, Nepal and China. If my predictions of the long-run forces of democratization prove correct, these are the countries where the most substantial movements toward democracy should be visible in the future.

The country which would most profoundly affect the world order if it were to democratize is of course China. What would make China democratize? According to my results, sustained economic growth will *not* be the trigger of democratization in this country, contrary to what traditional modernization theorists and even recent scholars have proclaimed for the particular case of China (Rowen 2007). We should instead expect democratic advances to occur if China's impressive growth rate starts to dwindle, perhaps at some time point turning into an economic recession. This could also be the spark for a peaceful popular uprising which, contrary to the failed Tiananmen Square protests of 1989, could stand the chance of reaching beyond student circles in Beijing by mobilizing large portions of the working population in the countryside. Other conditions favorable for democratization are that the Chinese economy is not highly dependent on trade, and that its neighboring countries are more democratic than China itself.

Excessive optimism about the future of democracy in China is, however, not warranted. China is a large and militarily powerful country and will thus not be easily pressured to democratize from abroad. As Figure 7.4 also makes clear, the expected long-run equilibrium level of democracy in China is only little more than halfway to "full" democracy in the basic sense (the prediction is at 6.29). Even this prediction disregards the fact that China's authoritarian system is institutionalized through single-party rule. As this study shows, this is the form of autocracy most resilient to democratization, both in and of itself and as a response to possible future exogenous shocks.

Appendix A
Data and variable definitions

The large-*n* analysis of this study is based on a cross-sectional time-series database covering 196 countries in the world from 1972 to 2006. They include all countries in the world recognized by the United Nations during this time period, plus Taiwan, but excluding countries having fewer than 100,000 inhabitants and no statistical data on GDP in the World Bank World Development Indicators (leaving out Andorra, Liechtenstein, Monaco, Nauru, San Marino and Tuvalu). With respect to countries that have merged or split during the period of observation, I follow the standards applied in Teorell *et al.* (2009). With respect to countries that have split, this means I treat Ethiopia as a distinct case after the secession of Eritrea, Russia as distinct from the USSR, Serbia-Montenegro as distinct from the People's Republic of Yugoslavia, and the Czech and Slovak Republics from Czechoslovakia. (I do, however, treat Indonesia as the same case before and after the secession of Timor-Leste.)

Due to missing data, however, the most general estimation sample used throughout this book (except in the multiple imputation model 7 in Table C.1) consists of 165 countries. The following thirty-one countries are *not* included in the estimation sample: Afghanistan, Cuba, Czechoslovakia, Equatorial Guinea, Ethiopia before the secession of Eritrea in 1993, East and West Germany, Iraq, Kiribati, North Korea, Laos, Libya, Marshall Islands, Mauritania, Micronesia, Myanmar, Palau, Sao Tome and Principe, Serbia and Montenegro, Somalia, Taiwan, Timor-Leste, North and South Vietnam, USSR, Uzbekistan, Vanuatu, North and South Yemen, the Republic of Yemen, and the People's Republic of Yugoslavia.

The following variable definitions and sources are used, approximately in the order of their appearance in the book:

Democracy: The graded measure from Freedom House (2009) is computed by taking the average of their 1–7 ratings of *Political*

Rights and *Civil Liberties*, and then inverting and transforming this scale to run from 0 to 10. The graded measure from Polity is the *Revised Combined Polity Score* (Marshall and Jaggers 2009) transformed to run from 0 to 10. These two graded measures are then averaged into a combined index running from 0 to 10. I have imputed missing values by regressing the average FH/Polity index on the FH scores, which have better country coverage than Polity.

Colonial origin: I employ dummy variables for countries that are a former Western overseas colony. I thus follow the practice of Bernard *et al.* (2004) in exclusively focusing on a particular form of colonial legacy (Western overseas colonialism), and also by excluding the "settler colonies" from the group of British colonies (including the US, Canada, Australia, New Zealand and Israel). Each country is coded as a colony that was colonized after 1700. In cases of several colonial powers, the last one is counted, if it lasted for 10 years or longer.

Five colonial powers were coded separately, based on *Encyclopedia Britannica* and *Atlas till Världshistorien* (Stockholm: Svenska bokförlaget, 1963): *British* (Antigua and Barbuda, The Bahamas, Bahrain, Bangladesh, Barbados, Belize, Bhutan, Botswana, Brunei, Cyprus, Dominica, Egypt, Eritrea, Fiji, Gambia, Ghana, Grenada, Guyana, India, Iraq, Jamaica, Jordan, Kenya, Kiribati, Kuwait, Lesotho, Malawi, Malaysia, Maldives, Mauritius, Myanmar, Namibia, Nigeria, North Yemen, Oman, Pakistan, Qatar, Republic of Yemen, Samoa, Seychelles and Tonga, Sierra Leone, Singapore, Solomon Islands, South Africa, South Yemen, Sri Lanka, St. Kitts and Nevis, St. Lucia, St. Vincent and the Grenadines, Sudan, Swaziland, Tanzania, Trinidad and Tobago, Uganda, United Arab Emirates, Zambia, Zimbabwe); *Spanish* (Argentina, Bolivia, Chile, Colombia, Costa Rica, Cuba, Dominican Republic, Ecuador, Equatorial Guinea, El Salvador, Guatemala, Honduras, Mexico, Nicaragua, Panama, Paraguay, Peru, Uruguay and Venezuela); *French* (Algeria, Benin, Burkina Faso, Cambodia, Cameroon, Central African Republic, Chad, Côte d'Ivoire, Comoros, Djibouti, Gabon, Guinea, Haiti, Laos, Lebanon, Morocco, Madagascar, Mali, Mauritania, Niger, The Republic of Congo, Senegal, Syrian, Togo, Tunisia, Vietnam, North and South Vietnam); *Portuguese* (Angola, Brazil, Cape Verde, Guinea-Bissau, Mozambique, Sao Tome and Principe); as well as *Dutch/ Belgian/Italian* (Burundi, the Democratic Republic of Congo, Indonesia,

Libya, Rwanda, Somalia, and Suriname). A residual colonial category of *French-British/Australian/American* origin (Marshall Islands, Micronesia, Palau and the Philippines, Papua New Guinea, Vanuatu) was excluded due to data limitations (only three countries included in the estimation sample).

Religious denomination: The data on religious denominations has been collected from David Barrett *et al.* (2001). The data is an estimate of the fraction of the population as of 1970 that are Catholics, Protestants, Orthodox, Other Christians, Muslims, Hindus, Buddhists, Other denominations (including miscellaneous East Asian religions and Jews), and Non-religious.

Fractionalization: I employ data on *ethnolinguistic* and *religious fractionalization* collected by Alberto Alesina *et al.* (2003), with data compiled in Teorell *et al.* (2009), reflecting the probability that two randomly selected individuals from a population belong to different groups. The figures on ethnolinguistic fractionalization are based on 650 distinct ethnic groups (ethnicity being defined in either racial or linguistic terms), and those on religious fractionalization on 294 different religions. Although the underlying data only pertain to one year for any given country (in most instances from the 1990s or around 2000), I treat these figures as constants over the entire time period 1972–2006. Although this of course might distort real-world developments and cause problems of endogeneity, I concur with Alesina *et al.*'s claim that treating these figures as constants "seems a reasonable assumption at the 30 year horizon" (2003, p. 160).

Size: In order to measure country *size*, I use the log of the area in 1,000s of square kilometers from Banks (2009). In Chapter 2, I also use the log of *population*, again with data from Banks. The log of *population density* is simply this latter measure over the former.

Female-to-male education ratio: Measured as the gross secondary school enrollment rate of women over men, with data taken from the WDI (2009). Missing observations are filled in by linear yearly imputation (country by country).

Women in parliament: The share of women among members of the legislature, expressed as fractions. Original source is Melander (2005), with data compiled in Teorell *et al.* (2009).

Island: A country is defined as an island if it, according to Douglas Stinnett *et al.*'s (2002) direct contiguity data, shares no land or river border with any other country. There are three exceptions to this operationalization, which are also coded as islands: the United Kingdom, Ireland and Indonesia.

Socioeconomic modernization: The indicators combined into this index are: (1) *industrialization*, measured as the net output of the *non*-agricultural sector expressed as a percentage of GDP; (2) *education*, measured as the gross secondary school enrollment ratio; (3) *urbanization*, measured as the urban percentage of the total population; (4) *life expectancy* at birth (in years); (5) the inverse of *infant mortality* (per 1,000 live births); (6) the log of *GDP per capita*, expressed in current US dollars (to maximize coverage); (7) the number of *radios* per capita; (8) the number of *television sets* per capita; and (9) *newspaper* circulation per capita. The source of indicators (1)–(6) is WDI (2009), of indicators (7)–(9) Banks (2009). I used linear intrapolation, country by country, to fill in missing years for secondary school enrollment, life expectancy and infant mortality. The secondary school enrollment ratio was used since it has the strongest correlation with the Barro and Lee's (2001) indicators of "average years of primary schooling in the total population," although with more extensive country coverage.

The principal component factor loadings for these nine indicators are (n = 3,269):

Industrialization	.83
Education	.91
Urbanization	.84
Life expectancy	.92
Inverse infant mortality	.90
ln(GDP/capita)	.94
Radios	.81
TVs	.89
Newspapers	.78

The eigenvalue of this first dimension is 6.80, explaining 75.5 percent of the variation in the indicators across time and space. The eigenvalue of the second component is only .68, strongly supporting unidimensionality.

The factor loadings are extremely similar if computed at any given year instead of pooled across all years. The index of socioeconomic modernization is computed by taking the factor scores of the above pooled solution, and then using imputation on the regression line with all nine indicators as regressors.

Apart from the theoretical argument proffered in the text, there are two more technical reasons why I base my results on this summary measure instead of any or some of its constituent parts, which has been the dominant approach in the field. First, since my index is based on multiple indicators it should have a reliability edge over any of its subcomponents. Second, all of the indicators used have a theoretical underpinning in the modernization literature. Yet when introduced separately into a regression equation (such as in Table 3.4), they introduce huge amounts of multicollinearity. I avoid this in my general estimation model by only including the summary index.

When subdividing this index into its components in Chapter 3, the *health indicators* are a factor index of life expectancy and infant mortality, whereas the *media proliferation* measure is a factor index of the number of radios, TVs and newspaper circulation per capita.

Economic performance: Following Gasiorowski (1995), I employ two measures of short-term economic performance (both based on WDI 2009): recessionary crises, measured as the annual *growth* rate of GDP per capita in fractions, and inflationary crises, measured as the annual *inflation* rate (based on the GDP deflator), also in fractions. This measure of inflation correlates at .99 with the one based on the consumer price index, but has larger country coverage. Based on these indicators, I compute two measures of economic performance among neighboring countries in Chapter 4: their average level of growth, and their average level of inflation.

Fuel and minerals: Following Ross (2001), *fuels* is the export value of mineral-based fuels (petroleum, natural gas and coal), and *minerals* is the export value of non-fuel ores and metals, both expressed as fractions of GDP, based on data from WDI (2009). Also following Ross (2001, p. 358), I replaced the values for Singapore, as it is a transshipment port with no natural resources on its own, by .001. Unlike Ross, however, I have *not* replaced the values for Trinidad and Tobago, which are actually a possessor of both fuels and mineral deposits. Instead I replace the value on fuels for the Bahamas by .001, since the Bahamas much like Singapore is merely a transshipment port for oil and natural gas. I have filled in missing values by yearly linear imputation (country by country).

Income inequality: Measured as Gini coefficients, expressed as fractions, from Galbraith and Kum (2003), with data compiled in Teorell *et al.* (2009). James Galbraith and Hyunsub Kum (2003) estimate these Gini coefficients through an equation whereby the Deininger and Squire (1996) high-quality dataset is regressed on a measure of manufacturing pay inequality, the ratio of manufacturing employment to population, and three dummies for data sources of the Deininger and Squire measures (income vs. expenditure, gross vs. net of taxes, household vs. personal unit of analysis). Apart from providing substantially enhanced coverage, Galbraith and Kum (2003) argue that this estimated income inequality measure produces better comparability both across countries and over time.

Economic freedom: Measured through the Fraser Institute's (chain-linked) Economic Freedom of the World Index (Gwartney and Lawson 2006), with data compiled in Teorell *et al.* (2009) and missing observations for 5-year intervals replaced by linear yearly imputation (country by country). The index comprises twenty-one components designed to identify the consistency of institutional arrangements and policies with economic freedom in five major areas: size of government, legal structure and security of property rights, access to sound money, freedom to trade internationally, as well as regulation of credit, labor and business. The index ranges from 0 to 10 where 0 corresponds to "less economic freedom" and 10 to "more economic freedom."

No. of successful coups: As measured by Banks (2009): "The number of extraconstitutional or forced changes in the top government elite and/or its effective control of the nation's power structure in a given year ... Unsuccessful coups are not counted."

Trade volume: Defined as "the sum of exports and imports of goods and services measured as a share of gross domestic product," expressed as a fraction of GDP (with data from WDI 2009). In Chapter 4, I control for bilateral trade volume with the US, UK, France, China and USSR/Russia, with data from Gleditsch (2002).

International capital flows: Following Li and Reuveny (2003; 2009), foreign direct investment is measured as the yearly value of net inflows of foreign direct investment as a fraction of a country's GDP, and portfolio investments as the yearly value of net inflows of portfolio investment as a fraction of GDP (excluding liabilities constituting foreign authorities' reserves). Both are based on data from WDI (2009).

Diffusion effects: I employ three proxies for diffusion effects. They are composed of mean scores of the combined democracy index computed at three different spatial levels. The most proximate level is that of neighboring countries. Neighbors are defined as countries separated by a land or river border, or by 400 miles of water or less, using Stinnett *et al.*'s (2002) direct contiguity data. The rationale behind the water contiguity distance is that 400 miles is the maximum distance at which two 200-mile exclusive economic zones can intersect (2002, p. 62). This criterion creates the maximum number of contiguous states in the world system, only leaving New Zealand and Iceland without any defined neighboring countries at any time. Countries that lack neighbors in a particular year are scored zero; instead, a dummy variable is entered scored 1 for these countries, 0 for all others. Beyond contiguous neighbors, I also test whether diffusion effects operate at the regional (regions being defined below) and global level. Both these measures are computed as yearly means.

Regional organizations: Following Pevehouse (2005), I compute the average degree of democracy among the countries belonging to the same regional organization. For countries belonging to more than one regional organization, only the score for the most democratic regional organization is included. Countries not belonging to any regional organization in a particular year are scored zero; instead, a dummy variable is entered scored 1 for these countries, 0 for all others. Data on membership in regional organizations is provided by Pevehouse *et al.* (2004). Again following Pevehouse (2005, pp. 49–50, 67–70), I have only included political, economic and/ or military intra-regional organizations, thus excluding inter-regional organizations and international financial institutions, as well as cultural, technical and environmental organizations. To the list of regional organizations existing up until 1992 provided by Pevehouse, I have added a small number of organizations formed afterwards (namely, the Association of Caribbean States, the Caribbean Financial Action Task Force, the Central Asian Economic Community, the Communauté économique et monétaire d'Afrique central, the Conference of African Ministers Responsible for Sustainable Development, the Group of Three, the North American Free Trade Agreement, the Union économique et monétaire Oest Africaine, and the Vision and Strategies around the Baltic Sea 2010), for a total of sixty-three international regional organizations.

Foreign intervention index: I employ the annual data on hostile military interventions in 1972–1996 provided by Pickering and Peceny (2006), and the data on economic sanctions in 1978–2000 from Hufbauer *et al.* (2009) provided by Dan Cox and Cooper Drury (2006). I only code economic sanctions with a democratic sender, operationalized equivalently to Pickering and Peceny, that is, countries having a Polity score of at least 6.

Popular mobilization: I use Banks' (2009) data on the yearly number of *demonstrations*, defined as "any peaceful gathering of at least 100 people for the primary purpose of displaying or voicing their opposition to government policies or authority, excluding demonstrations of a distinctly anti-foreign nature"; *riots*, defined as "any violent demonstration or clash of more than 100 citizens involving the use of physical force"; and *strikes*, defined as "any strike of 1000 or more industrial or service workers that involves more than one employer and that is aimed at national government policies or authority." Based on these indicators, I compute three measures of popular mobilization among neighboring countries in Chapter 4: their average number of demonstrations, riots and strikes.

According to Banks (2009), all of these figures are "derived from the daily files of *The New York Times*." This could be a source of bias, since press coverage of protest events is known to overestimate events in geographical proximity, and underestimate events of minor intensity. In my case, however, I believe the potential geographical bias makes my tests of the mobilization variables conservative, since there is smaller variation in the dependent variable in the West. Moreover, the fact that minor protests are underreported might seem less of a problem from a theoretical point of view, since one could argue that only large-scale events should stand any chance to affect regime change (see Ulfelder 2005, p. 321, for a similar conclusion).

Civil conflict: Conflicts between the government of a state and internal opposition groups incurring at least twenty-five battle-related deaths per year, with or without the intervention of other states. Original source is the UCDP/PRIO Armed Conflict Dataset (Gleditsch *et al.* 2002), with data compiled in Teorell *et al.* (2009).

Authoritarian regime types: Data on authoritarian regime types is from Hadenius and Teorell (2007), mostly based on updated and revised data from Banks. This typology of authoritarian regimes is based on a distinction between three modes of political power maintenance: hereditary succession (lineage), corresponding to *monarchies*; the actual or threatened use of military force, corresponding to *military* regimes; and popular elections, designating electoral regimes. Among the latter in Hadenius and Teorell distinctions are made among *no-party* regimes (for which there are no observations in my estimation sample), *one-party* regimes (where all but one party is prohibited), and "limited multiparty regimes," in this book termed *multiparty autocracies* (where multiple parties are allowed but the system still does not pass as democratic). A subtype of military regimes is coded "rebel regimes," where a rebel movement has taken power by military means. Several minor types of regimes are also coded, here treated as *others*: "theocracies," "transitional" regimes, "civil war," foreign "occupation" and a residual category. Using the mean of the Freedom House and Polity scales, the line between *democracies* and autocracies is drawn at 7.5. This threshold value was chosen by estimating the mean cut-off point separating democracy from autocracy in five well-known categorical measures of democracy: those of Przeworski *et al.* (2000), Mainwaring *et al.* (2001), and Reich (2002), together with Freedom House's and Polity's own categorical thresholds for democracy. The twelve *transition dummies* capture movements into and out of the six generic regime types described above. Moreover, the *size of the largest party* measures the largest party's number of seats divided by the legislative assemblies' total within multiparty autocracies. Finally, the *mean executive turnover* captures the total number of changes of the chief executive during the regime spell divided by the years of regime-spell duration. The effective executive may be the president, prime minister, leader of the ruling party, the monarch or the ruling military junta, or someone else, working behind political figureheads.

Regional effects: As a check on the robustness of my findings, I include dummy variables for six world "regions": Eastern Europe and Central Asia, Latin America and the Caribbean, Middle East and North Africa, Asia and the Pacific, the West, and Sub-Saharan Africa.

Appendix B
Statistical model

Let $D_{i,t}$ be the democracy index of country i at time t. I then model $D_{i,t} - D_{i,t-1}$, or ΔD_i for short, as a function of $\mathbf{x}$, a vector of explanatory variables. Most of these variables vary over time, in which case I have lagged them one year as a partial check on endogeneity bias. Moreover, I control for previous levels of democracy, $D_{i,t-1\,\ldots\,q}$, that is, $D_{i,t}$ lagged up to a maximum of q years.

There are numerous reasons to include lagged values of the dependent variable. First, as argued in the text, a lagged dependent variable may work as an explanatory factor in itself. Second, including lagged values of the dependent variable in the model helps to control for the possibility of endogeneity bias, that is, causality running in the direction from democracy to the explanatory variables instead of vice versa. Lagging the explanatory variables is only a first step toward this control. By also including lagged values of D_i on the righthand side of the equation the model assures that any effects of D_i on $\mathbf{x}_i$ occurring previous to t–q is controlled for. For example, the inclusion of $D_{i,t-1}$ rules out any effects due to the path $D_{i,t} \leftarrow D_{i,t-1} \leftarrow D_{i,t-2} \rightarrow \mathbf{x}_{i,t-1}$ (see, e.g., Finkel 1995, pp. 24–31). More generally, since the lagged dependent variables work as a composite measure of *all* factors contributing to the level of democracy up until time t–q, including them works as a proxy control for other potential determinants not included in the model. Third, and finally, lagging the dependent variable helps to control for serial correlation in the error term (Beck and Katz 1996).

In sum, this yields the model:

$$D_{i,t} - D_{i,t-1} = \sum_{\lambda=1}^{q} \phi_\lambda D_{i,t-\lambda} + \mathbf{x}_{i,t-1}\beta + \varepsilon_{i,t}, \tag{1}$$

where ϕ_λ and the β-vector contain the short-run effect parameters to be estimated, and $\varepsilon_{i,t}$ is the error term. It turns out that two lagged values of the dependent variable are required to purge the residuals from serial autocorrelation in my data.[1] In other words, $q = 2$ in the analyses reported here.

Although OLS should yield consistent estimates of β, there are a number of statistical problems involved in estimating its standard errors on time-series cross-section data: most notably, serial and spatial autocorrelation as well as panel heteroskedasticity (Beck and Katz 1995). I control for the first of these problems, as already noted, by controlling for lagged values of the dependent variable, and for the second and the third through panel corrected standard errors, as recommended by Beck and Katz (1995; 1996). Since I also model spatial dependence directly by controlling for diffusion effects, my reported estimates should err on the conservative side.

For each determinant in **x**, I systematically check the sensitivity of the estimates in β to relatively extreme influential observations. Following John Fox (1991, p. 19), I do this by computing the $dfbetas_{i,t}$, defined as $(\beta\text{-}\beta_{-i,-t})/\text{se}(\beta_{-i,-t})$ where $\beta_{-i,-t}$ is the estimate of β produced when the i,t^{th} observation is omitted. I then plot this measure against the rank order of all $dfbetas_{i,t}$ (at both extremes, thus taking into account both influential confirming and influential disconfirming outliers).[2] Relative extremeness is indicated by a steep slope that levels off sharply after a few observations. The absence of relative outliers, by contrast, is apparent in a smooth plot where each additional observation exerts a level of influence that decreases at a steady rate.

There is considerable variation among the determinants in **x** with respect to their changeability over time. Some determinants are event-like, with a within-country variation that by far exceeds the cross-country variation (e.g., growth, inflation, demonstrations, riots and strikes). In some cases, moreover, I have been able to induce over-time variation by including the (lagged) yearly change in the variable (neighbor diffusion and regional organizations). Most of the determinants in **x**, however, only enter the estimation equation in levels. This obviously applies for the country constants (colonial heritage, religion and

[1] The estimated value of the autocorrelation coefficient ρ from the Lagrange multiplier test recommended by Beck and Katz (1996, p. 9) is .092 and statistically significant when only one lag of the democracy index is introduced on my estimations sample (n = 3,795). With two lags ρ = .048 and is not statistically significant.

[2] For determinants that are country constants, I have performed the same procedure by computing country-level *dfbetas* (Chaterjee and Hadi 1988, p. 200).

fractionalizations), but also for a host of other determinants that change through time so slowly that they vary between countries to a much larger extent than they vary within countries over time (size, socioeconomic modernization, fuels, minerals, trade volume, regional and global level of democracy).

Although this needs to be held in mind when interpreting the results, there is nothing inherently wrong in trying to explain changes (in the level of democracy) through levels (in most of the determinants). In the end it all comes down to what counterfactual claims one wants to make. When cross-country variation dominates, one can mostly make inferences of the type "had country A been more similar to country B in this regard, the expected change in its level of democracy would have been so and so much higher" (i.e., the standard operating procedure in all cross-sectional analyses). When within-country variation comes to the fore, on the other hand, one can add inferences of the type "had country A been more similar to itself at time *t*, its expected rate of democratization would have been so and so much smaller." Although I generally prefer the latter inference to the former, there is no logical flaw in the former. Moreover, as I show by including fixed effects in the robustness test in Appendix C, most of my results apply even when based on the within-country variation only.

Related to the issue of temporal stability is that of a causal ordering among the determinants. To the extent that some determinants are caused by other determinants, I introduce bias in the estimation of the latter by controlling for the former. In other words, I would ideally like to estimate both direct and indirect effects of the determinants in $\mathbf{x}$. Lacking an adequate theory of the relationships among determinants, however, I have refrained from this. What judgments can be made on this issue can be made from two properties of the data: historical priority and temporal stability. One could argue, for example, that a determinant such as colonial origin is historically prior to, say, the trade volume as of last year. Or, that an event-like determinant such as peaceful demonstrations would be more likely to have been caused by than being a cause of a slow-moving characteristic such as socioeconomic modernization.

Evident as this may sound, the inclusion of the lagged dependent variable in my models makes both these judgments dubious. The reason is that, as stated above, including the lagged dependent variables works as a composite control for *all* factors affecting the level of democracy up until time $t-q$. What I estimate from equation (1) with colonial origin on the righthand side is thus not the unmediated effect of this historical event on the present rate of democratization. This unmediated, historical effect is already picked up by the lagged dependent variable. What remains to be estimated for a historical variable, then, is a potential *legacy* of colonial origin that somehow (organizationally, institutionally, culturally, etc.) survives in the country in question and thereby may exert a causal influence at present. The implication of this, however, is that I cannot use historical priority to determine the causal ordering of the explanatory variables. I simply cannot say whether the proxied legacy of colonialism sustains itself in a way that makes it causally prior or antecedent to, say, trade volume. The same applies for the criterion of temporal stability. Since all variables in equation (1) are only able to exert their influence over a one-year period (from $t-1$ to t), their temporal stability – which, as a rule, is computed over a large number of consecutive years – is not necessarily indispensable proof of their relative causal ordering.

The one exception to this absence of a causal ordering among the variables is of course when I test for mechanisms, where I test a *theoretical* argument that the impact of a certain determinant should be mediated by another variable.

In order to gauge the long-run performance of my models, I make use of the fact that the lagged values of the dependent variable also alter the way our **x**-variables affect democracy over time. If one assumes a sustained one unit increase at time t in one of these explanatory variables, say x_j, the immediate impact occurring over the following year $t+1$ is of course this variable's corresponding short-term β-coefficient, that is β_j. Due to the first lagged value of the dependent variable, however, an effect of the magnitude $(1+\phi_1) \times \beta_j$ will then be induced over the year $t+2$. In the following year (i.e., at $t+3$) up to two lagged values of the dependent variable will influence the effect, which now amounts to $[(1+\phi_1)^2 + \phi_2] \times \beta_j$ and so on. The result will be a dissipating effect slowly leaving the system.

The solid line of Figure B.1 depicts this dissipating effect when simulated over a 50-year time period from the parameter estimates of the two lagged dependent variables of my model. The dashed line, by contrast, shows the cumulative effect of a sustained unit increase (for tractability expressed as a fraction of the long-run coefficient θ, see below). According to these estimates, about 36 percent of the

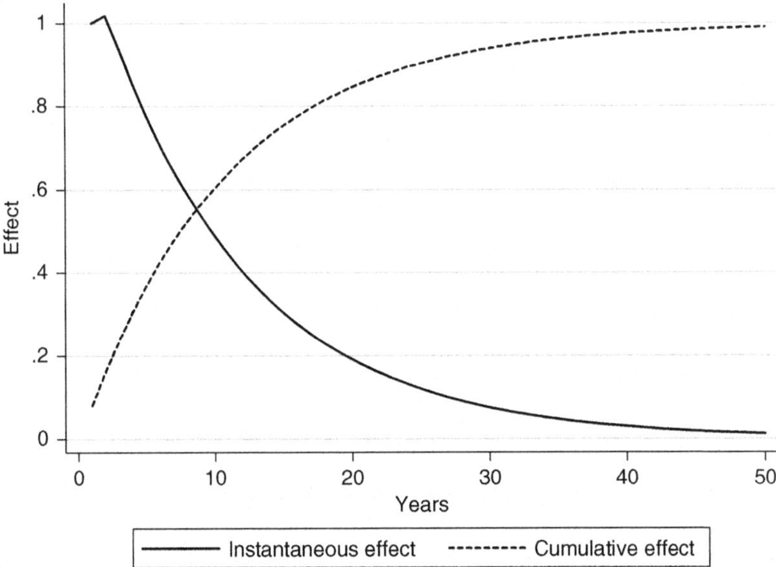

Figure B.1 Projected Response to a Sustained Unit Level Shock
Note: Simulations based on the parameter values of .018 and –.098 for the first and second lag of the dependent variable in the estimation sample (n=3,795).

adjustment back to equilibrium occurs over a 5-year period, some 60 percent over a 10-year period, and around 84 percent over 20 years. Only after 50 years, does the adjustment reach 99 percent. I may thus conclude that it takes approximately 50 years for the full long-run effects in my models to occur.[3]

In order to obtain the long-term estimates for each determinant I project the behavior of the short-run coefficients according to this logic as t goes to infinity. As long as the usual stationarity conditions are satisfied (i.e., that the roots of the characteristic equation for $\phi_1 \ldots_n$ lie outside the unit root circle; see, e.g., Green 1997, p. 829), one may compute the long-run impact multipliers according to the formula

[3] These calculations were made by plugging in the coefficients for the lags of the dependent variable in the estimated model into a purely autoregressive equation, and then simulating the projected response to a one-unit change at time t = 0 as t goes from 0 to 50.

$$\theta = -\beta/\phi^*, \tag{2}$$

where $\phi^* = \sum_{\lambda=1}^{q} \phi_\lambda$, and β and $\phi_{1...q}$ are estimated through equation (1). Since θ is a ratio of coefficients there is no general formula for its exact variance. Following Gunnar Bårdsen (1989), a large sample approximation formula can, however, be obtained by

$$\text{var}(\theta) \cong (\phi^*)^{-2}[\text{var}(\beta) + \theta^2\text{var}(\phi^*) + 2\theta\text{cov}(\beta, \phi^*)], \tag{3}$$

where the variances and covariances in my case are panel corrected.[4]

In order to assess long-term predictive performance, I proceed as follows. The long-term projections discussed above are based on the notion of a static equilibrium, determined by the **x**-vector of explanatory variables, toward which each system is attracted. One may think of such an equilibrium in terms of a state where any inherent tendency to change has ceased, that is, as the estimated level of democracy that would arise in the long-run if all explanatory variables were held fixed at their current values. In the present context one can compute this long-run equilibrium level of democracy for each country and year as:

$$D^*_{i,t} = \mathbf{x}_{i,t}\theta \tag{4}$$

I then simply regress the actual level of democracy for each country and year on this projected long-run equilibrium level, and assess model fit.

The reduction in predicted error variance is computed as

$$RPE = (s_y - \sigma)/s_y, \tag{5}$$

where s_y is the standard deviation of the dependent variable ($\Delta D_{i,t}$, $\Delta D+_{i,t}$, $\Delta D-_{i,t}$, or $D_{i,t}$, depending on what model is being assessed), and σ is the standard error of the regression.

Finally, there is the issue of how to separate effects on movements toward versus away from democracy. With a dichotomous measure of democracy, this is straightforward since, given a certain starting point, change may only occur in a single direction. By limiting the sample of cases to countries that are authoritarian at time t–1, the results that ensue pertain to effects on transitions toward democracy. Similarly, when the results are based on countries that are democratic at time

[4] These estimates have been computed by the xtpcse and nlcom commands of Stata 10.0.

t–1, the estimates pertain to transitions toward autocracy, or inversely, to democratic survival. With a graded measure of democracy, however, things are not quite as simple since both the starting points (the level of democracy at time t–1) and the direction of change may vary. Should one model the extent to which different determinants have different effects at different starting points or the extent to which they have different effects on different directions of change? Ideally both, of course, but in this book I take the simpler approach by limiting my attention to the latter.[5] Formally, following Acemoglu *et al.* (2007), this means that I apart from equation (1) run

$$D^{+}_{i,t} - D_{i,t-1} = \sum_{\lambda=1}^{q} \phi^{+}_{\lambda} D_{i,t-\lambda} + \mathbf{x}_{i,t-1}\beta^{+} + \varepsilon^{+}_{i,t} \qquad (6)$$

for movements toward the democratic end of the scale, referred to as *upturns*, and

$$D^{-}_{i,t} - D_{i,t-1} = \sum_{\lambda=1}^{q} \phi^{-}_{\lambda} D_{i,t-\lambda} + \mathbf{x}_{i,t-1}\beta^{-} + \varepsilon^{-}_{i,t} \qquad (7)$$

for movements toward the authoritarian end of the scale, or *downturns*, where $D^{+}_{i,t} = \max\{D_{i,t}, D_{i,t-1}\}$ and $D-_{i,t} = \min\{D_{i,t}, D_{i,t-1}\}$. Essentially this means that I distinguish cases of $\Delta D_i>0$ (upturns) from cases of $\Delta D_i<0$ (downturns). When the former are being modeled, I simply s*et all* cases of downturns to zero, and vice versa.

The aim of this exercise is to compare β (from equation 1) with β^{+} and β^{-}. Considering the possibility that each one of these three sets of coefficients may be significantly larger than zero, significantly lower than zero or insignificantly different from zero, there are in theory $3^3 = 27$ theoretical combinations to consider per variable. Some of these are logically impossible, and some empirically highly unlikely, however, which means that I can focus on three general scenarios. The first is where $\beta = 0$, that is, there is no statistically significant effect

[5] In Hadenius and Teorell (2005a) the cultural theory of democratization is tested by using the former approach, that is, by separating different causal effects at different initial levels of democracy. This would, however, be a highly intractable strategy with the very large number of determinants tested here, essentially requiring one interaction effect to be estimated per explanatory variable. I do, however, make use of this estimation strategy in Chapter 6, where I can focus on a more restrictive set of explanatory factors.

when both upturns and downturns are considered. Apart from the general null result ($\beta^+ = 0; \beta^- = 0$), this still leaves open the possibility that there is an effect on upturns but not on downturns ($\beta^+ \neq 0; \beta^- = 0$), an effect on downturns but not on upturns ($\beta^+ = 0; \beta^- \neq 0$), or even that the determinant in question has an effect on downturns and upturns that are unequally signed ($\beta^+>0; \beta^-<0$, or $\beta^+<0; \beta^->0$). In the second scenario, where $\beta >0$, the most likely outcomes are an effect on both ($\beta^+>0; \beta^->0$) or either ($\beta^+>0; \beta^- = 0$, or $\beta^+ = 0; \beta^->0$). Inversely, in the third scenario ($\beta<0$), the most likely outcomes are the same ($\beta^+<0; \beta^-<0$, $\beta^+<0; \beta^- = 0$, or $\beta^+ = 0; \beta^-<0$). I must, however, also consider the possibility that no discernible effect appears on either upturns or downturns ($\beta^+ = 0; \beta^- = 0$), despite β being positive or negative. The reason for this is that what equations (4) and (5) in essence imply is that I limit the variation in the dependent variable. This leads to the well-known statistical tendency to push the coefficients toward zero. In case this occurs, my preferred interpretation is that the determinant in question affects both upturns and downturns, but that the magnitude of these effects is only so large as to be statistically discernible in the full sample.

Appendix C
Robustness tests

Apart from the general results reported in the text, I have performed a number of robustness checks. Table C.1 displays the results of these tests for the determinants reported in the text to have statistically significant effects that do not depend on variable-specific extreme outliers (as diagnosed by *dfbetas*, see Appendix B above). The first test deletes ten observations that exert an extreme influence on the performance of the entire model, as diagnosed by both *Cook's D* and *dffits* (Fox 1991, 30).[1]

In the second test, I exclude all Western countries from the estimation sample. Since most (but not all) of these countries democratized before the third wave, one could otherwise fear that their inclusion would bias my results.

Third, I control for six world "regions": Eastern Europe and Central Asia, Latin America and the Caribbean, the Middle East and North Africa, Asia and the Pacific, the West, and Sub-Saharan Africa. I call this the model of "region-fixed effects," since it means that any region-specific determinants of democratization, left out from our models, are in effect controlled for. In other words, it leaves room for the explanatory variables only to affect democratization within world regions (and over time).

The fourth test involves adding year-fixed effects (one dummy variable per year in the estimations sample save one). This essentially works as a check on the ability of the panel-corrected standard errors to correct for spatial autocorrelation, since the year-fixed effects control for any unobserved characteristics that are common for all countries in a given year.

[1] Regardless of what diagnostic tool is used, these observations are Haiti 1991, Suriname 1980, Turkey 1980, Thailand 1976, Indonesia 1999, Thailand 2006, Nicaragua 1989 and 1990, Gambia 1994 and Greece 1974.

Table C.1 *Robustness Tests*

	(1) *Deleting extreme outliers*	(2) *Deleting Western countries*	(3) *Region-fixed effects*	(4) *Year-fixed effects*	(5) *Country-fixed effects*	(6) *Year- & country-fixed effs*	(7) *Missing value imputation*	(8) *FH Political Rights*	(9) *FH Civil Liberties*	(10) *Polity score*
Muslim population (general)	–.174***	–.206**	–.103	–.214***	–	–	–.297***	–.307***	–.259***	–.267***
	(.055)	(.081)	(.095)	(.069)			(.088)	(.100)	(.093)	(.081)
Size (upturns)	–.015***	.060***	–.013**	–.014***	.080	.123	–.047***	–.014**	–.010	–.026***
	(.005)	(.018)	(.006)	(.005)	(.359)	(.359)	(.006)	(.006)	(.007)	(.009)
Socioeconomic modernization (downturns)	.045***	.060***	.065***	.057***	.102**	.037	.065***	.095***	.085***	.057***
	(.013)	(.018)	(.017)	(.014)	(.046)	(.054)	(.012)	(.023)	(.017)	(.016)
Growth (upturns)	–.530***	.060***	–.522***	–.614***	–.486***	–.572***	–.349***	–.549**	–.233	–.809***
	(.198)	(.018)	(.194)	(.189)	(.186)	(.190)	(.158)	(.256)	(.222)	(.282)
Fuels (upturns)	–.189**	.060***	–.177**	–.169**	–.012	.100	–.143	–.318***	–.218**	–.136
	(.074)	(.018)	(.078)	(.070)	(.172)	(.175)	(.087)	(.107)	(.103)	(.105)

Trade volume (upturns)	–.081**	.060***	–.076**	–.066**	–.054	–.012	–.071*	–.093**	–.053	–.085
	(.036)	(.018)	(.037)	(.031)	(.058)	(.059)	(.036)	(.047)	(.038)	(.058)
Democratization among neighbors (upturns)	.073***	.060***	.076***	.071***	.075***	.067***	.055**	.037*	.009	.093***
	(.024)	(.018)	(.024)	(.025)	(.023)	(.023)	(.023)	(.022)	(.023)	(.035)
Prior level of democracy of regional organization (upturns)	.035***	.060***	.032***	.036***	.024*	.028**	.030***	.032***	.024***	.039***
	(.007)	(.018)	(.007)	(.007)	(.014)	(.014)	(.009)	(.009)	(.008)	(.011)
Peaceful demonstrations (upturns)	.029***	.060***	.040***	.041***	.040***	.042***	.056***	.040***	.021***	.045***
	(.007)	(.018)	(.007)	(.007)	(.007)	(.007)	(.009)	(.010)	(.008)	(.009)
No. of observations	3,785	3,073	3,795	3,795	3,828	3,828	5,554	3,801	3,801	3375
No. of countries	165	141	165	165	169	169	196	165	165	144
Mean years per country	22.9	21.8	23.0	23.0	22.6	22.6	28.3	23.0	23.0	23.4

Table C.1 (*cont.*)

	(1) *Deleting extreme outliers*	(2) *Deleting Western countries*	(3) *Region-fixed effects*	(4) *Year-fixed effects*	(5) *Country-fixed effects*	(6) *Year- & country-fixed effs*	(7) *Missing value imputation*	(8) *FH Political Rights*	(9) *FH Civil Liberties*	(10) *Polity score*
Economic Freedom (downturns)	.050*** (.014)	.047*** (.018)	.041*** (.014)	.046*** (.018)	.058*** (.016)	.056*** (.016)	.015 (.012)	.055** (.022)	.048*** (.016)	.048*** (.017)
No. of observations	2,820	2,138	2,827	2,827	2,844	2,844	5,554	2,828	2,828	2,702
No. of countries	119	95	119	119	120	120	196	119	119	113
Mean years per country	23.7	22.5	23.8	23.8	23.7	23.7	28.3	23.8	23.8	23.9
Multiparty Autocracy (upturns)	.166*** (.063)	.164** (.073)	.170*** (.062)	.171** (.068)	.191** (.077)	.207*** (.078)	.320*** (.064)	.293*** (.073)	.010 (.070)	.288*** (.089)
No. of observations	3,638	2,948	3,647	3,647	3,678	3,678	5,554	3,653	3,653	3,248
No. of countries	165	141	165	165	169	169	196	165	165	144
Mean years per country	22.0	2.9	22.1	22.1	21.8	21.8	28.3	22.1	22.1	22.6

* significant at the .10-level, ** significant at the .05-level, *** significant at the .01-level.

Note: Entries are unstandardized regression coefficients with standard errors in parentheses. Standard errors are panel-corrected in all models except (2), where only panel heteroskedasticity is being corrected for, and models (4)–(6), where OLS standard errors are reported. All models include two lags of the dependent variable and the determinants in Table 2.1, 3.1, 4.1 and 5.1 as controls.

An even stricter test, in the fifth model, restricts the model to explain within-country variation over time (country-fixed effects). This of course means I have to drop all variables that do not vary over time (but only across countries), such as the share of Muslims in the population. In the sixth model, I apply year- and country-fixed effects simultaneously.

Seventh, I attempt to remedy the missing data problem caused by patchy data on the explanatory variables. This is done through multiple imputation, essentially a technique through which all non-missing information in the data is used to fill in the missing parts, while at the same time recognizing the estimation uncertainty inherent in this endeavor (King *et al.* 2001).[2] As can be seen this results in an increase in the estimation sample size of about 50 percent, leaving us with valid observations for 31 more countries, that is, all 196 countries in all years for which there is Freedom House data on democracy after the year of independence.

The three final tests disaggregate my dependent variable into its three constitutive components: the two Freedom House measures of Political Rights and Political Liberties, and the Revised Combined Polity Score.

[2] I imputed five datasets using AmeliaView II. The regression estimates were obtained by use of the MI program for Stata developed by Kenneth Scheve. All software is available at Gary King's website: http://gking.harvard.edu/amelia/ (accessed May 24, 2007).

Appendix D
The pathway criterion

Gerring and Seawright define a *pathway case* as "a case where the causal effect of one factor can be isolated from other confounding factors," and suggest two criteria for how to single out such a case: (1) that it is "not an extreme outlier," and (2) "that its score on the outcome ... is strongly influenced by the theoretical variable of interest ... taking all other factors into account" (2007, pp. 122, 126). In operational terms, the latter criterion implies a case that is close to the regression surface (has a small residual) when the causal variable under consideration is included in the model, but far from the regression surface (has a large residual) when it is not controlled for.

Although I find Gerring and Seawright's approach promising, I take issue with their first criterion, and instead add a new one. Gerring and Seawright provide no substantial arguments for why a pathway case should not be an outlier (or at least not an extreme outlier). One could of course argue that there is some general value in studying a case that is well accounted for by the entire causal model. But that is not directly relevant to the issue of whether a *specific* causal variable works as posited or not. One could thus envision a case where one particular mechanism is strong and present, but where the outcome is still not fully accounted for (that is, a case with a large residual). For this reason, I do not address the issue of outliers in my case selection criterion. There is, instead, another criterion that needs to be added: that the case in question actually experiences the outcome that should be explained. It makes little sense to trace the mechanisms causing democratization, for example, in a case that never democratized. Unfortunately, Gerring and Seawright forget this crucial aspect of how to select a good pathway case.[1]

[1] In their more informal treatment on how to select pathway cases with dichotomous causal factors, however, they imply this third criterion by only considering cases where *Y* experienced the outcome (Gerring and Seawright 2007, p. 124).

Although alternative ways to incorporate this third consideration might be envisioned, I propose a slight modification of Gerring and Seawright's (2007, p. 127) pathway case criterion that takes it into account: to simply multiply the pathway measure with the absolute magnitude of change in the democracy score for that same year. Formally, a pathway case is then a case that maximizes the function

$$\text{Pathway} = |\text{Res}_{\text{reduced}} - \text{Res}_{\text{full}}| \times |\Delta D|, \text{if} |\text{Res}_{\text{reduced}}| > |\text{Res}_{\text{full}}|, \quad (8)$$

where Res_{full} is the residuals from the "full model" (i.e., the model with all relevant variables included), $\text{Res}_{\text{reduced}}$ is the residuals from the "reduced model" (i.e., the model with all variables included except the one which causal pathway one wants to explore), and ΔD is the change in the democracy score for each given year. In effect, a pathway case is thus a case where the causal factor under study contributes by drawing the case to the regression surface *and* where a substantial upturn or downturn in the level of democracy occurred.

References

Acemoglu, Daron, Simon Johnson and James A. Robinson. 2001. "The Colonial Origins of Comparative Development: An Empirical Investigation." *The American Economic Review* **91**(5): 1,369–401

2002. "Reversal of Fortune: Geography and Institutions in the Making of the Modern Income Distribution." *The Quarterly Journal of Econometrics* **118**: 1,231–94

Acemoglu, Daron, Simon Johnson, James A. Robinson and Pierre Yared. 2005. "From Education to Democracy." *American Economic Review* **95**(2): 44–49

2007. "Reevaluating the Modernization Hypothesis." MIT, Department of Economics Working Paper Series 07–23

2008. "Income and Democracy." *American Economic Review* **98**(3): 808–42

Acemoglu, Daron and James Robinson. 2006. *Economic Origins of Dictatorship and Democracy*. Cambridge: Cambridge University Press

Alesina, Alberto, Arnaud Devleeschauwer, William Easterly, Sergio Kurlat and Romain Wacziarg. 2003. "Fractionalization." *Journal of Economic Growth* **8**: 155–94

Alesina, Alberto and Enrico Spolaore. 1997. "On the Number and Size of Nations." *The Quarterly Journal of Economics* **112**: 1,027–56

Alexander, Gerard. 2002. *The Sources of Democratic Consolidation*. Ithaca and London: Cornell University Press

Anckar, Dag. 2002. "Why Are Small Island States Democracies?" *The Round Table* **365**: 375–90

Anckar, Dag and Carsten Anckar. 1995. "Size, Insularity and Democracy." *Scandinavian Political Studies* **18**(4): 211–29

Armony, Ariel. 2004. *The Dubious Link: Civic Engagement and Democratization*. Stanford: Stanford University Press

Ash, Timothy Garton. 1990. *We the People: The Revolution of '89*. London: Granta Books

Banks, Arthur. 2009. *Cross-National Time-Series Data Archive*. Jerusalem: Databanks International

Bårdsen, Gunnar. 1989. "Estimation of Long Run Coefficients in Error Correction Models." *Oxford Bulletin of Economics and Statistics* **51**(2): 345–50

Barrett, David B., George Thomas Kurian and Todd M. Johnson. 2001. *World Christian Encyclopedia: A Comparative Survey of Churches and Religions in the Modern World*, 2nd edition. Oxford: Oxford University Press

Barro, Robert. 1997. *Determinants of Economic Growth: A Cross-Country Empirical Study*. Cambridge: The MIT Press

1999. "Determinants of Democracy." *Journal of Political Economy* **107**(6, pt. 2): S158–83

Barro, Robert and Jong-Wha Lee. 2001. "International Data on Educational Attainment: Updates and Implications." *Oxford Economic Papers* **53**(3): 541–63

Beck, Nathaniel and Jonathan Katz. 1995. "What To Do (and Not To Do) with Time-Series Cross-Section Data." *American Political Science Review* **89**(3): 634–47

1996. "Nuisance vs. Substance: Specifying and Estimating Time-Series Cross-Section Models." *Political Analysis* **6**(1): 1–36

Beissinger, Mark. 2007. "Structure and Example in Modular Political Phenomena: Bulldozer/Rose/Orange/Tulip Revolutions." *Perspectives on Politics* **5**(2): 259–76

2008. "A New Look at Ethnicity and Democratization." *Journal of Democracy* **19**(3): 85–97

Bellin, Eva. 2000. "Contingent Democrats: Industrialists, Labor, and Democratization in Late-Developing Countries." *World Politics* **52**(January): 175–205

Benhabib, Jess and Adam Przeworski. 2005. "The Political Economy of Redistribution under Democracy." *Economic Theory* **29**: 271–90

Bermeo, Nancy. 1997. "Myths of Moderation: Confrontation and Conflict during Democratic Transitions." *Comparative Politics* **29**(3): 305–22

2003a. *Ordinary Citizens in Extraordinary Times: The Citizenry and the Breakdown of Democracy*. Princeton and Oxford: Princeton University Press

2003b. "What the Democratization Literature Says – or Doesn't Say – About Postwar Democratization." *Global Governance* **9**: 159–77

Bernard, Michael, Christopher Reenock and Timothy Nordstrom. 2001. "Economic Performance, Institutional Intermediation, and Democratic Survival." *Journal of Politics* **63**(3): 775–83

2003. "Economic Performance and Survival in New Democracies: Is There a Honeymoon Effect?" *Comparative Political Studies* **36**(4): 404–31

2004. "The Legacy of Western Overseas Colonialism on Democratic Survival." *International Studies Quarterly* **48**: 225–50

Boix, Carles. 2003. *Democracy and Redistribution*. Cambridge: Cambridge University Press

Boix, Carles and Susan Stokes. 2003. "Endogenous Democratization." *World Politics* 55(July): 815–49

Bollen, Kenneth. 1983. "World System Position, Dependency, and Democracy: The Cross-National Evidence." *American Sociological Review* **48**(August): 468–79

Bollen, Kenneth and Robert Jackman. 1985. "Political Democracy and the Size Distribution of Income." *American Sociological Review* **60**: 983–89

1995. "Income Inequality and Democratization Revisited: Comment on Muller." *American Sociological Review* **50**: 438–57

Boniface, Dexter. 2007. "The OAS's Mixed Record," in T. Legler, S. Lean and D. Boniface (eds.), *Promoting Democracy in the Americas*. Baltimore: The Johns Hopkins University Press

Brady, Henry and David Collier (eds.). 2004. *Rethinking Social Inquiry: Diverse Tools, Shared Standards*. Lanham: Rowman & Littlefield

Bratton, Michael and Nicholas van de Walle. 1997. *Democratic Experiments in Africa: Regime Transitions in Comparative Perspective*. Cambridge: Cambridge University Press

Brinks, Daniel and Michael Coppedge. 2006. "Diffusion Is No Illusion: Neighbor Emulation in the Third Wave of Democracy." *Comparative Political Studies* **39**(4): 463–89

Brooker, Paul. 2000. *Non-Democratic Regimes: Theory, Government and Politics*. New York: St. Martin's Press

Brownlee, Jason. 2002. ". . . And Yet They Persist: Explaining Survival and Transition in Neopatrimonial Regimes." *Studies in Comparative International Development* **37**(3): 35–63

2007. *Authoritarianism in the Age of Democratization*. Cambridge: Cambridge University Press

2009. "Portents of Pluralism: How Hybrid Regimes Affect Democratic Transitions." *American Journal of Political Science* **53**(2): 515–32

Brunk, Gregory, Gregory Caldeira and Michael Lewis-Beck. 1987. "Capitalism, Socialism, and Democracy: An Empirical Inquiry." *European Journal of Political Research* **15**: 459–70

Bueno de Mesquita, Bruce and George Downs. 2006. "Intervention and Democracy." *International Organization* **60**: 627–49

Bueno de Mesquita, Bruce, Alastair Smith, Randolph Siverson and James Morrow. 2003. *The Logic of Political Survival*. Cambridge: The MIT Press

Bunce, Valery. 2000. "Comparative Democratization: Big and Bounded Generalizations." *Comparative Political Studies* **33**(6/7): 703–34

2003. "Rethinking Recent Democratization: Lessons from the Postcommunist Experience." *World Politics* 55(January): 167–92

Burkhart, Ross. 1997. "Comparative Democracy and Income Distribution: Shape and Direction of Causal Arrow." *Journal of Politics* 59(1): 148–64

2000. "Economic Freedom and Democracy: Post–cold war tests." *European Journal of Political Research* 37: 237–53

Burkhart, Ross and Michael Lewis-Beck. 1994. "Comparative Democracy: The Economic Development Thesis." *American Political Science Review* 88(4): 903–10

Cameron, Maxwell. 1998. "Latin American *Autogolpes*: Dangerous Undertows in the Third Wave of Democratisation." *The Third World Quarterly* 19(2): 219–39

Carothers, Thomas. 2002. "The End of the Transition Paradigm." *Journal of Democracy* 13(1): 5–21

2007. "How Democracies Emerge: The Sequencing Fallacy." *Journal of Democracy* 18(1): 12–27

Casper, Gretchen and Michelle Taylor. 1996. *Negotiating Democracy: Transitions from Authoritarian Rule*. Pittsburgh: University of Pittsburgh Press

Chatterjee, Samprit and Ali Hadi. 1988. *Sensitivity Analysis in Linear Regression*. New York: John Wiley

Cheibub, José Antonio. 2007. *Presidentialism, Parliamentarism, and Democracy*. Cambridge: Cambridge University Press

Chen, Baizhu and Yi Feng. 1999. "Economic Development and the Transition to Democracy: A Formal Model." *Social Choice and Welfare* 16: 1–16

Clague, Christopher, Suzanne Gleason and Stephen Knack. 2001. "Determinants of Lasting Democracy in Poor Countries: Culture, Development, and Institutions." *Annals of the American Academy of Political and Social Science* 573(1): 16–41

Cohen, Youssef. 1994. *Radicals, Reformers, and Reactionaries: The Prisoner's Dilemma and the Collapse of Democracy in Latin America*. Chicago and London: The University of Chicago Press

Collier, David and Robert Adcock. 1999. "Democracy and Dichotomies: A Pragmatic Approach to Choices about Concepts." *Annual Review of Political Science*, 2: 537–65

Collier, Ruth Berins. 1999. *Paths Toward Democracy: The Working Class and Elites in Western Europe and South America*. Cambridge. Cambridge University Press

Colomer, Josep. 2000. *Strategic Transitions: Game Theory and Democratization*. Baltimore and London: The Johns Hopkins University Press

Cooper, Andrew and Thomas Legler. 2001. "The OAS in Peru: A Model for the Future?" *Journal of Democracy* 12(4): 123–36

Coppedge, Michael. 2003. "Book Review: Przeworski *et al.*, *Democracy and Development: Political Institutions and Well-Being in the World, 1950–1990.*" *Studies in Comparative International Development* **38**(1): 123–27

2005. "Explaining Democratic Deterioration in Venezuela Through Nested Induction," in F. Hagopian and S. Mainwaring (eds.), *The Third Wave of Democratization in Latin America*, pp. 289–316. Cambridge: Cambridge University Press

forthcoming. *Approaching Democracy: Research Methods in Comparative Politics*. Cambridge: Cambridge University Press

Coppedge, Michael and Wolfgang Reinicke. 1990. "Measuring Polyarchy." *Studies in Comparative International Development* **25**(1): 51–72

Cox, Dan and Cooper Drury. 2006. "Democratic Sanctions: Connecting the Democratic Peace to Economic Sanctions." *Journal of Peace Research* **43**(6): 709–22

Crescenzi, Mark. 1999. "Violence and Uncertainty in Transitions." *Journal of Conflict Resolution* **43**(2): 192–212

Cutright, Phillips. 1963. "National Political Development: Measurement and Analysis." *American Sociological Review* **28**: 253–64

Dagi, Ishan. 1996. "Democratic Transition in Turkey, 1980–83: The Impact of European Diplomacy." *Middle Eastern Studies* **32**(2): 124–41

Dahl, Robert. 1971. *Polyarchy*. New Haven: Yale University Press

Dahl, Robert and Edward Tufte. 1973. *Size and Democracy*. Stanford: Stanford University Press

Deininger, Klaus and Lyn Squire. 1996. "A New Data Set Measuring Income Inequality." *The World Bank Economic Review* **10**(3): 565–91

Deutsch, Karl. 1961. "Social Mobilization and Political Development." *American Political Science Review* **55**(3): 493–514

Diamond, Larry. 1992. "Economic Development and Democracy Reconsidered," in Gary Marks and Larry Diamond (eds.), *Reexamining Democracy: Essays in Honor of Seymour Martin Lipset*, pp. 93–139. Newbury Park: Sage Publications

2002. "Thinking About Hybrid Regimes." *Journal of Democracy* **13**(2): 21–35

1999. *Developing Democracy Towards Consolidation*. Baltimore: The Johns Hopkins University Press

Diaz-Cayeros, Alberto and Beatriz Magaloni. 2001. "Party Dominance and the Logic of Electoral Design in Mexico's Transition to Democracy." *Journal of Theoretical Politics* **13**(3): 271–93

Donno, Daniela and Bruce Russett. 2004. "Islam, Authoritarianism, and Female Empowerment: What Are the Linkages?" *World Politics* **56**(July): 582–607

Doorenspleet, Renske. 2005. *Democratic Transitions: Exploring the Structural Sources of the Fourth Wave*. Boulder and London: Lynne Rienner

Doorenspleet, Renske and Petr Kopecký. 2008. "Against the Odds: Deviant Cases of Democratization." *Democratization* **15**(4): 697–713

Doorenspleet, Renske and Cas Mudde. 2008. "Upping the Odds: Deviant Democracies and Theories of Democratization." *Democratization* **15**(4): 815–32

Downing, Brian. 1992. *The Military Revolution and Political Change: Origins of Democracy and Autocracy in Early Modern Europe*. Princeton: Princeton University Press

Drake, Paul. 1998. "The International Causes of Democratization, 1974–1990," in P. Drake and M. McCubbins (eds.), *The Origins of Liberty: Political and Economic Liberalization in the Modern World*, pp. 70–91. Princeton: Princeton University Press

Drazen, Allan. 2000. *Political Economy in Macroeconomics*. Princeton: Princeton University Press

Dunning, Thad. 2006. "Conditioning the Effects of Aid: Cold War Politics, Donor Credibility, and Democracy in Africa." *International Organization* **58**: 409–23

2008. *Crude Democracy: Natural Resource Wealth and Political Regimes*. Cambridge: Cambridge University Press

Eisenstadt, Todd. 2004. *Courting Democracy in Mexico: Party Strategies and Electoral Institutions*. Cambridge: Cambridge University Press

Elster, Jon. 1983. *Explaining Technical Change: A Case Study in the Philosophy of Science*. Cambridge: Cambridge University Press

Epstein, David, Robert Bates, Jack Goldstone, Ida Kristensen and Sharyn O'Halloran. 2006. "Democratic Transitions." *American Journal of Political Science* **50**(3): 551–69

Evin, Ahmet. 1994. "Demilitarization and Civilianization of the Regime." in M. Heper and A. Evin (eds.), *Politics in the Third Turkish Republic*, pp. 23–40. Boulder: Westview Press

Feng, Yi and Paul Zak. 1999. "The Determinants of Democratic Transitions." *Journal of Conflict Resolution* **43**(2): 162–77

Finkel, Steven. 1995. *Causal Analysis with Panel Data*. Thousand Oaks: Sage Publications

Finkel, Steven, Aníbal Pérez-Liñán and Mitchell Seligson. 2007. "The Effects of U.S. Foreign Assistance on Democracy Building, 1990–2003." *World Politics* **59**(April): 404–39

Fish, Steven. 1998. "Democratization's Requisites: The Postcommunist Experience." *Post-Soviet Affairs* **14**(3): 212–47

2002. "Islam and Authoritarianism." *World Politics* **55**(October): 4–37

Fish, Steven and Robin Brooks. 2004. "Does Diversity Hurt Democracy?" *Journal of Democracy* **15**(1): 154–66

Fish, Steven and Omar Choudhry. 2007. "Democratization and Economic Liberalization in the Postcommunist World." *Comparative Political Studies* **40**(3): 254–82

Foweraker, Joe and Todd Landman. 1997. *Citizenship Rights and Social Movements: A Comparative and Statistical Analysis.* Oxford: Oxford University Press

Fox, John. 1991. *Regression Diagnostics.* Newbury Park: Sage Publications

Freedom House. 2009. *Freedom of the World.* Washington: Freedom House. Available online at: http://www.freedomhouse.org

Galbraith, James and Hyunsub Kum. 2003. "Inequality and Economic Growth: A Global View Based on Measures of Pay." *CESifo Economic Studies* **49**(4): 527–56

Gandhi, Jennifer. 2008. *Political Institutions under Dictatorship.* Cambridge: Cambridge University Press

Gandhi, Jennifer and Ellen Lust-Okar. 2009. "Elections under Authoritarianism." *Annual Review of Political Science* **12**: 403–22

Gandhi, Jennifer and Adam Przeworski. 2006. "Cooperation, Cooptation, and Rebellion under Dictatorship." *Economics & Politics* **18**(1): 1–26

2007. "Authoritarian Institutions and the Survival of Autocrats." *Comparative Political Studies* **40**(11): 1,279–301

Gasiorowski, Mark. 1988. "Economic Dependence and Political Democracy: A Cross-National Study." *Comparative Political Studies* **20**(4): 489–515

1995. "Economic Crisis and Political Regime Change: An Event History Analysis." *American Political Science Review* **89**(4): 882–97

1996. "An Overview of the Political Regime Dataset." *Comparative Political Studies* **29**(4): 469–83

Gasiorowski, Mark and Timothy Power. 1998. "The Structural Determinants of Democratic Consolidation: Evidence from the Third World." *Comparative Political Studies* **31**(6): 740–71

Gates, Scott and Brian Humes. 1997. *Games, Information, and Politics: Applying Game Theoretic Models to Political Science.* Ann Arbor: The University of Michigan Press

Geddes, Barbara. 1999. "What Do We Know about Democratization after Twenty Years?" *Annual Review of Political Science* **2**: 115–44

Geddes, Barbara. 2002. "The Effect of Foreign Pressure on the Collapse of Authoritarian Regimes." Paper presented to the Annual Meeting of the American Political Science Association, Boston

2003. *Paradigms and Sand Castles: Theory Building and Research Design in Comparative Politics.* Ann Arbor: Michigan University Press

George, Alexander and Andrew Bennet. 2005. *Case Studies and Theory Development in the Social Sciences*. Cambridge: The MIT Press

George, Alexander and Timothy McKeown. 1985. "Case Studies and Theories of Organizational Decision Making," in Robert Coulam and Richard Smith (eds.), *Advances in Information Processing in Organizations*, vol. **2**, pp. 21–58. Santa Barbara: JAI Press

Gerring, John. 2001. *Social Science Methodology: A Criterial Framework*. Cambridge: Cambridge University Press

Gerring, John and Jason Seawright. 2007. "Techniques for Choosing Cases," in John Gerring, *Case Study Research: Principles and Practices*. Cambridge: Cambridge University Press

Giavazzi, Francesco and Guido Tabellini. 2005. "Economic and Political Liberalizations." *Journal of Monetary Economics* **52**: 1,297–330

Gill, Graham. 2000. *The Dynamics of Democratization: Elites, Civil Society and the Transition Process*. Houndmills and London: MacMillan

Glaeser, Edward, Giacomo Ponzetto and Andrei Shleifer. 2007. "Why Does Democracy Need Education?" *Journal of Economic Growth* **12**(7): 77–99

Gleditsch, Kristian Skrede. 2002. "Expanded Trade and GDP Data." *Journal of Conflict Resolution* **46**(5): 712–24

Gleditsch, Kristian Skrede and Michael Ward. 2006. "Diffusion and the International Context of Democratization." *International Organization* **60**: 911–33

Gleditsch, Nils Petter, Peter Wallensteen, Mikael Eriksson, Margaretha Sollenberg and Håvard Strand. 2002. "Armed Conflict 1946–2001: A New Dataset." *Journal of Peace Research*, **39**(5): 615–37

Goldsmith, Arthur. 2001. "Donors, Dictators and Democrats in Africa." *Journal of Modern African Studies* **39**(3): 411–36

Gonick, Lev and Robert Rosh. 1988. "The Structural Constraints of the World Economy on National Political Development." *Comparative Political Studies* **21**(2): 171–99

Gourevitch, Peter. 1978. "The Second Image Reversed: the International Sources of Domestic Politics." *International Organization* **32**(4): 881–911

2002. "Domestic Politics and International Relations," in W. Carlsnaes, T. Risse and B. Simmons (eds.), *Handbook of International Relations*, pp. 309–28. London: Sage

Gradstein, Mark and Branko Milanovic. 2004. "Does Liberté=Egalité? A Survey of the Empirical Links Between Democracy and Inequality with Some Evidence on the Transition Economies." *Journal of Economic Surveys* **18**(4): 515–37

Green, Andrew and Richard Kohl. 2007. "Challenges of Evaluating Democracy Assistance: Perspectives from the Donor Side." *Democratization* **14**(1): 151–65

Green, Kenneth. 2007. *Why Dominant Parties Lose: Mexico's Democratization in Comparative Perspective*. Cambridge: Cambridge University Press

Green, William. 1997. *Econometric Analysis*. Upper Saddle River: Prentice-Hall

Grimm, Sonja. 2008. "External Democratization after War: Success and Failure." *Democratization* 15(3): 525–49

Gwartney, James and Robert Lawson. 2006. *Economic Freedom of the World: 2006 Annual Report*. Vancouver: The Fraser Institute

Hadenius, Axel. 1992. *Democracy and Development*. Cambridge: Cambridge University Press

Hadenius, Axel and Jan Teorell. 2005a. "Cultural and Economic Prerequisites of Democracy: Reassessing Recent Evidence." *Studies in Comparative International Development* **39**(4): 87–106

2005b. "Assessing Alternative Indices of Democracy." *Concepts & Methods Working Papers* **6**, IPSA. Available online at: www.concepts-methods.org/papers.php

2007. "Pathways from Authoritarianism." *Journal of Democracy* **18**(1): 143–56

Haggard, Stephan and Robert Kaufman. 1995. *The Political Economy of Democratic Transitions*. Princeton: Princeton University Press

1997. "The Political Economy of Democratic Transitions." *Comparative Politics* **29**(3): 263–83

Helliwell, John. 1994. "Empirical Linkages between Democracy and Economic Growth." *British Journal of Political Science* **24**: 225–48

Herb, Michael. 1999. *All in the Family: Absolutism, Revolution, and Democracy in the Middle Eastern Monarchies*. Albany: State University of New York Press

Herbst, Jeffrey. 2004. *States and Power in Africa: Comparative Lessons in Authority and Control*. Princeton: Princeton University Press

Hiscox, Michael and David Lake. 2001. "Democracy and the Size of States." Unpublished paper. Department of Political Science, University of California, San Diego

Hofmann, Steven Ryan. 2004. "Islam and Democracy: Micro-Level Indications of Compatibility." *Comparative Political Studies* **37**(6): 652–76

Horowitz, Donald. 1985. *Ethnic Groups in Conflict*. Berkeley: University of California Press

Howard, Marc Morjé and Philip Roessler 2006. "Liberalizing Electoral Outcomes in Competitive Authoritarian Regimes." *American Journal of Political Science* **50**(2): 365–81

Hufbauer, Gary Clyde, Jeffrey Schott, Kimberly Ann Elliott and Barbara Oegg. 2009. *Economic Sanctions Reconsidered*. 3rd edition. Washington: Peterson Institute for International Economics

Huntington, Samuel. 1991. *The Third Wave: Democratization in the Late Twentieth Century*. Norman and London: University of Oklahoma Press

Hyde-Price, Adrian. 1994. "Democratization in Eastern Europe: The External Dimension," in G. Pridham and T. Vanhanen (eds.), *Democratization in Eastern Europe: Domestic and International Perspectives*, pp. 220–52. London and New York: Routledge

Inglehart, Ronald. 1997. *Modernization and Postmodernization: Cultural, Economic, and Political Change in 43 Societies*. Princeton: Princeton University Press

Inglehart, Ronald and Christian Welzel. 2005. *Modernization, Cultural Change, and Democracy: The Human Development Sequence*. Cambridge: Cambridge University Press

Karl, Terry Lynn. 1990. "Dilemmas of Democratization in Latin America," in D. Rustow and K. Erickson (eds.), *Comparative Political Dynamics: Global Research Perspectives*, pp. 163–91. New York: Harper Collins

Karl, Terry Lynn and Philippe Schmitter. 1991. "Modes of Transition in Latin America, Southern and Eastern Europe." *International Social Science Journal* **128**: 269–84

King, Gary, James Honaker, Anne Joseph and Kenneth Scheve. 2001. "Analyzing Incomplete Political Science Data: An Alternative Algorithm for Multiple Imputation." *American Political Science Review* **95**(1): 49–69

King, Gary, Robert Keohane and Sidney Verba. 1994. *Designing Social Inquiry: Scientific Inference in Qualitative Research*. Princeton: Princeton University Press

Kitschelt, Herbert. 1992. "Political Regime Change: Structure and Process-Driven Explanations?" *American Political Science Review* **86**(4): 1,028–34

Knack, Stephen. 2004. "Does Foreign Aid Promote Democracy?" *International Studies Quarterly* **48**: 251–66

Kopecký, Petr and Cas Mudde. 2003. "Rethinking Civil Society." *Democratization* **10**(3): 1–14

Kopstein, Jeffrey and David Reilly. 2000. "Geographic Diffusion and the Transformation of the Postcommunist World." *World Politics* **53**(October): 1–37

Kurzman, Charles. 1998. "Waves of Democratization." *Studies in Comparative International Development* **33**(1): 42–64

Lacy, Dean and Emerson Niou. 2004. "A Theory of Economic Sanctions and Issue Linkage: The Roles of Preferences, Information, and Threats." *Journal of Politics* **66**(1): 25–42

Langston, Joy. 2006. "Elite Ruptures: When Do Ruling Parties Split?", in A. Schedler (ed.), *Electoral Authoritarianism: The Dynamics of Unfree Competition*. Boulder and London: Lynne Rienner

Legler, Thomas. 2003. "Peru Then and Now: The Inter-American Democratic Charter and Peruvian Democratization." *Canadian Foreign Policy* **10**(3): 61–73

Lerner, Daniel. 1958. *The Passing of Traditional Society*. Glencoe: The Free Press

Levitsky, Steven and Lucan Way. 2002. "The Rise of Competitive Authoritarianism." *Journal of Democracy* **13**(2): 51–65

Levitt, Barry. 2006. "A Desultory Defense of Democracy: OAS Resolution 1080 and the Inter-American Democratic Charter." *Latin American Politics and Society* **48**(3): 93–123

Li, Quan and Rafael Reuveny. 2003. "Economic Globalization and Democracy: An Empirical Analysis." *British Journal of Political Science* **33**: 29–54

2009. *Democracy and Economic Openness in an Interconnected System: Complex Transformations*. Cambridge: Cambridge University Press

Lieberman, Evan. 2005. "Nested Analysis as a Mixed-Method Strategy for Comparative Research." *American Political Science Review* **99**(3): 435–52

Lijphart, Arendt. 1977. *Democracy in Plural Societies: A Comparative Exploration*. New Haven: Yale University Press

Lindberg, Staffan. 2006. *Democracy and Elections in Africa*. Baltimore: The Johns Hopkins University Press

Linz, Juan. 1978. *The Breakdown of Democratic Regimes: Crisis, Breakdown, and Reequilibrium*. Baltimore and London: The Johns Hopkins University Press

Lipset, Seymour Martin. 1959. "Some Social Requisites of Democracy: Economic Development and Legitimacy." *American Political Science Review* **53**: 69–105

1994. "The Social Requisites of Democracy Revisited." *American Sociological Review* **59**(1): 1–22

Lipset, Seymour Martin, Kyoung-Ryung Seong and John Charles Torres. 1993. "A Comparative Analysis of the Social Requisites of Democracy." *International Social Science Journal* **45**: 155–75

Londregan, John and Keith Poole. 1996. "Does High Income Promote Democracy?" *World Politics* **49**: 1–30

Luebbert, Gregory. 1991. *Liberalism, Fascism, or Social Democracy: Social Classes and the Political Origins of Regimes in Interwar Europe*. Oxford: Oxford University Press

Lust-Okar, Ellen. 2006. "Elections under Authoritarianism: Preliminary Lessons from Jordan." *Democratization* **13**(3): 456–71

Lust-Okar, Ellen and Amaney Ahmad Jamal. 2002. "Rulers and Rules: Reassessing the Influence of Regime Type on Electoral Law Formation." *Comparative Political Studies* **35**(3): 337–66

MacMillan, John and Pablo Zoido. 2004. "How to Subvert Democracy: Montesinos in Peru." *Journal of Economic Perspectives* **18**(4): 69–92

Magaloni, Beatrice. 2006. *Voting for Autocracy: Hegemonic Party Survival and Its Demise in Mexico*. Cambridge: Cambridge University Press

2008. "Credible Power-Sharing and the Longevity of Authoritarian Rule." *Comparative Political Studies* **41**(4–5): 715–41

Mahoney, James. 2003. "Knowledge Accumulation in Comparative Historical Research: The Case of Democracy and Authoritarianism," in J. Mahoney and D. Rueschemeyer (eds.), *Comparative Historical Analysis in the Social Sciences*, pp. 131–74. Cambridge: Cambridge University Press

Mainwaring, Scott, Daniel Brinks and Aníbal Pérez-Liñán. 2001. "Classifying Political Regimes in Latin America, 1945–1999." *Studies in Comparative International Development* **36**(1): 37–65

Mainwaring, Scott and Aníbal Pérez-Liñán. 2003. "Level of Development and Democracy: Latin American Exceptionalism, 1945–1996." *Comparative Political Studies* **36**(9): 1,031–67

2005a. "Latin American Democratization since 1978: Democratic Transitions, Breakdowns, and Erosions," in F. Hagopian and S. Mainwaring (eds.), *The Third Wave of Democratization in Latin America*, pp. 14–59. Cambridge: Cambridge University Press

2005b. "Why Regions of the World Are Important: Regional Specificities and Region-Wide Diffusion of Democracy." Kellogg Institute Working Paper Series 322, University of Notre Dame, October 2005

Markoff, John. 1996. *Waves of Democracy: Social Movements and Political Change*. Thousand Oaks: Pine Forge Press

Marshall, Monty and Keith Jaggers. 2009. "Polity IV Project: Political Regime Characteristics and Transitions, 1800–2007." George Mason University: Center for Global Peace. Available online at: www.systemicpeace.org/polity/polity4.htm

Mauceri, Philip. 1997. "Return of the *Caudillo*: Autocratic Democracy in Peru." *The Third World Quarterly* **18**(5): 889–911

McClintock, Cynthia. 2001. "The OAS in Peru: Room for Improvement." *Journal of Democracy* **12**(4): 137–40

McFaul, Michael. 2002. "The Fourth Wave of Democracy *and* Dictatorship: Noncooperative Transitions in the Postcommunist World." *World Politics* **54**: 212–44

Melander, Erik. 2005. "Gender Equality and Intrastate Armed Conflict." *International Studies Quarterly* **49**(4): 695–714

Meltzer, Allan and Scott Richard. 1981. "A Rational Theory of the Size of Government." *Journal of Political Economy* **89**(5): 914–27

Moore, Barrington. 1966. *Social Origins of Dictatorship and Democracy: Lord and Peasant in the Making of the Modern World*. Boston: Beacon Press

Moore, Mick. 2004. "Revenues, State Formation, and the Quality of Governance in Developing Countries." *International Political Science Review* **25**(3): 297–319

Morton, Rebecca. 1999. *Methods and Models: A Guide to the Empirical Analysis of Formal Models in Political Science*. Cambridge: Cambridge University Press

Mozaffar, Shaheen and Richard Vengroff. 2002. "A 'Whole Systems' Approach to the Choice of Electoral Rules in Democratizing Countries: Senegal in Comparative Perspective." *Electoral Studies* **21**(4): 601–16

Muller, Edward. 1988. "Democracy, Economic Development, and Income Inequality." *American Sociological Review* **53**: 50–68

1995a. "Economic Determinants of Democracy." *American Sociological Review* **60**: 966–82

1995b. "Income Inequality and Democratization." *American Sociological Review* **60**: 990–96

Mulligan, Casey, Ricard Gil and Xavier Sala-i-Martin. 2004. "Do Democracies Have Different Public Policies than Nondemocracies?" *Journal of Economic Perspectives* **18**(1): 51–74

Munck, Gerardo and Richard Snyder. 2007. "Debating the Direction of Comparative Politics." *Comparative Political Studies* **40**(1): 5–31

Munck, Gerardo L. and Jay Verkuilen. 2002. "Conceptualizing and Measuring Democracy: Evaluating Alternative Indices." *Comparative Political Studies* **35**(1): 5–34

Neubauer, Deane. 1967. "Some Conditions of Democracy." *American Political Science Review* **61**: 1,002–9

Nordlinger, Eric. 1977. *Soldiers in Politics: Military Coups and Governments*. Englewood Cliffs: Prentice-Hall

Norris, Pippa. 2008. *Driving Democracy: Do Power-Sharing Institutions Work?* Cambridge: Cambridge University Press

Norris, Pippa and Ronald Inglehart. 2004. *Sacred and Secular: Religion and Politics Worldwide*. Cambridge: Cambridge University Press

O'Donnell, Guillermo. 1979. *Modernization and Bureaucratic-Authoritarianism: Studies in South American Politics*. Berkeley: Institute of International Studies

2001. "Democracy, Law, and Comparative Politics." *Studies in Comparative International Development* **36**(1): 7–36

O'Donnell, Guillermo and Philippe Schmitter. 1986. *Transitions from Authoritarian Rule: Tentative Conclusions about Uncertain Democracies*. Baltimore and London: The Johns Hopkins University Press

O'Donnell, Guillermo, Philippe Schmitter and Laurence Whitehead. 1986. *Transitions from Authoritarian Rule: Prospects for Democracy*. Baltimore and London: The Johns Hopkins University Press

O'Loughlin, John, Michael Ward, Corey Lofdahl, Jordin Cohen, David Brown, David Reilly, Kristian Gleditsch and Michael Shin. 1998. "The Diffusion of Democracy, 1946–1994." *Annals of the Association of American Geographers* **88**(4): 545–74

Olsen, Marvin. 1968. "Multivariate Analysis of National Political Development." *American Sociological Review* **35**: 699–712

Parajulee, Ramjee. 2000. *The Democratic Transition in Nepal*. Lanham: Rowman & Littlefield

Paris, Roland. 2004. *At War's End: Building Peace After Civil Conflict*. Cambridge: Cambridge University Press

Paxton, Pamela. 2002. "Social Capital and Democracy: An Interdependent Relationship." *American Sociological Review* **67**(April): 254–77

Pearl, Judea. 2000. *Causality: Models, Reasoning, and Inference*. Cambridge: Cambridge University Press.

Perotti, Roberto. 1996. "Growth, Income Distribution, and Democracy: What the Data Say." *Journal of Economic Growth* **1**: 149–87

Persson, Torsten and Guido Tabellini. 2003. *The Economic Effects of Constitutions*. Cambridge: The MIT Press

2009. "Democratic Capital: The Nexus of Political and Economic change." *American Economic Journal* **1**(2): 88–126

Pevehouse, Jon. 2005. *Democracy from Above: Regional Organizations and Democratization*. Cambridge: Cambridge University Press

Pevehouse, Jon, Timothy Nordstrom and Kevin Warnke. 2004. "The Correlates of War 2. International Governmental Organizations Data Version 2.0." *Conflict Management and Peace Science* **21**: 101–19

Pickering, Jeffrey and Emizet Kisangani. 2006. "Political, Economic, and Social Consequences of Foreign Military Intervention." *Political Research Quarterly* **59**(3): 363–76

Pickering, Jeffrey and Mark Peceny. 2006. "Forging Democracy at Gunpoint." *International Studies Quarterly* **50**: 539–59

Plümper, Thomas and Vera Troeger. 2007. "Efficient Estimation of Time Invariant and Rarely Changing Variables in Panel Data Analysis with Unit Effects." *Political Analysis* **15**(2): 124–39

Posusney, Marsha Pripstein. 2002. "Multi-Party Elections in the Arab World: Institutional Engineering and Oppositional Strategies." *Studies in Comparative International Development* **36**(4): 34–62

Price, Robert. 1991. *The Apartheid State in Crisis: Political Transformation in South Africa, 1975–1990*. New York and Oxford: Oxford University Press

Przeworski, Adam. 1991. *Democracy and the Market: Political and Economic Reforms in Eastern Europe and Latin America*. Cambridge: Cambridge University Press

2005. "Democracy as an Equilibrium." *Public Choice* **123**: 253–73

Przeworski, Adam, Michael Alvarez, José Antonio Cheibub and Fernando Limongi. 2000. *Democracy and Development: Political Institutions and Well-Being in the World, 1950–1990*. Cambridge: Cambridge University Press

Rabushka, Alvin and Kenneth Shepsle. 1972. *Politics of Plural Societies: A Theory of Democratic Instability*. Ohio: Merrill

Randall, Vicky. 1993. "The Media and Democratisation in the Third World." *Third World Quarterly* **14**(3): 625–46

Reich, Gary. 2002. "Categorizing Political Regimes: New Data for Old Problems." *Democratization* **9**: 1–24

Remmer, Karen. 1996. "The Sustainability of Political Democracy: Lessons From South America." *Comparative Political Studies* **29**(6): 611–34

Rigobon, Roberto and Dani Rodrik. 2005. "Rule of Law, Democracy, Openness, and Income." *Economics of Transition* **13**(3): 533–64

Robinson, James. 2006. "Economic Development and Democracy." *Annual Review of Political Science* **9**: 503–27

Rogowski, Ronald. 1998. "Democracy, Capital, Skill, and Country Size: Effects of Asset Mobility and Regime Monopoly on the Odds of Democratic Rule," in P. Drake and M. McCubbins (eds.), *The Origins of Liberty: Political and Economic Liberalization in the Modern World*, pp. 48–69. Princeton: Princeton University Press

Rose, Richard. 2002. "How Muslims View Democracy: Evidence from Central Asia." *Journal of Democracy* **13**(4): 102–11

Rosendorff, Peter. 2001. "Choosing Democracy." *Economics & Politics* **13**(1): 1–29

Ross, Michael. 2001. "Does Oil Hinder Democracy?" *World Politics* **53**(April): 325–61

2004. "Does Taxation Lead to Representation?" *British Journal of Political Science* **34**: 229–49

2006. "Is Democracy Good for the Poor?" *American Journal of Political Science* **50**(4): 860–74

2008. "Oil, Islam, and Women." *American Political Science Review* **102**(1): 107–23

Rowen, Henry. 2007. "When Will the Chinese People Be Free?" *Journal of Democracy* **18**(3): 38–52

Rudra, Nita. 2005. "Globalization and the Strengthening of Democracy in the Developing World." *American Journal of Political Science* **49**(4): 704–30

Rueschemeyer, Dietrich, Evelyn Huber Stephens and John D. Stephens. 1992. *Capitalist Development and Democracy*. Chicago: The University of Chicago Press

Rustow, Dankwart. 1970. "Transitions to Democracy: Toward a Dynamic Model." *Comparative Politics* **2**: 337–63

Saxonberg, Steven. 2001. *The Fall: A Comparative Study of the End of Communism in Czechoslovakia, East Germany, Hungary and Poland.* Amsterdam: Harwood Academic

Schedler, Andreas. 1998. "What is Democratic Consolidation?" *Journal of Democracy* **9**(2): 91–107

2002a. "The Nested Game of Democratization by Elections." *International Political Science Review* **23**(1): 103–22

2002b. "The Menu of Manipulation." *Journal of Democracy* **13**(2): 36–50

2006. "The Logic of Electoral Authoritarianism," in A. Schedler, (ed.), *Electoral Authoritarianism: The Dynamics of Unfree Competition.* Boulder and London: Lynne Rienner

Schmitter, Philippe. 1995. "Transitology: The Science or the Art of Democratization?", in Joseph Tulchin with Bernice Romero (eds.), *The Consolidation of Democracy in Latin America*, pp. 11–41. Boulder and London: Lynne Rienner

Schock, Kurt. 2005. *Unarmed Insurrections: People Power Movements in Nondemocracies.* Minneapolis and London: University of Minnesota Press

Shin, Doh Chull. 1994. "On the Third Wave of Democratization: A Synthesis and Evaluation of Recent Theory and Research." *World Politics* **47**: 135–70

Slater, Dan 2009. "Revolutions, Crackdowns, and Quiescence: Communal Elites and Democratic Mobilization in Southeast Asia." *American Journal of Sociology* **115**(1): 203–54

Smithey, Lee and Lester Kurtz. 1999. "'We Have Bare Hands': Nonviolent Social Movements in the Soviet Bloc," in S. Zunes, L. Kurtz and S. B. Asher (eds.), *Nonviolent Social Movements: A Geographical Perspective.* Malden and Oxford: Blackwell

Snyder, Richard. 1998. "Paths out of Sultanistic Regimes: Combining Structural and Voluntarist Perspectives," in H. E. Chehabi and J. Linz (eds.), *Sultanistic Regimes*, pp. 49–81. Baltimore and London: The Johns Hopkins University Press

Snyder, Richard and James Mahoney. 1999. "The Missing Variable: Institutions and the Study of Regime Change." *Comparative Politics* **32**(1): 103–22

Sollenberg, Margareta. 2008. "From Bullets to Ballots: Using the People as Arbitrators to Settle Civil Wars," in M. Öberg and K. Strøm (eds.), *Resources, Governance, and Civil Conflict*, pp. 178–204. London: Routledge

Starr, Harvey. 1991. "Democratic Dominoes: Diffusion Approaches to the Spread of Democracy in the International System." *Journal of Conflict Resolution* **35**(2): 356–81

Starr, Harvey and Christina Lindborg. 2003. "Democratic Dominoes Revisited: The Hazards of Governmental Transition." *Journal of Conflict Resolution* **47**(4): 490–519

Stepan, Alfred with Graeme Robertson. 2003. "An 'Arab' More Than A 'Muslim' Electoral Gap." *Journal of Democracy* **14**(3): 30–44

2004. "Arab, Not Muslim, Exceptionalism." *Journal of Democracy* **15**(4): 140–46

Stinnett, Douglas, Jaroslav Tir, Paul F. Diehl, Philip Schafer and Charles Gochman. 2002. "The Correlates of War (COW) Project Direct Contiguity Data, Version 3.0." *Conflict Management and Peace Science* **19**(2): 59–67

Sutter, Daniel. 2000. "The Transition from Authoritarian Rule: A Game Theoretic Approach." *Journal of Theoretical Politics* **12**(1): 67–89

Swaminathan, Siddharth. 1999. "Time, Power, and Democratic Transitions." *Journal of Conflict Resolution* **43**(2): 178–91

Teorell, Jan. 2006. "Political Participation and Three Theories of Democracy: A Research Inventory and Agenda." *European Journal of Political Research* **45**(5): 787–810

Teorell, Jan, Nicholas Charron, Marcus Samanni, Sören Holmberg and Bo Rothstein. 2009. "The Quality of Government Dataset, version 17June09." University of Gothenburg: The Quality of Government Institute. Available online at: www.qog.pol.gu.se

Teorell, Jan and Axel Hadenius. 2006. "Democracy without Democratic Values: A Rejoinder to Welzel and Inglehart." *Studies in Comparative International Development* **41**(3): 95–111

2007. "Determinants of Democratization: Taking Stock of the Large-N Evidence," in D. Berg-Schlosser (ed.), *Democratization: The State of the Art*, pp. 69–95. Opladen and Farmington Hills: Barbara Budrich Publishers

2009. "Elections as Levers of Democratization: A Global Inquiry," in S. Lindberg (ed.), *Democratization by Elections: A New Mode of Transition*. Baltimore: The Johns Hopkins University Press

Tessler, Mark. 2002a. "Islam and Democracy in the Middle East: The Impact of Religious Orientations on Attitudes towards Democracy in Four Arab Countries." *Comparative Politics* **34**(3): 337–54

2002b. "Do Islamic Orientations Influence Attitudes Toward Democracy in the Arab World? Evidence from Egypt, Jordan, Morocco, and Algeria." *International Journal of Comparative Sociology* **43**(3–5): 229–49

Tessler, Mark and Eleanor Gao. 2005. "Gauging Arab Support for Democracy." *Journal of Democracy* **16**(3): 83–97

Therborn, Göran. 1977. "The Rule of Capital and the Rise of Democracy." *New Left Review* **I/103**: 3–41

Thompson, Marc. 1995. *The Anti-Marcos Struggle: Personalistic Rule and Democratic Transition in the Philippines*. New Haven and London: Yale University Press

2004. *Democratic Revolutions: Asia and Eastern Europe*. London: Routledge

Tilly, Charles. 2004. *Contention and Democracy in Europe, 1650–2000*. Cambridge: Cambridge University Press

2007. *Democracy*. Cambridge: Cambridge University Press

Tucker, Joshua. 2007. "Enough! Electoral Fraud, Collective Action Problems, and Post-Communist Colored Revolution." *Perspectives on Politics* 5(3): 535–51

Ulfelder, Jay. 2005. "Contentious Collective Action and the Breakdown of Authoritarian Regimes." *International Political Science Review* **26**(3): 311–34

van de Walle, Nicolas. 2006. "Tipping Games: When Do Opposition Parties Coalesce?", in A. Schedler (ed.), *Electoral Authoritarianism: The Dynamics of Unfree Competition*, pp. 77–92. Boulder and London: Lynne Rienner

Wantchekon, Leonard. 2004. "The Paradox of 'Warlord' Democracy: A Theoretical Investigation." *American Political Science Review* **98**(1): 17–33

Wantchekon, Leonard and Zvika Neeman. 2002. "A Theory of Post-Civil War Democratization." *Journal of Theoretical Politics* **14**(4): 439–64

Way, Lucan. 2005. "Authoritarian State Building and the Sources of Regime Competitiveness in the Fourth Wave: The Cases of Belarus, Moldova, Russia, and Ukraine." *World Politics* 57(January): 231–61

WDI 2009. World Development Indicators Database Online. The World Bank Group. Available for subscribers online at: http://publications.worldbank.org/WDI/

Weingast, Barry. 1997. "The Political Foundations of Democracy and the Rule of Law." *American Political Science Review* **91**(2): 245–63

Welzel, Christian and Ronald Inglehart. 2006. "Emancipative Values and Democracy: Response to Hadenius and Teorell." *Studies in Comparative International Development* **41**(3): 74–94

Whitehead, Lawrence. 1986. "Bolivia's Failed Democratization, 1977–1980," in G. O'Donnell, P. Schmitter and L. Whitehead (eds.), *Transitions from Authoritarian Rule: Latin America*. Baltimore: The Johns Hopkins University Press

1996. "Three International Dimensions of Democratization," in L. Whitehead (ed.), *The International Dimensions of Democratization: Europe and the Americas*, pp. 3–25. Oxford: Oxford University Press

1997. "East-Central Europe in Comparative Perspective," in Pridham, G., E. Herring and G. Sanford (eds.), *Building Democracy? The International Dimension of Democratization in Eastern Europe*. Second edition, pp. 30–55. London and Washington: Leicester University Press

Winham, Gilbert. 1970. "Political Development and Lerner's Theory: Further Test of a Causal Model." *American Political Science Review* **64**: 810–18

Wintrobe, Ronald. 1990. "The Tinpot and the Totalitarian." *American Political Science Review* **84**(3): 850–72

1998. *The Political Economy of Dictatorship*. Cambridge: Cambridge University Press

Wood, Elisabeth Jean. 2000. *Forging Democracy from Below: Insurgent Transitions in South Africa and El Salvador*. Cambridge: Cambridge University Press

2001. "An Insurgent Path to Democracy: Popular Mobilization, Economic Interests, and Regime Transition in South Africa and El Salvador." *Comparative Political Studies* **34**(8): 862–88

Wright, Joseph. 2009. "How Foreign Aid Can Foster Democratization in Authoritarian Regimes." *American Journal of Political Science* **53**(3): 552–72

Zak, Paul and Yi Feng. 2003. "A Dynamic Theory of the Transition to Democracy." *Journal of Economic Behavior & Organization* **52**: 1–25

Zunes, Stephen. 1999. "The Role of Non-violent Action in the Downfall of Apartheid." *Journal of Modern African Studies* **37**(1): 137–69

Index

Lightning Source UK Ltd.
Milton Keynes UK
UKOW06f2050180817
307474UK00010B/222/P

9 780521 139